KNOWING RELIGIOUSLY

BOSTON UNIVERSITY STUDIES IN PHILOSOPHY AND RELIGION

General Editor: Leroy S. Rouner

Volume Seven

Knowing Religiously

Edited by
Leroy S. Rouner

UNIVERSITY OF NOTRE DAME PRESS
Notre Dame, Indiana 46556

The essay "Reconceiving God for a Nuclear Age" by
Gordon D. Kaufman is adapted from chapter three of
Theology for a Nuclear Age by Gordon D. Kaufman.
Copyright © 1984 Gordon D. Kaufman. Adapted and
used by permission of the Westminster Press, Philadel-
phia, Pa.

Library of Congress Cataloging-in-Publication Data

Main entry under title:

Knowing religiously.

(Boston University studies in philosophy and
religion ; 7)
  Includes index.
  1. Knowledge, Theory of (Religion) — Addresses, essays,
lectures.   2. Religion — Philosophy — Addresses, essays,
lectures.   I. Rouner, Leroy S.   II. Series: Boston
University studies in philosophy and religion ; v. 7.
BL51.K614   1985   200'.1   85-8689
ISBN 0-268-01224-5

Manufactured in the United States of America

Contents

Preface

Boston University Studies in Philosophy and Religion is a joint project of the Boston University Institute for Philosophy and Religion and the University of Notre Dame Press. While these Studies may eventually include occasional volumes by individual authors dealing with critical issues in the philosophy of religion, it is presently focused on an annual volume edited from the previous year's Institute lecture program. The Director of the Institute, who also serves as editor of these Studies, chooses a theme and invites participants to lecture at Boston University in the course of the academic year. These public lectures are on Wednesday evenings, chaired by faculty from the various schools and departments within the university which jointly sponsor the Institute. There is a critical respondent to each paper and general discussion by the audience. The papers are then revised by their authors, and the editor selects and edits the papers to be included in these Studies. In preparation is a volume on civil religion/political theology.

The Boston University Institute for Philosophy and Religion is sponsored jointly by the Graduate School, the School of Theology, the Department of Philosophy, and the Department of Religion at Boston University. As an interdisciplinary and ecumenical forum it does not represent any philosophical school or religious tradition. Within the academic community it is committed to open interchange on questions of value, truth, reality, and meaning which transcend the narrow specializations of academic life. Outside the university community it seeks to recover the public tradition of philosophical discourse which was a lively part of American intellectual life in the early years of this century before the professionalization of both philosophy and religious studies. This

vii

volume, perhaps more than its predecessors, makes specific a conception of the philosophy of religion which has informed the series as a whole. As the Introduction makes clear, we are committed to a renewal of the philosophy of religion as it was understood by Harvard philosophers from James and Royce to Hocking, and by Boston University philosophers from Bowne and Brightman to Bertocci.

Our themes are intentionally broad and inclusive in order to provide a home for a variety of views and projects. Our essays focus on the analysis of quite specific issues within the theme, however, and we encourage our authors to make an autobiographical connection with their analysis. We also emphasize the need for comparative studies. Religious and cultural pluralism is now the inescapable context for all work in the philosophy of religion.

It is our hope that these volumes will provide a resource for critical reflection on fundamental human issues of meaning and value both within academic communities and beyond.

In memory of
Bernard J. F. Lonergan, S.J.

kindly priest, intellectual giant, and pioneer spirit in philosophical theology. A complex and challenging writer, his Institute lectures were nevertheless models of clarity, graced with charm, wit, and, above all, insight.

Acknowledgments

Once again I have the privilege of thanking those who have helped prepare this book. Our authors have been gracious in response to my insistence that clarity and conciseness should be hallmarks of a consistent style in this series. Even extensive revisions were accomplished with a patient cooperation for which I am especially grateful. Irena Makarushka and Rosalind Carey did the first round of copy editing with their usual care and attention to detail, and my Administrative Assistant, Barbara Darling Smith, was once again responsible for final preparation of the manuscript for the publishers. This requires a sure and certain knowledge of everything from Sanskrit diacritical marks to the subtleties of the English subjunctive, and Barbara's happy expertise in these matters is rapidly making her a legend in her own time.

Greg Rockwell reviewed the manuscript for the University of Notre Dame Press, and he and Barbara ironed out the last details before Ann Rice began shepherding it through the actual publication process. Although she must do this on a very tight schedule, since our annual publication party date is fixed before the book ever gets to the printer, Ann's unflappable competence and professionalism are a constant source of reassurance to us all. Beth Preuss and Ellen Akins have been imaginative and tireless in publicizing the series and arranging reviews for the finished book, and we are increasingly grateful to them. Finally, while Jim Langford is only occasionally involved in the detailed process of turning the manuscript into a book, he is a major resource in planning the volumes, offering ideas for future volumes in the series, suggesting names of potential participants, and helping in innumerable ways to make the series widely known. He is an ideal publisher and there is no way to thank him adequately.

Contributors

ELIOT DEUTSCH is Professor of Philosophy at the University of
Hawaii and Editor of *Philosophy East and West*. He studied
at the University of Wisconsin, the University of Chicago, and
Harvard University, receiving his Ph.D. from Columbia University in 1960. As a Faculty Fellow of the American Institute
of Indian Studies, he studied in India 1963–64. He has also
been the New York State Faculty Scholar in International
Studies (1965–67), and Senior Fellow of the National Endowment for the Humanities (1973–74). Among his many guest
lectureships are those at the University of Chicago, the University of London, Lucknow University, Oxford University,
and Harvard University. His books include: *Advaita Vedānta*:
A Philosophical Reconstruction (1969); *Humanity and Divinity*: *An Essay in Comparative Metaphysics* (1970); *On Truth*:
An Ontological Theory (1979); and *Personhood, Creativity,
and Freedom* (1982).

J. N. FINDLAY is University Professor and Borden Parker Bowne
Professor of Philosophy at Boston University. He has studied
at Transvaal University College, South Africa; and at Balliol
College, Oxford. His doctorate is from the University of Graz,
Austria, in 1933. Professor Findlay has written numerous
books, including *Meinong's Theory of Objects* (1933), *Hegel*:
A Reexamination (1958), *Values and Intentions* (1961), two
series of Gifford Lectures entitled *The Discipline of the Cave*
(1966) and *The Transcendence of the Cave* (1967), *Ascent to
the Absolute* (1970), *Plato: The Written and Unwritten Doctrines* (1974), and *Kant and the Transcendental Object* (1981).

Professor Findlay is a Fellow of the British Academy and of the American Academy of Arts and Sciences.

ANTONY FLEW is Professor of Philosophy at York University. He was Professor of Philosophy at the University of Reading from 1973 to 1982 and Professor of Philosophy at the University of Keele from 1954 to 1971. He is the author of *A New Approach to Psychical Research* (1953), *Hume's Philosophy of Belief* (1961), *God and Philosophy* (1966), *Evolutionary Ethics* (1967), *An Introduction to Western Philosophy* (1971), *Crime or Disease?* (1973), *God, Freedom, and Immortality* (1984), *God: A Critical Enquiry* (1984), and other books. In addition, he has edited *Malthus: An Essay on the Principle of Population* (1971) and various philosophical anthologies, including (with Alasdair MacIntyre) *New Essays in Philosophical Theology* (1955). His university study was at Oxford University, where he received the M.A. (1949); Keele University awarded him a D.Litt. in 1974.

LANGDON GILKEY studied at Harvard University (A.B.) and at Union Theological Seminary/Columbia University (A.M., Ph.D.). He is Shailer Mathews Professor of Theology at the University of Chicago, where he has taught since 1963. His many theological books include *Maker of Heaven and Earth* (1959), *Naming the Whirlwind: The Renewal of God-Language* (1969), *Religion and the Scientific Future* (1970), *Reaping the Whirlwind: A Christian Interpretation of History* (1977), and *Society and the Sacred: Towards a Theology of Culture in Decline* (1981). He has also written *Shantung Compound* (1968) about his experience as a Japanese prisoner in Shantung Province, China, during World War II. He received a Fulbright Scholarship, a Guggenheim Fellowship, and a Fulbright Teaching Fellowship.

NAOMI R. GOLDENBERG is Associate Professor of Religious Studies at the University of Ottawa, where she has taught since 1977. She is the author of many articles about Jungian theory, Freudian theory, and feminism, and of the following books: *Changing of the Gods: Feminism and the End of Traditional Religions* (1971), *The End of God: Important Directions for a Feminist Critique of Religion in the Works of Sigmund Freud and Carl Jung* (1982), and *Psychoanalysis, Feminism, and the Perception of Body* (forthcoming). Professor Goldenberg has studied at Douglass College, Princeton University (B.A.), C. G. Jung Institute in Zurich, Switzerland, and Yale University (M.A., M.Phil., Ph.D.).

CHARLES HARTSHORNE is a Fellow of the American Academy of Arts and Sciences. Educated at Harvard, he received his Ph.D. there in 1923. Honorary degrees have been conferred on him by Haverford College (1967), Emory University (1969), Episcopal Seminary of the Southwest (1977), and the University of Louvain, Belgium (1978). Professor Hartshorne is the author of over four hundred articles and his books include *The Philosophy and Psychology of Sensation* (1934); *The Divine Relativity* (1948); *Reality as Social Process* (1953); *The Logic of Perfection* (1962), for which he won the Lecomte du Noüy Award; and *Aquinas to Whitehead: Seven Centuries of Metaphysics of Religion* (1976). He is also the editor (with Paul Weiss) of *The Collected Papers of Charles S. Peirce*.

GORDON D. KAUFMAN is the author of *Relativism, Knowledge, and Faith* (1960), *Systematic Theology: A Historicist Perspective* (1968, 1978), *God the Problem* (1972), *An Essay on Theological Method* (1975, 1979), *The Theological Imagination: Constructing the Concept of God* (1981), and other books. He received the A.B. degree from Bethel College (Kansas), an M.A. in sociology from Northwestern University, and the B.D. and Ph.D. in philosophical theology from Yale University. He has taught at Harvard University since 1963 and has been Edward Mallinckrodt, Jr., Professor of Divinity there since 1969. The recipient of a Fulbright Fellowship and a Guggenheim Fellowship, he has been Visiting Professor at the United Theological College in Bangalore, India (1976–77) and at Doshisha University in Kyoto, Japan (1983).

JÜRGEN MOLTMANN was educated at the University of Göttingen where he received his Ph.D. in 1955 and his Habilitation in 1957. He is also the recipient of several honorary degrees and the Elba Library Prize. He is Professor of Systematic Theology at the University of Tübingen. Among his many books are *Theology of Hope* (1967), *The Crucified God* (1974), *The Church in the Power of the Spirit* (1977), *The Future of Creation* (1979), *The Trinity and the Kingdom* (1981), and *On Human Dignity: Political Theology and Ethics* (1984).

KAI NIELSEN is Professor of Philosophy at the University of Calgary, where he has taught since 1970. Prior to that he taught at Amherst College and New York University. He is the author of numerous reviews and essays, and is coeditor of *Philosophy and Political Action*. His books include: *Contemporary Critiques of Religion* (1971), *Reason and Practice, Ethics without God* (1973), and *An Introduction to the Philosophy of Religion* (1982). He received his Ph.D. degree in philosophy from Duke University.

WOLFHART PANNENBERG is Professor of Theology at the University of Munich. He edited *Revelation as History* (1968). Among his many books which have appeared in English are *Theology and the Kingdom of God* (1969), *Basic Questions in Theology*, 2 vols. (1970), *The Idea of God and Human Freedom* (1973), *Jesus, God and Man* (1977), *Theology and the Philosophy of Science* (1977), *Human Nature, Election, and History* (1977), *Faith and Reality* (1977), *Ethics* (1981), *The Church* (1983), and *Christian Spirituality* (1983).

LEROY S. ROUNER is Professor of Philosophical Theology at Boston University, Director of the Institute for Philosophy and

Religion, and general editor of Boston University Studies in Philosophy and Religion. He graduated from Harvard College (A.B., 1953), Union Theological Seminary (B.D., *summa cum laude*, 1958), and Columbia University (Ph.D., 1961). He was Assistant Professor of Philosophy and Theology at the United Theological College, Bangalore, India, from 1961 to 1966. He is editor of the Hocking Festschrift, *Philosophy, Religion, and the Coming World Civilization* (1969), and (with John Howie) of *The Wisdom of William Ernest Hocking* (1978), as well as author of *Within Human Experience: The Philosophy of William Ernest Hocking* (1969) and *Return Home in Peace: The Christian Contribution to a World Community* (forthcoming). He was Visiting Professor of Philosophy at the University of Hawaii in 1982.

NINIAN SMART, Honorary Professor of Religious Studies at the University of Lancaster and Professor of Religious Studies at the University of California at Santa Barbara, was born in England and educated at Queen's College, Oxford. In 1968 he was awarded an honorary doctorate from Loyola University in Chicago. He has taught at London University and was the H. G. Wood Professor of Theology at Birmingham University. Professor Smart has written and reviewed extensively for numerous journals, and his books include: *Reasons and Faiths* (1958), *Philosophers and Religious Truth* (1964, 1969), *The Religious Experience of Mankind* (1969, 1976), *Beyond Ideology: Religion and the Future of Western Civilization* (1981 — these were the Gifford Lectures), and *World Views: Cross-Cultural Explorations of Human Beliefs*. He has also served as editorial consultant for the British Broadcasting Company's television series *The Long Search*.

CORNEL WEST received the A.B. from Harvard College (*magna cum laude*, 1973) and the M.A. and Ph.D. from Princeton University (1975, 1980). He has authored *Prophesy Deliverance! An Afro-American Revolutionary Christianity* (1982) as well as many articles on Marxist theory, Afro-American experience, Nietzsche studies, and revolutionary theory. He is Associate Professor of Philosophy of Religion at Yale University. Prior to going to Yale in 1984 Professor West taught philosophy of religion at Union Theological Seminary, as Assistant Professor and then Associate Professor on the Endowment of the Marcellus Hartley Professorship of Philosophy of Religion.

Introduction

LEROY S. ROUNER

DO WE KNOW GOD, or do we only feel God's presence? The distinction between idea and feeling has been critical for the philosophy of religion. Unlike the psychology or sociology of religion, the philosophy of religion must defend the idea of God in the philosophical marketplace of ideas. If the transcendent is available only through feeling, or sense, or awareness, and not through ideas, then a philosophy of religion is not possible.

As an academic discipline, the philosophy of religion is the product of the European Enlightenment, where the humanistic Greek notion of reason had been refined and sharpened into the modern scientific notion of logical rationality. When David Hume wrote his *Dialogues Concerning Natural Religion* and Immanuel Kant proposed to view *Religion within the Bounds of Reason Alone*, they were no longer thinking of reason in Aristotelian terms as the human capacity to discover the hidden but inherent intelligibility in life's various processes. For Hume and Kant modern scientific thinking had grounded the notion of truth in logical consistency and empirical fact. And their logical categories — especially the idea of an *idea* — were more in tune with Plato than with Aristotle. Plato, influenced by Pythagoras, used the immaculate purity of number as his model for idea, and the process of mathematical figuring as the ultimate form of reason. Aristotle, on the other hand, was more biologist than mathematician; more interested in the development of living things than in the purity of mathematical relationships. The father of pragmatists and problem solvers everywhere, Aristotle had functional and developmental models for his idea of an idea. And reasoning, for him, was less a pure form of mathematical *figuring* than it was a living process of *figuring out* the reasons why things are as they are.

1

Since its modern inception the philosophy of religion has been defensive. It must prove that the idea of God, and the religious ways of knowing that idea, are philosophically legitimate, in a philosophical climate which makes that task especially difficult. Religion is always a passionate business, and any idea of God devoid of feeling for God might win grudging admiration from scientific philosophers but could not win recognition from religious believers. In fact, most of our major philosophers of religion, from Hume and Kant to James and Royce, have been more than a little ambivalent about their personal religious beliefs. The defensive struggle continues, and both Antony Flew and Kai Nielsen represent long-standing criticisms of the philosophy of religion. However, that particular conversation has many fewer participants than it did when Flew and Alasdair MacIntyre published their influential *New Essays in Philosophical Theology* some thirty years ago. As Cornel West points out, analytical philosophy has lost much of its earlier influence. Further, the reexamination of scientific method popularized in Thomas Kuhn's book *The Structure of Scientific Revolutions* shows scientific ideas and scientific reasoning to be less pristine and more historically influenced than had once been thought. What West calls the "historicist turn" in philosophy of religion is paralleled by the recognition of growth, development, and change in the philosophy and history of science. At the same time, philosophies of culture are newly confronted by bewildering varieties in our rapidly shrinking global village. The threat of atomic holocaust lends moral urgency to a method of understanding which will do justice to the distinctive differences among the various controlling cultural conceptions of God, person, truth, community, the good life, and so forth. It also sharpens the need to understand various ways in which different peoples think about these fundamental ideas. The result has been a philosophic turn toward the ragged dynamics of experience, and away from the clean structure of pure concepts. Aristotle's biocentric agenda now comes to the forefront of much contemporary philosophy of religion.

This is not to say that the changeless and absolute are now irrelevant, or that pluralism and relativism are necessarily answers to our fundamental human questions about the reality of God and the meaning of life. Charles Hartshorne and Wolfhart Pannenberg both argue that philosophies of science, culture, and religion all require grounding in concepts which are historically and culturally adaptive precisely because they continue to be self-consistent. The botanist's discovery of a new variety of tree enhances, but does not negate, the essential notion of tree-ness. So with the philosophy of religion. Gordon Kaufman's reconception of God for a nuclear age, for example, still requires an essential notion of God in order for his reconception to be comprehensible. What is new in this philosophic turn toward the ragged dynamics of history and cultural pluralism is a refusal to live with the old conceptual dichotomy between idea and feeling and the personal schizophrenia of a stated philosophy which cannot articulate private belief. Kai Nielsen's passionate atheism and Jürgen Moltmann's passionate Christian faith both witness to this philosophic turn. Hume's combination of Calvinism and skepticism is no longer honorable. Philosophy of religion is in search of a new integrity.

But this is not to say that philosophy of religion must become theology, taking its point of departure uncritically from a tradition of faith and doctrine which is off limits to skeptical philosophical questioning. The philosophical agenda is unchanged. The theory of knowledge, which is our focus here, still concerns the nature of ideas and the process by which we know the things we most need to know. But our authors tend toward a reconception of basic concepts and a reexamination of the knowing process as historically dynamic, focusing on our experience of cultural and religious pluralism. Naomi Goldenberg's feminist concern for a psychoanalytic theory of the body as knower; Ninian Smart's conjoining of genuine knowledge with actual uncertainty; and John Findlay's exploration of the varieties of religious knowing are all contributions in this direction.

An especially vivid example of renewed confidence and seriousness in the philosophy of religion is Eliot Deutsch's "Knowing Religiously" with which we begin Part One, on "The Nature of Religious Knowledge." I have used the title of his paper as the title for the book because it embodies the new turn in religious philosophy. Eschewing the old defensiveness, he argues that aesthetic and religious considerations are not peripheral to philosophy but are at the heart of the philosophic enterprise. In the past, issues such as causality and the nature of language have been primary, and then applied to problems of aesthetics and the philosophy of religion. Deutsch goes at it the other way around. "If we can understand creativity, we might then be able to understand causality; if we can understand what religious language is, we will then be able to understand better what a proposition is." His basic thesis is one William James would have found sympathetic. Our most fundamental experience of knowing comes not when we have clarified the cognitive status of specific concepts. It is not factual or formal or strategic or praxis-oriented. "Knowing religiously" is not a skill; it does not grasp empirical truth or logical rules and systems. It does not conceive strategies or achieve goals. Knowing religiously is an attentiveness to one's world in the spirit of what Aristotle called philosophic wonder. This fundamental awareness is not subject/object-bound, and it conjoins idea with feeling in the knowing process. For Deutsch, religious knowledge is not characterized by its object but by the style and manner of knowing which involves wonder, openness, insight, and love. It is the key to human creativity because it transforms ordinary knowledge and leads to the kind of "unknowing knowing" which is necessary for the direction of creative instinct.

Knowing religiously is nonegocentric. Whereas most modern Western epistemologies present individual minds hard at work grasping and shaping sense impression to structure concepts and create knowledge, Deutsch turns to Śaṁkara and the Hindu philosophy of Advaita Vedānta for a realization of the simplicity of being, once we stop setting our ego over against its world of objects. When one adds care or concern to this nonegocentric approach to experience, the thinking process becomes liberated for creative imagination which is as much a form of play as it is work. Deutsch also turns to the Chinese tradition to argue that truth and the nature of language are both dependent upon the personhood of the knower, at least in those utterances arising from the liberated creativity of knowing religiously.

Cornel West is less radical than Deutsch. He focuses on developments in recent American philosophy. Whereas Deutsch presents a universal epistemology drawing on Indian and Chinese as well as Western sources, West finds his place in a specific national tradition. He argues, however, that in the philosophy of religion no other national philosophical tradition compares with the outpouring of American philosophy of religion from William James's book *The Varieties of Religious Experience* in 1902 to Edgar Sheffield Brightman's work *A Philosophy of Religion* in 1940. That outpouring served to challenge the subjectivism of European philosophy and its assumption that philosophical reflection begins inside the heads of individual thinkers. Pragmatism, especially, promoted an intersubjectivity which emphasized the social and communal character of knowledge. But the Golden Age of American philosophy of religion was cut short by the increasing professionalization of philosophy and the rise of logical positivism. West laments that, in recent years, philosophy in America has lost touch with its own tradition.

West sees a resurgence of American philosophy, however, resulting from the criticisms which Quine, Goodman, and Sellars made of the three fundamental tenets of logical positivism. Those were: that truth and meaning are characteristics of individual, isolated sentences; that sentences about physical objects are properly reduced to sentences about sense data; and that the meaning of a sentence can be verified only if there is observable empirical evidence for its claim. Quine countered the first of these assertions with his insistence that it is systems of sentences — that is, theories — which are the basic units of empirical significance. Goodman countered the second by noting the theory-laden character of all observation, thus making the positivist's reduction impossible. And Sellars condemned the empiricist grounding of knowledge claims by denying that any such given foundation could properly precede the actual process of logical exploration. These developments have opened up the possibility of a historicist philosophy of religion which can recapture the experiential focus of the Golden Age. West argues that a historicist view must strengthen the moral content of philosophy's social and cultural criticism and engage various religious world views, in order to understand human experience more fully and to transform the structures of human oppression.

Charles Hartshorne has been a major figure in the later years of the Golden Age in American philosophy of religion which Cornel West celebrates. While best known as a process philosopher in the tradition of Whitehead, Hartshorne has been much influenced by C. S. Peirce and has been a student of scientific logic.

His major study of the ontological argument for the existence of God, *The Logic of Perfection*, proposed a form of that argument which can withstand criticism. The ontological argument has long been the classical test for philosophy of religion, and the fact that so many philosophers of religion have been unable to accept the argument as valid has contributed to the turn toward experience, history, and culture in current philosophies of religion. Hartshorne has stood his ground, however, persuaded that the logic of religious philosophy was better than most of its practitioners realized. Like Eliot Deutsch, he is much interested in Asian philosophy; unlike Deutsch, however, he has not adopted the holism of much Eastern thought but continues to refine the classical categories of traditional Western religious epistemology. He does come close to Deutsch in many of his refinements. He begins, for example, by arguing that all knowledge is either empirical or a priori (metaphysical). Later, however, he admits that truths about God are neither exclusively empirical nor exclusively metaphysical although the metaphysical aspect has priority. He notes, wryly, "The biblical saying 'The heavens declare the glory of God' was written by a believer whose belief was not derived from the heavens." The manner in which the metaphysical is apprehended here is not altogether unlike Deutsch's "knowing religiously," but Hartshorne says little about that.

After reviewing some of the fundamental arguments of his neoclassical theism, Hartshorne declares that his favorite arguments for belief in God are the argument from order and the argument from the rational aim, or what rational beings could reasonably accept as the final purpose of their existence. His view requires not an absolute order but one where the risks of conflict are justified by the opportunities for harmony. The argument concerning the rational aim notes that individuals are fragments of reality and that God as the coherence of the whole of things makes it possible for us to understand how there can be meaning and order in our fragmentary existence.

Hartshorne quotes John Findlay on several occasions in his essay, and Findlay's own essay reveals their common commitment to traditional conceptions of reason and its logical tasks. While Hartshorne's style is spare, even skeletal, Findlay never sits down to write without his robust wit engaged. And Findlay entertains a rational mysticism which occasionally puts him more in touch with Deutsch's understanding of how we know religiously than it does with Hartshorne's less transcendental logic. Findlay regards religion as a basic human enterprise on the same level as science, aesthetics, politics, and other rational human enterprises. While he acknowledges that there is much in religion which has been bad, he regards the good in religion as the supreme achievement of our value consciousness. He is persuaded that religious ideas and feelings are conjoined. Values, Findlay tells us, are rationally validated by "the fact that we always feel ourselves to be one among others, that our inner life always spills over and informs the acts and gestures of others, and that we can only be conscious of ourselves and our needs and aversions in a context of actual or possible others." Here Findlay makes common cause with Cornel West and American pragmatism.

Findlay also echoes Deutsch's call for nonegocentric approaches to philosophy of religion when he argues that "we and our emotional-practical orientations become mere values of variables for which any emotional-practical subject could be substituted." Here Findlay's Neoplatonism and Deutsch's empathy for Advaita Vedānta join hands. But Findlay's approach to the ultimate is thoroughly rationalistic, in contrast to Deutsch's humanism, and here Findlay renews his bonds with Hartshorne. The philosophic validation of religion depends on the "category in which we must put the object of religion." But after much rumination, Findlay chooses to put this category "*hors Catégorie*, as they say of very good French hotels." Both Saint Thomas and Hegel, whom Findlay regards as chief among Western theologians, argue that the conceptual category for God is beyond all other categories of human reason. This emphasis moves Findlay's philosophy toward a rational mysticism.

Findlay confesses that his own philosophy of religion "has patches of Upanishadic and Buddhistic and Neoplatonic influences to weave into it." He insists that the philosophy of religion is itself part of religious knowing, so there can be no radical distinction between philosophic method and personal religious belief. Our universities still harbor philosophers of religion who find the religious phenomenon "interesting" yet who are not, themselves, religiously interested, but Findlay is not among them.

We conclude this section with Ninian Smart's intriguing assertion that knowing religiously includes knowing some things that are uncertain. He begins with a paradox: nothing seems more certain than faith or more compelling than religious experience, yet nothing seems less certain than any one belief system, since there are so many vital and serious alternatives. Smart proposes a "soft epistemology" in dealing with religious matters, but it is not relativistic, in spite of his openness to the truth claims of various religious traditions. He argues that we can have reason to believe in one world view rather than another. Any knowledge of the ultimate is necessarily fragmentary, but Smart argues that this is nevertheless a real fragment of a real ultimate. Smart also rejects absolutism as well, since we have no basis for asserting that one world view is exclusively and comprehensively true. What the fundamental resources of religious insight — revelation, reason, and religious experience — do give us is a reasonable basis for the claim that a particular world view is as true a one as can be found, and better than others. The appropriate epistemological stance in a religiously pluralistic situation is therefore what Smart calls a "soft nonrelativism."

Charles Hartshorne continues to explore a "hard epistemology," but Deutsch and West are clearly on the side of an epistemology which takes its categories more from interpersonal, historic, and aesthetic experience than from the canons of the hard physical sciences, and this is part of what Smart means with his soft epistemology. Findlay's system, like Hartshorne's, is not "soft" in Smart's sense, because he does not understand his fundamental concepts and arguments to be only approximations of truth. Like Hartshorne, Findlay is persuaded that it is possible to know some things definitely and for sure. Smart's extensive examination of various world religious traditions has led him to think in terms of more and less. His epistemology must be soft because we get closest to the truth when we know how to weight a certain argument or idea in relation to others, but that weighting can never be more than approximate, and the results never absolutely certain.

With Kai Nielsen and Antony Flew we begin our Part Two, "Religious Truth Claims Reconsidered," and we are back in the world of hard epistemologies and the traditional criticisms of religious philosophy. Ninan Smart noted that the fundamental sources of religious insight are revelation, reason, and religious experience. Nielsen begins with the observation that reason and religious experience no longer weigh heavily as proofs for God. Very few philosophers are defending the classical rational proofs, and the appeal to religious experience, while not quite dead, is seldom used to establish the existence of God as an objective supernatural fact. So Nielsen is persuaded that the relevant argument with religious believers is over the philosophical status of revelation and the validity of the religious philosophy based on it. He calls this philosophy fideism and takes Alasdair MacIntyre's *Difficulties in Christian Belief* as a clear and forceful defense of it. The nub of that argument is that the freedom to accept or reject God would be vitiated by logical proofs of God's existence. For Nielsen, such religious belief cannot be validated by demonstrative knowledge and has neither metaphysical nor epistemological foundations. Nevertheless, he observes, lots of people want to live that way, separating head from heart with a leap of religious faith. His question is whether there is good reason for everyone doing so, and his answer is no.

Hartshorne has already touched on the question whether life can have meaning apart from religious faith, and that question comes up later in Pannenberg's essay. Nielsen focuses first on the foundations of morality. Does the believer have a way of understanding and justifying moral action which the atheist does not have? He offers a close examination of this question and concludes that the believer does not. His second question is whether the believer's hope for eternal life makes life on earth more meaningful. His concluding pages are a personal answer to this question. Distinguishing between wishes, which can be for anything, and hopes, which must involve some conception of hoped-for possibility, Nielsen admits that he sometimes does wish that he could live forever, but he does not hope for this because he knows it to be fanciful and therefore distracting from the important issues of living. He ends with the warning that fideists should not assume that all atheists are tortured souls yearning for the absolute, or that fideists have deeper and more humane resources for nonevasive reflection about the human condition.

Antony Flew's philosophical stance is not unlike Nielsen's in his criticism of religious truth claims. He begins his essay on "The

Burden of Proof" with Descartes's view that philosophy must challenge current theological belief. Descartes had argued that successful response to such a challenge would require adequate reasons for holding theological belief, and for the superiority of this belief over different and often contradictory ones. Flew's thesis is that philosophy ought to presume atheism, and that the burden of proof is therefore on the argument for God. Atheism, as Flew uses the term, is not the view that there is no God. It is simply a view which does not include belief in God. In this sense, the theist is not asked to overcome criticisms of theism so much as he or she is asked to build a case for God from the ground up.

Flew defends his well-known demand that religious statements be verified. Any proposition must be equal to the negation of its own negation, and it is here that he finds theism garbled. His famous critical question asks simply, "What would have to occur, or to have occurred, to constitute for you a disproof of the love of, or of the existence of, God?" Those who respond that religious truth claims do not concern matters of fact, Flew brands as heretics; and those who insist that he present a theory of meaning before attacking particular questions of significance he repudiates on the ground that we could never then test whether any theory was adequate to the facts it was supposed to explain. True to the spirit of his definition of atheism, Flew is not concerned to disprove the theistic claim. The burden of his essay "The Burden of Proof" is to lay the ground rules for a theistic statement which could possibly meet Descartes's two criteria for successful response to the philosophic presumption of atheism.

With Naomi Goldenberg's essay on "The Body of Knowledge" we move to a rather different criticism of traditional religious ideas. She is not concerned with the logic of theological propositions. Her interest is in the effect of religious ideas on what she calls "strategies for living." Because she opposes mechanism as dehumanizing, and because she interprets transcendent notions of the saving God as a machine fantasy (Deus ex machina), she rejects the notion of a transcendent godhead. She looks, instead, for a salvific religious message in psychoanalysis and feminism. The effect of theology's mechanistic notion of God has been a rejection of the human body. Goldenberg argues that the body is a rich resource for an optimistic view of human possibility. Theology illustrates the way a patriarchal society splits mind from body and celebrates mind as knower. Goldenberg's thesis is that the body has its own distinctive knowledge.

Psychoanalysis is a resource because it finds intellect, morality, and aesthetic sensibility all grounded in bodily sources. Is this reductionism itself dehumanizing? Goldenberg responds that psychoanalysis has actually elevated the body by granting it all the qualities which most Western philosophy reserves for the mind. Freud's notion of the unconscious is not a mental notion but a somatic one. The body, for Freud, is the complex context of all experience. She suggests this notion of the body as matrix of human cognition is necessary if contemporary philosophy is to foster respect for life. Later in her essay, however, she admits that psychoanalysis has a small, esoteric audience and is not in a position to influence intellectual life the way feminism is. Feminism and psychoanalysis are both philosophies of sexuality, and hence both are led back to the body. Goldenberg calls for a rationality which is rooted in emotion, and here she joins with Deutsch, West, Findlay, and Smart, in conjoining idea and feeling in contemporary philosophy, even though hers is a materialist criticism of the philosophy of religion.

Gordon Kaufman's "Reconceiving God for a Nuclear Age" criticizes traditional conceptions of God from within the Christian tradition. He is motivated by a moral concern for human survival and a growing awareness of religious and cultural pluralism. Unlike Smart, however, who is trying to clarify categories for interreligious conversation, Kaufman is trying to restructure Christian theology itself in the light of new historical demands. While his essay makes some radical proposals, his method honors the traditional Christian concern for discovering what God is doing in history and continually recasting doctrine in the light of these ongoing discoveries. Kaufman's theology is an "imaginative construction" of the notions of God, world, and humankind in order to provide significant orientation for contemporary life. The principal criteria for this constructive work are the relativizing and humanizing functions of an ultimate: relativizing because every finite thing has its being relative to the ultimate, and humanizing because God as ultimate creates and cares for the world and all its creatures.

Since biological evolution and historical development are the conditions under which human life has been humanized and relativized, it is from these sources, Kaufman argues, that we must take our metaphors and images for God. There has been a creativity working in and through both history and biology which has made life distinctively human, and this creativity is the reality which Kaufman calls God. But if God is only the creativity at work in the world, why speak of God at all? Here Kaufman argues, as Hartshorne was not quite willing to do, that God is necessary for life to have meaning. Here Kaufman and Nielsen are totally at odds. Kaufman insists that "*God* is that of which above all else we must be aware, and that to which above all else we must attend, if in our conscious reflection and in our action we are to be properly oriented in life and in the world." Nuclear holocaust would be a disaster for God as well as for humankind. For Kaufman, devotion to God means taking full accountability for the continuance of life on earth.

Kaufman's essay leads us readily into our final section on "Philosophy of Religion and Contemporary Culture," beginning with Wolfhart Pannenberg's study of meaninglessness in the modern world. Pannenberg's essay is, in effect, a detailed response, not only to Kai Nielsen's atheism and Naomi Goldenberg's materialism, but also to Charles Hartshorne's view that the idea of God does not make life meaningful but rather makes us understand how life is meaningful. Pannenberg begins by asking whether meaning is something we construct, in somewhat the way Kaufman argues that we construct the notion of God, or is meaning a reality which we discover? Put baldly, is meaning subjective or objective? As a paradigm case Pannenberg explores the philosophy of language. Since language is a human activity one could argue that linguistic meaning is always a human product. Pannenberg notes, however, that *true* assertions are true in relation to the reality of the asserted state of affairs. The words may be human constructs, but their meaning has been discovered, not bestowed. Following Dilthey, Pannenberg argues that meaning in life is not bestowed by a human subject but results from the relationship of life's momentary experiences to the whole of the life context. And siding with both Schleiermacher and Tillich, Pannenberg notes that all individual meaning is conditioned by a context of meaning which in turn rests on an unconditioned ground of meaning. Tillich noted that this unconditioned ground of meaning only becomes an explicit topic for the religious consciousness.

Referring to his book on *Theology and the Philosophy of Science*, Pannenberg recapitulates an argument first stated in that volume, that the religious consciousness deals explicitly with the totality of meaning implicit in all everyday experience. Here he finds common ground with Kaufman in asserting that religious traditions must prove themselves by integrating the relations of meaning in everyday experience with an encompassing context which grounds it, or, as Kaufman would say, symbolizes it. Finally, Pannenberg notes that the question of meaning is inseparable from the question of truth. While warning against the dangers of human presumption in enquiring into the meaning of the whole of reality, Pannenberg nevertheless defends the question as theologically legitimate. God is distinct from human subjectivity, but the concept of God always comes also as an answer to the question of the meaning of reality as a whole. Here Pannenberg seems more ready than Kaufman to affirm the objective reality of a God who is distinct even from the constructive imagination of theologians.

Langdon Gilkey takes us from general theoretical and methodological considerations to the creationist controversy as it was argued in the Arkansas courts in 1981. Gilkey shares Kaufman's fear that religious fanaticism and scientific destructive know-how may lead to atomic holocaust. He is also clearly fascinated with what this case revealed (he was a participant) about the complex relations among various kinds of religion and various kinds of science in our advanced scientific culture. His initial example of this complexity and confusion is that those arguing for teaching biblical literalism as creation science were largely natural scientists with advanced degrees holding tenured positions in reputable universities, while those opposed to teaching the Bible as creation science were largely church groups, clergy, and ministerial associations. He also notes that science is now thoroughly established as queen of our contemporary culture, in much the same role that theology occupied in the high Middle Ages. Dominance of this sort means power, and an inevitable issue is the misuse of power. In this case, the misuse has been in the way science has used the teaching of science to identify scientific knowledge with total knowledge. Creationism, as he understands it, has a measure of legitimacy as a reaction to this dismissal of religion as primitive, prescientific, and false. (Readers of volume six in this series, *On Nature*, will remember Huston's Smith's "Two Evolutions" in which he made the same point.)

Because science influences every level of our culture, popular science now appears in myriad forms in much the same way that popular religion takes on local, age-old, often deviant or bizarre, syncretistic forms in a culture where a given religious tradition has been long established. Gilkey notes that different cultures with different ideologies incorporate science and technology in different ways. Khomeini's Iran may yet prove to be the most bizarre of all. "Surely we cannot be so naive as to think that the vast number of Sunni and Shi'ite students at our technological and engineering schools will return to their lands to reproduce there MIT and the Charles River Basin rather than to help create an *Islamic* form of modern culture and so of science." Our liberal understanding of science and technology reveals itself not as a guaranteed or necessary form of scientific culture but as only one option developed by the liberal ideology of the European Enlightenment.

Gilkey notes the persistence of religion in a scientific culture, especially in times of trouble when new anxieties have arisen, not despite our scientific culture but because of it. Religious fundamentalism is an inevitable response. The destructive dangers of a science which has done us so much good are matched by the fanatical dangers of a religion which has also done us much good. Gilkey's message is that the uses of science depend on the character and intentions of its users, and that we are dependent on their moral and spiritual capacities. Unless religion and science unite in reasonable and humane ways they will unite as partners in disintegration.

My own essay on Tillich's philosophy of religion returns to the search for common ground among the world's religious believers, with their conflicting truth claims. Eliot Deutsch proposes a nondualistic religious metaphysics which unites transcendentalist elements from India, China, and the West with common aesthetic insights and common human concerns. He focuses on the process of knowing religiously, however, rather than on the objective reality of the transcendent. Wolfhart Pannenberg uses the existential quest for a meaningful life to establish the cultural relevance of Christianity's revelation of God in Christ. I have argued that the nondualism which informs religious philosophies such as Deutsch's, and the qualified dualism which informs religious philosophies such as Pannenberg's, are the two fundamental metaphysical options for any philosophy of religion, and that Tillich's attempt to integrate them represents a significant contribution to interreligious understanding. I have argued further that both of these perspectives are grounded in common human experience, so that this intercultural issue is reflected in any philosophy of religion which takes experience seriously. As an illustration of the problem I have taken Whitehead's engaging statement of perplexity: "Sometimes I think that I am in the world; and sometimes I think that the world is in me." Put in traditional philosophical terms, this is a conflict between an objective natural realism and subjective idealism.

I have focused on Tillich's doctrine of the Fall for several reasons. With atomic holocaust threatening us all, each religion owes us all its best account of what it is in humankind that makes monumental evil possible. The Christian doctrine of sin, however, is probably the most controversial issue in interreligious dialogue. Hinduism, Buddhism, Taoism, and Confucianism have differences among themselves, but they are unanimous in rejecting the Christian doctrine of sin. Most importantly, however, Tillich's account of what he calls the transition from essence to existence is a particularly vivid illustration of his attempt to conjoin naturalism and idealism, or a qualified dualism with a nondual understanding of God as Being Itself. Tillich rejects the idealistic reading of the Fall, which reduces it to the difference between the ideal and the real, where reality points to the ideal and the Fall is not a genuine break between the realms of essence and existence but an imperfect fulfillment of essence in existence. But Tillich also rejects the realistic meaning of the Fall in which humankind has no predicament. In this reading evil is not a problem of human responsibility but simply a fact of existence. Tillich proposes a "half-way demythologization of the Fall" in which the "moment" of creation, the transition from essence to existence, is also the "moment" of Fall, the transition from "dreaming innocence" to the awareness of sin.

We conclude with Jürgen Moltmann's essay on Ernst Bloch, the Marxist and Jewish philosopher whose philosophy of hope is set within an overarching perspective of messianism. As a Christian theologian whose theology of hope has had considerable impact, Moltmann finds Bloch a particular challenge to Jewish and Christian theology. Bloch's work *The Principle of Hope* (1959) offers a messianic interpretation of the great religions. His key phrase is, "Where hope is, there is religion." But Bloch is ambivalent. The opposite is also valid: "Where hope is, there is atheism," since atheism criticizes religion in this same spirit of messianic expectation, the "human-eschatological, in which a messianism ready to explode is set." Bloch's messianism is aimed at utopia, but the utopias of history, of scientific socialism, are only partial. His "totum of utopia" is not a real-world social or political utopia. This notion is so central to his thought that Moltmann regards him as "not just a metaphysician, but also a metaethicist, metasocialist, metareligionist." Bloch's atheism, like Marx's, is a functional criticism of religion, not a criticism of the essence of the religious. Had experience shown that belief in God had actually helped liberate people from poverty then this functional criticism would not have been necessary. Moltmann clearly regards Bloch's atheism as a prophetic criticism with serious religious concern.

But Moltmann is also mindful of the cost of messianism. Bloch's absorption with the "totum of utopia" is subject to the same weakness which Gershom Scholem noted in his tract on "The Messianic Idea in Judaism." That weakness is that dreams of the future drain off energy for living in the present. Moltmann comments that "the messianic idea has the weakness of the preliminary and provisional which does not give of itself, but preserves itself, which cannot die because it refuses to live." Bloch's philosophical messianism puts the world in a state of suspension, and Moltmann presses his criticism. In such a situation every word remains open, every thought remains fluid. The core of existence cannot be defined because it is yet to appear. Where does the conclusive, the non-evasive, the ability to die, come into this continually preliminary-because-hopeful messianic life and thought? This, for Moltmann, is the philosophical significance of Christ's death on the cross. "There is then no transcending of hope without the paradoxical counter-movement of the incarnation of love, no breaking out to new horizons without the sacrifice of life, no anticipating of the future without first investing in it."

As the philosophy of religion moves away from the tight logical constraints of analytical philosophy and the tight professional constraints of ever-narrowing departmentalization, it runs the risk of becoming conceptually amorphous and logically sloppy. Ninian Smart, for example, retains the blessed gift of clarity which has been the glory of British empiricism and was an awesome feature of logical positivism, but he would be the first to admit that a "soft epistemology" is fraught with philosophical dangers. Nevertheless, he runs that risk in what seems to me a good cause which he shares with a number of our authors. Here I should point out that they were invited to participate in the Institute's program because of their distinction and diversity, not because they represented a particular school of thought. But there are two features of their essays, taken collectively, which seem to me significant for the future of the philosophy of religion.

The first of these—the "good cause" which Smart and others serve—is a focus on the fundamental experiences of contemporary life. Moral concern, social awareness, aesthetic sensibility, human feeling, care; these are evident in the work of both theists and nontheists, and signal a new energy and seriousness in the discipline. The Golden Age of American philosophy of religion was influential in American life because its philosophy had this same concern with fundamental issues of human experience.

The second feature follows from the first. If philosophy of religion is to concern itself once again with a philosophical analysis of contemporary human experience in its religious depth, then its practitioners may well include those from other academic departments who share its concerns and accept its disciplines. This may lead to looser conceptualization, softer logic, and a blurring of academic fields, but the result will be a new vitality and relevance which is already evident in the essays before you.

PART I

The Nature of
Religious Knowledge

1

Knowing Religiously

ELIOT DEUTSCH

IN HIS VERY KIND letter inviting me to participate in the Institute program this year Professor Rouner asked that I weave into my paper some autobiographical statements concerning how and why I developed the position set forth there and — that by working, as I have further been asked to do, in an intercultural framework — to indicate some of the sources of my views in various traditions.

Like many other philosophers in what William James once referred to as the "tender-minded" (Platonic) tradition, as opposed to the hard-headed, "tough-minded," empirical (Aristotelian) tradition, I have been uneasy about the conspicuous absence of the religious spirit in so much of twentieth-century philosophy. The obsessive concern for solid facts, technical subtlety, and explanatory certainty, the search for *the* method of philosophy, whether analytic or phenomenological, as though knowledge and truth were to be had like pressing buttons on a machine, betrays not only a lack of confidence in the potentialities of the creative human spirit but a view of the world that deprives that world of what is most valuable in it. I believe that philosophy has its greatest natural kinship with those spiritual activities like art and religion that address our deepest concerns and give expression to the most valuable aesthetic and ethical features of the world. This belief has motivated and informed my interest in non-Western as well as Western traditions, for it seems clear to me that human experience is not the exclusive possession of that small and historically limited phenomenon which we call Western civilization. The great traditions of Asian thought have much to teach us in dealing both with technical philosophical matters in areas such

21

as ontology and epistemology and with the larger issues of the spirit.

In my own philosophy I have tried to work in an unself-conscious, spontaneous way from the background of both Western and non-Western traditions and in what I would like to think is a religious spirit. I have tried to see how aesthetic and religious experience, rather than being peripheral areas that one turns to after one has done one's real work, can be brought into the very center of philosophy. If one can begin to understand the deepest, richest, and most valuable of our experiences, one can then go a long way toward understanding other issues. If we can understand creativity, we might then be able to understand causality; if we can understand what religious language is, we will then be able to understand better what a proposition is; if we can understand what it means to achieve freedom of consciousness, we can understand what free will means, and so on.

I begin, then, with a quotation from that wonderful California-Cambridge philosopher Josiah Royce, who combined a kind of East-West of the times and who, in his work *The Religious Aspect of Philosophy*, wrote: "Deliberately insincere, dishonest thinking is downright blasphemy."[1]

Most often today discussion and analysis of the so-called problem of religious knowledge is concerned to determine such things as the cognitive status of religious language, the criteria for the truth of religious claims, the definition of religious belief, and the nature of religious symbolism. It seems to me that underlying them is a more basic, primordial, experiential situation — one that makes possible a dynamic bringing together of knowledge and religion — and it is that experiential situation which I am calling "knowing religiously." My general thesis is that religious knowledge doesn't so much have a distinctive or special object as it has a unique style or manner. Knowing religiously, I shall argue, is a reverential knowing that is centered in reality. It involves wonder, openness, insight, and love; it brings about a transformation of our ordinary knowledge and the achievement of a kind of "unknowing knowing" that issues in a liberated creativity.

I propose to proffer a rather concise description or characterization of "knowing religiously"; and for the sake of clarity I will present this characterization in ideal terms, realizing of course that it is something to which we only approximate in our actual experience. I will conclude the paper with some reflections on the problem of truth as it relates to this activity. I will argue that the criterion for the truth of utterances originating from knowing religiously has to do in an important way with the personhood of the (religious) knower.

I

Before presenting the descriptive characterization, however, it might be useful to relate what I am calling "knowing religiously" with other kinds of knowing in order to see, in a preliminary and rather elementary way, what it is not. Without going into elaborate or technical detail we can, I think, recognize clearly enough the meaningfulness of distinguishing between the following: factual knowing, praxis knowing, formal knowing, and strategic knowing. These are not placed in any hierarchy and are not, of course, intended to exhaust all possible kinds of knowing. In the actual world these modes overlap, intertwine, and mesh together in a variety of complex ways.

By "factual knowing" I mean simply a "knowing *what*" (like knowing the name of the capital of Brazil). Factual knowing is a public, learned, empirical, fact-oriented knowing; the sort of knowing that one can easily be tested on, for it is a kind of possession. Knowing religiously, it will be entirely evident, is not a having of a special kind of factual understanding. When knowing religiously the knower is not in any special position to announce empirical truths.

"Praxis knowing" is knowing *how* to do something or other (like knowing how to drive a car). Most praxis knowing is also learned behavior, the acquiring of certain bodily-mental skills that enable one to perform various tasks. Although knowing religiously does involve discipline and always issues in a kind of action it is not itself a praxis knowing. It doesn't reduce essentially to a skill; it cannot be taught as such; it cannot be practiced simply in a habitual way.

Neither does it involve formal principles as such. By "formal knowing" I mean a kind of "knowing *that*" (like knowing that if

$A > B$ and $B > C$ then $A > C$). Formal knowing involves rules, systems, principles. It is that mode of knowing, of reaching conclusions, that is usually taken as the paradigm of rational knowing. Now although there is nothing irrational or illogical about knowing religiously, it is clearly not itself to be placed within a category of formal knowing. Knowing religiously is not a knowing that can be carried out simply by any rational mind who has mastered various semantic and syntactic principles.

Lastly, knowing religiously is not to be identified with what I have called "strategic knowing," by which I mean a "knowing *if*" (like knowing if I move my rook three places forward I should be able to capture your queen in five moves). Strategic knowing involves a grasping of causal connections, a manipulation of objects and situations; it involves the ability to predict, to control, to seize upon opportunities, and so on. Knowing religiously, as we will see, in contrast to this, does not intend the achievement of some specific goal or the realization of some particular purpose. It is not a knowing directed toward the satisfaction of an immediate need or desire, or the resolution of what Dewey was so fond of calling a "problematic situation."

Knowing religiously is thus different in kind from these more ordinary modes of knowing and has a distinctive character of its own.

Aristotle, as we know, spoke of wonder as the impetus to philosophy. Today, with our passion for those bits and pieces of knowledge that we call information, we have reduced wonder to curiosity. Educators constantly tell their students that they should be curious about this or that — but not that they should stand in wonderment. By *wonder* I mean essentially an openness, a "letting be" in the profound sense in which Heidegger used the expression. To wonder means to acknowledge fully the mystery of being. To be in wonderment does not mean, though, that one stands unequally in awe before some overpowering reality or being (that would be a kind of astonishment); to be in wonderment means that one attends freely in consciousness to a reality to which one feels one belongs. I don't so much wonder *at* something as *with* something. In wonderment one feels a kinship with the being of that wonderful thing.

To wonder requires, then, a kind of nonegoistic availing of

self. When obsessed with oneself, one is alienated from being. Withdrawn, one is simply not available to what is.

Knowing religiously is then first of all a concentrated attentiveness — an open sensitivity to, a belonging with, being. And it also involves, I believe, an insight into the utter simplicity of being.

This is not the occasion to elaborate an ontology or metaphysics, but it should be noted that one of the conditions for knowing religiously is precisely the realization of the utter simplicity of being. By this I mean a non-subject/object-bound awareness of reality. Now there have been many ways in which this awareness has been analyzed and understood in diverse philosophical and religious traditions. I have found that one of the most interesting ways to understand the nature of this insight into the simplicity of being is to be had in the analysis of ignorance (*avidyā, ajñāna*) put forward in the classical Indian system of Advaita Vedānta.[2]

According to Advaita Vedānta, what stands in the way of our having an insight into reality and an adequate self-knowledge is a fundamental and pervasive confounding of self and world which is of our own making. We incessantly — and, according to Śaṁkara, the leading exponent of Advaita, quite naturally — misidentify ourselves, wrongly attributing to ourselves characteristics which properly belong to the nonself and attributing to the nonself qualities which properly belong to ourselves. In our ordinary ego-based consciousness we "superimpose" (*adhyāsa*) attributes of the nonself onto the self and of the self onto the nonself. Śaṁkara writes:

> It is a matter not requiring any proof that the object and the subject, whose respective spheres are the notion of the 'Thou' (the Non-Ego) and the Ego, and which are opposed to each other as much as darkness and light are, cannot be identified. All the less can their respective attributes be identified. Hence it follows that it is wrong to superimpose upon the subject — whose Self is intelligence, and which has for its sphere the Ego — the object whose sphere is the notion of the Non-Ego, and the attributes of the object; and vice versa to superimpose the subject and the attributes of the subject on the object. In spite of this it is on the part of man a natural procedure. . . .[3]

> This superimposition thus defined, learned men consider
> to be Nescience (*avidyā*), and the ascertainment of the true
> nature of that which is (the Self) by means of the discrimi-
> nation of that (which is superimposed on the Self) they call
> knowledge (*vidyā*).[4]

For example:

> Extra-personal attributes are superimposed on the Self,
> if a man considers himself sound and entire, or the contrary,
> as long as his wife, children, and so on are sound and entire
> or not. Attributes of the body are superimposed on the Self,
> if a man thinks of himself (his Self) as stout, lean, fair, as stand-
> ing, walking, or jumping. . . .[5]

In other words, we quite naturally misidentify ourselves by
wrongly mixing ourselves up as "subjects" with a world taken to
be entirely constituted by diverse "objects." We scatter ourselves,
as it were, about the world, and then come to believe that its limitations are our own. To know religiously, to gain insight into the
simplicity of being, requires that we put aside that complexity and
recollect ourselves, recovering then the silence which is at the core
of our being. We must, the advaitin says, desuperimpose ourselves
from the world and realize its profound oneness. This, of course,
demands a great deal of hard mental work, for we need to dis-
criminate away all those misidentifications of self, such as that I
am my body, or my mental capacities, or my willing, emotional
nature. Advaita Vedānta insists that it requires a complete mental-
spiritual discipline which it calls *jñāna-yoga*. This discipline of
mental concentration and discrimination is said to yield that non-
subject/object-bound awareness of reality.

But something more is needed, I believe, for "knowing religiously"— and that is care or concern. In more traditional language
we might call it simply love. In the *Bhagavad-gītā*, Kṛṣṇa, the incarnate Lord, instructs Arjuna that the one who realizes one's own
true self will at the same time achieve the highest love or devotion.

> Having become Brahman, tranquil in the Self, he neither
> grieves nor desires. Regarding all beings as equal, he attains
> supreme devotion to Me (8.54).

Knowing religiously involves the whole person in his or her belonging with reality. The openness, the insight that we have briefly spoken of, must be thoroughly informed by love. The religious knower is not, in other words, an indifferent observer or collector of facts. Nor is the religious knower what Josiah Royce called a "theoretic knower" who wants knowledge whatever it may turn out to be; he or she is rather one who, as Royce says, wants to know the value of the truths being sought. Religious philosophy, he writes, "wants to know what in the world is worthy of worship as the good."[6] When one knows something religiously, I submit, one celebrates or affirms the thing for what it is in the fulness of its reality. One loves the being of the thing, but not as it is an object for possession or consumption; one reveres the thing as the thing that it is.

With love, knowing then becomes a kind of power — not in the coercive sense but, if I may so call it, in a transformative sense. In knowing religiously there is brought forth a fundamental change in the confidence we otherwise enjoy in the categories of our ordinary thinking and knowing, in particular in those time/space-bound, classifying, explanatory propensities of "rationality." In knowing religiously there is a transformation of ordinary knowing in virtue of the realization, in loving, insightful wonderment, of that which is incommensurable with that ordinary knowing. Simplicity is not the opposite of complexity, as it obtains at an entirely different level of being. In other words, knowing religiously is not just another kind of knowing to be set alongside other kinds, of the sort previously identified; rather it is radically different in kind from them. It opens up entirely new dimensions of being.

For this reason, in what is surely one of its highest forms, it is often referred to as a kind of unknowing. In the *Kena Upaniṣad* (2.3) it is said:

> To whomsoever it [Brahman] is not known, to him it is known: to whomsoever it is known, he does not know. It is not understood by those who understand it; it is understood by those who do not understand it.[7]

And from Meister Eckhart we hear that

> one must achieve this unself-consciousness by means of transformed knowledge. This *ignorance* does not come from lack

of knowledge, but rather it is from knowledge that we may achieve this ignorance.[8]

Knowing religiously is a kind of ignorance, a "learned ignorance," as Nicholas of Cusa called it. It is the ignorance of the wise, one which is free from all pretense. It is a knowing which is devoid of a distinctive subject matter — a knowing, however, which as part of its nature issues in a liberated creativity. By a "liberated creativity" in the context of knowing religiously, I mean a disciplined spontaneity which gives rise to a meaningful utterance that is in its own way right for itself.

Many theories of creativity in both philosophy and psychology lay stress on the self-expressive character of the creative act. Still largely under the influence of romanticism, these theories look to the creative agent as he or she embodies and expresses a unique imaginative force as the central focus for understanding creativity. The popular image of the artist as an inspired half-mad libertarian betrays this romantic notion. But this is surely an extremely naive understanding of creativity. Without having to deny that the creative process, especially in the arts, often has its roots in the shadowy recesses of one's being, we can nevertheless see how creativity at its best is a highly disciplined activity wherein the individual, isolated self, rather than being the heart and soul of the activity, turns itself over, as it were, to what is being created.

A creative person works with the material of the medium. He or she is neither a passive responder nor a forceful imposer. "Working with" implies a full cooperation, a controlling intelligence directing and, in turn, being directed by the medium — be it wood, stone, or words. I have argued elsewhere that genuine creativity always exhibits an immanent purposiveness, that "aiming at the fulfillment of only those ends which it itself defines and articulates, the creative act answers to no other guiding need or external *telos*. Its purpose is developed in the process itself; which is to say, a sense of rightness or appropriateness, within the context of the particular creative act, governs the artist's bringing his work to fulfillment or completion."[9] Creativity, then, requires discipline: the ordering of relations so as to achieve form. And it also requires spontaneity or freedom in action. Spontaneity is different from impulsiveness; for unlike impulsiveness, where one is a victim of the strongest force within one, spontaneity is a free bringing forth of one's essential nature as an expression of creative power.

Creativity at its best, then, or what I am calling in the context of knowing religiously a liberated creativity, is a non-self-obsessed sensitivity which allows a person to engage in thinking as a kind of play — not as a frivolous jumping about, but as a spontaneous activity that is carried out joyfully for its own sake. A liberated creativity is not a knowledge-gathering activity for the achieving of something else (for example, control over nature); it is rather a natural expression of that powerful harmony that obtains between the creative person and his or her world. A liberated creativity, with respect to thinking and utterance, is then as much a listening as it is a speaking. The listening is to and with that silence of being which is at the core of knowing religiously. It is a listening to and with that silence which provides a ground for all meaningful utterance and which thoroughly informs what is said.

It is not so much then a matter of "whatever is knowable is sayable," as that what is known religiously is always said in a manner entirely appropriate to it. In fact, we would have to go so far as to say that the manner of saying in knowing religiously is part and parcel of what is known. We don't, in other words, have two distinct acts, a knowing-act and a saying-act; rather the knowing and saying are part of the same creative activity. It is not that X knows Y and could then communicate, express, utter Y in a variety of different ways (as is the case to a considerable extent with simple empirical assertions); when X knows Y religiously the mode of utterance is inseparable from that which is known.

As a liberated creativity, knowing religiously is very much like poetry then in this, that its formed content is always a unique presentation, the particular how and what of speech being as-one. It is unlike poetry, though, insofar as whereas the poet may through the power of imagination create "character voices" that are not strictly speaking his or her own (for example, Shakespeare with his innumerable characters), the religious knower will always be present in the utterance. It will always reflect the knower's state of being. This is the case because that utterance is part and parcel of immediate experience. The utterance, in other words, is an integral part of the experience of the knower and will accordingly embody the degree to which he or she has achieved openness, sensitivity, insight. These are as much qualities of being as they are features of experience. Knowing religiously always culminates in expressive, insightful utterance — utterance which is inseparable from the knowing and which exhibits the state of the knower. And it is this which further distinguishes knowing religiously from pure intuition, which need not culminate in anything beyond itself. The religious knower is centered in reality, but does not simply remain there. One's knowing, one's experience, one's very being requires articulation.

II

This brings us to the problem of truth as it relates to knowing religiously. I want to argue for what will undoubtedly appear at first to be an outlandish thesis, one that goes entirely against the grain of modern epistemology, and that is that the criterion for the truth of statements originating from knowing religiously has always to do in an important way with the quality of personhood of the knower.[10] This means that the more genuine the person, the greater will be the truth-value of what he or she says, relative to knowing religiously. The latter qualification is needed, for I am not claiming that this variable truth value pertains to all forms of assertive utterance. If it is raining now outside, the statement "It is raining now" is not more or less true depending upon the quality of the person who utters it. Its meaning, as most of us now agree, might very well depend upon what the speaker intends by the utterance. One might, for example, intend it as a warning rather than as a simple factual assertion. It might even be used as a code for some entirely different kind of meaning. Its truth, however, is independent of the character of who says it.

But let us suppose that Joe Jones, an extremely unregenerate student of religious studies, were to utter "All is one" as an appropriate answer to some academic question asked by his professor. Let us further suppose that this utterance, taken propositionally, happens to convey a profound insight into reality (uttered, as it has been, by not a few sages in history). Is it not the case that in virtue of Joe Jones being the agent of the utterance the statement is not-true — or, at the least, that it cannot rightfully be taken as a statement in the first place? Or take a sentence like *tat tvam asi*, "Thou art that," one of the great *mahāvākyas* or "great sayings" of Vedānta which asserts the identity of the self and reality (*ātman* and Brahman). Is it not more or less true depending upon who says it, when, and in what manner? If the philosopher-sage utters *tat tvam asi* from the full authority of personal experience and achieved being to a well-prepared disciple, it means something very different from, say, if students in a course in Indian philosophy were asked on an examination to give an example of one of the *mahāvākyas* of Vedānta and answered *tat tvam asi*. Their answer might be correct, but it would not — if taken propositionally — be a truthful statement. Uninitiated students know not whereof they speak.

With our passion for the so-called objective and impersonal character of truth we still no doubt find this objectionable, if not downright unintelligible. But most of us are willing to accept the idea that meaning is closely related to a speaker's intention, and that the kind of utterance delivered reflects that intention. Meaning does not reside simply in the statement itself, a sentence oftentimes not involving a statement at all in its primary use or illocutionary force. If illiterate drunkard Ed Brown just before falling into a deep stupor were to utter "$E = MC^2$," we would not assume that he was in fact asserting something about the relation of energy and matter. We would, I gather, assume rather that he was mouthing some expression that he might have heard elsewhere, that he was just sounding off. We do indeed often assume that some relation obtains between who says what (in what context) in determining the meaning of what is said. I want to take this a step further and claim that with certain kinds of utterance, namely those arising from the liberated creativity of knowing religiously, the criterion for truth has to do with the quality of the personhood of the knower. We may look to a speaker's intention to determine partly the *meaning* of what is said. We may, I believe, look to the knower's being to determine partly the *truth* of what is said when what the speaker says issues from knowing religiously.

This is the case because with utterance which is an integral part of knowing religiously we don't in the first place look at some alleged isolable content of the utterance (the mere "what" that is said) in order to determine its truth. Rather, we respond to the utterance as precisely the utterance it is in the full richness of its nature. This nature, as we have seen, is a formed content (the "how" and "what" that is said being inseparable), and will necessarily embody the qualities of the being of the speaker. "Style is the person," it is often said, and the rightness of a style is grounded in the being of the person. One's religious language is thoroughly informed by who one is as a person; the manner of its utterance inescapably discloses the personhood of the speaker, the degree to which he or she is a consummate person who exhibits a loving sensitivity and has achieved freedom in being and in action.

In other words, when we respond to the utterance in the full richness of its nature we invariably respond as well to the person who utters it. We are attracted or repulsed to what amounts to an utterer's utterance as a conjoined entity. We recognize its rightness, if it possesses it, in terms of the quality of the knower as this is made evident in the utterance.[11]

The thinking, the utterance which derives from the liberated creativity of knowing religiously is not, then, concerned with making factual claims as such. Although there might be an assertive dimension present, its fundamental intentionality is that of speaking *with* reality, not *at* it. It is a speaking from the very being of the person.

This is a rather familiar position in Chinese philosophy, and so we might profitably look there for further elucidation. Confucianism in particular insists that moral utterance is true only insofar as it is spoken "sincerely." The concept of *sincerity* (*ch'eng*) is a very profound one in Confucian thought and points to the whole being (*jen*) of a person. It is not thus reducible to simple "honesty." In the *Chung-yung* or the *Doctrine of the Mean*, one of the major works of ancient Confucian literature, it is said:

> Sincerity (*ch'eng*) is the Way of Heaven. To think how to be sincere is the Way of man. He who is sincere is one who hits upon what is right without effort and apprehends without thinking.[12]

Tu Wei-Ming notes that the English word "sincere" does not encompass the many-leveled meanings of *ch'eng* and that the word in fact is often translated as "true." D. C. Lau, he notes, renders *ch'eng* as "true" in his translation of *Mencius*. Wing-tsit Chan likewise sometimes renders *ch'eng* as "true" in his translation of *Chung-yung*. In any event, as Tu Wei-Ming also observes:

> Whether it is translated as "true" or "sincere," *ch'eng* definitely points to a human reality which is not only the basis of self-knowledge but also the ground of man's identification with Heaven. [13]

And further:

> *Ch'eng* symbolizes not only what a person in an ultimate sense ought to be but what a person in a concrete way can eventually become. [14]

Confucianism thus clearly recognizes the intimate relationship that obtains between the quality of the person in realizing the supreme virtue of *jen* and the "truth" of knowing at the deepest levels of one's being. In the *Doctrine of the Mean* it is said that

> as there is sincerity, there will be its expression. As it is expressed, it will become conspicuous. As it becomes conspicuous, it will become clear. As it becomes clear, it will move others. As it moves others, it changes them. As it changes them, it transforms them. Only those who are absolutely sincere can transform others. [15]

This passage suggests one further point about the truth of religious language, and one which also fits well into the framework of contemporary speech-act philosophy of language, and that is the importance of the hearer or listener in determining the truth value of what is said. Although there is something irresistible about the language that issues from knowing religiously, its having a kind of compelling authority, a qualified hearer is clearly essential for recognizing and determining its truth. And this is hardly surprising. "One who has ears may listen" is stated in many cultures: only one who is properly receptive will be able to respond fully to what is said.

Knowing religiously, we might thus say, is in the final analysis a social or communal act. The religious knower does not know for his or her own sake alone, as it were, but finds the consummation of experience as that experience is taken up and embraced by others. A formed content is a form *for* someone; it does not stand isolated in a rarefied, pristine space. Knowing religiously intends to be shared; it fulfills itself as it moves, changes, and transforms others.

I have dealt with a very large topic and I have, of course, been able to treat it here in only a very brief and fragmentary way. My main goal was to try to articulate a special mode of knowing, which I have called knowing religiously, which differs in many significant ways from other modes of knowing. It is *sui generis*, but it is not in conflict with these other ways. It has no special subject matter of its own and it is not a way of knowing that admits of a formula or a recipe. The best one can do, I think, is to characterize it in a broad phenomenological way as having a certain style or manner which involves wonder, openness, insight, and love. It is a manner which brings about that transformation alluded to in Confucian philosophy and issues in what I have called a liberated creativity, a disciplined spontaneity. The creativity and the knowing are of a piece. Necessarily it is the experience of a person who is reflected in that which is uttered from the experience. The truth, then, of this kind of religious language will bear an intimate relationship to the character of the speaker. It will be true to the degree to which the speaker has achieved a loving sensitivity and that freedom of consciousness which is the truth of personhood.

NOTES

1. Josiah Royce, *The Religious Aspect of Philosophy* (1885; reprint ed., New York: Harper & Brothers, 1958), p. 7.
2. Advaita Vedānta is the nondualistic (*a-dvaita*) system of orthodox Indian philosophy which has had the largest influence in the Hindu tradition and which bases itself primarily on the ancient *Upaniṣads*. It remains today as one of the most important systems for contemporary Indian thinkers.

3. Śaṁkara, *Brahmasūtrabhāṣya*, trans. George Thibaut, *The Vedānta-sūtras with the Commentary of Śankarācharya*, vol. 35 of *The Sacred Books of the East*, ed. Max Muller (Oxford: Clarendon Press, 1890), p. 3.

4. Ibid., p. 6.

5. Ibid., pp. 8–9.

6. Royce, *Religious Aspect of Philosophy*, p. 8.

7. Sarvepalli Radhakrishnan, trans., *The Principal Upaniṣads* (New York: Harper & Brothers, 1953).

8. Meister Eckhart, *Meister Eckhart*, trans. Raymond B. Blakney (New York: Harper & Brothers, 1941), p. 107.

9. Eliot Deutsch, *Personhood, Creativity, and Freedom* (Honolulu: University of Hawaii Press, 1982), pp. 69–74.

10. See ibid., chap. 1, for a fuller discussion of what it means to achieve personhood.

11. It is interesting to note that the opposite of truth in knowing religiously is thus not falsity as such, but inauthenticity, pretense, insincerity.

12. Tu Wei-Ming, *Centrality and Commonality: An Essay on Chung-yung*, Society for Asian and Comparative Philosophy no. 3 (Honolulu: University Press of Hawaii, 1976), p. 107.

13. Ibid., p. 109. The character *ch'eng*, I am told by my colleague Roger T. Ames, is constituted of "to speak" and "to complete, to realize," and therefore suggests "to realize that which is spoken."

14. Ibid., p. 122.

15. Wing-tsit Chan, ed., *A Source Book of Chinese Philosophy* (Princeton: Princeton University Press, 1963), p. 108.

2

The Historicist Turn in Philosophy of Religion

CORNEL WEST

> From the disintegration of Hegelianism derives
> the beginning of a new cultural process, different
> in character from its predecessors, a process in
> which practical movement and theoretical thought
> are united (or are trying to unite through a strug-
> gle that is both theoretical and practical). . . . Out
> of the critique of Hegelianism arose modern ideal-
> ism and the philosophy of praxis. Hegelian imma-
> nentism becomes historicism, but it is absolute
> historicism only with the philosophy of praxis.
> . . . One should not be surprised if this beginning
> arises from the convergence of various elements,
> apparently heterogeneous. . . . Indeed it is worth
> noting that such an overthrow could not but have
> connections with religion.
> —Antonio Gramsci, *Prison Notebooks*

IN THE PAST FEW DECADES philosophy of religion has suffered decline as a discipline. The synoptic vision of Edgar Sheffield Brightman, the tough-minded empiricism of Henry Nelson Wieman, and
the magisterial metaphysics of Alfred North Whitehead are now
distant memories for present-day participants in this discipline.
In this essay I shall sketch a brief account of this decline and, more
important, suggest a new conception of philosophy of religion which
warrants serious attention. This new conception promotes a historicist turn in philosophy of religion which remains within yet deepens
the American grain — empirical, pluralist, pragmatic, and activist.[1]

The Golden Age of philosophy of religion

The Enlightenment critiques of religious thought — such as David Hume's *Dialogues concerning Natural Religion* and Immanuel Kant's chapter on "The Ideal of Pure Reason" in his *Critique of Pure Reason* — set the terms for the modern philosophical debate concerning the status of religious beliefs. These terms accepted the subjectivist turn which puts philosophical reflection first and foremost within the immediate awareness or self-consciousness. Undergirded by the rising authority of science — with its probabilistic reasoning and fallibilistic conclusions — post-Humean and post-Kantian philosophers of religion were forced either to give up or to redefine the scientific character of religious beliefs and thereby to conceptually redescribe such beliefs in moral, affective, aesthetic, or existential terms. In other words, one became a neo-Kantian, Schleiermachean, Hegelian, or Kierkegaardian. Whether such descriptions yielded epistemic status to religious beliefs became the question for modern philosophy of religion.

Yet this question was not the central issue for the masters of European philosophy in the late nineteenth century. Karl Marx, John Stuart Mill, and Friedrich Nietzsche were obsessed primarily with the nature of modern science and the character of modern society and culture. Modern theologians were preoccupied with the epistemic status of religious beliefs but this preoccupation signified their marginality in European intellectual life.

In stark contrast to their European counterparts, religious concerns loomed large in the first significant American philosophical response to modernity. The first generation of American pragmatists, especially Charles Peirce and William James, attempted not only to demythologize modern science but also to update religion. For American pragmatists, religious beliefs were not simply practical postulates for moral behavior, pietistic modes of self-consciousness, pictorial representations of absolute knowledge, or anxiety-ridden, self-involving choices. Religious beliefs were on the same spectrum as any other beliefs — always linked to experience. The pragmatism of Peirce and James incredibly seized the imagination of a whole generation of American philosophers, including idealist philosophers like Josiah Royce, William Ernest Hocking, and Edgar Sheffield Brightman — thereby initiating the

Golden Age of philosophy of religion in modern Euro-American thought.

Nowhere in the modern world did philosophers take religion more seriously than in the United States between 1900 and 1940. No other national philosophical tradition compares with the set of American texts such as William James's book *The Varieties of Religious Experience* (1902), John Elof Boodin's *Truth and Reality* (1911), William Ernest Hocking's work *The Meaning of God in Human Experience* (1912), Josiah Royce's text *The Problem of Christianity* (1913), Douglas Clyde MacIntosh's *Theology as an Empirical Science* (1919), Henry Nelson Wieman's *Religious Experience and Scientific Method* (1926), Alfred North Whitehead's *Process and Reality* (1929), Shailer Mathews's book *The Growth of the Idea of God* (1931), John Dewey's work *A Common Faith* (1934), and Edgar Sheffield Brightman's text *A Philosophy of Religion* (1940).

There are complex sociological and historical reasons which account for this phenomenon. My basic point is simply that for the first four decades of this century most of the major American philosophers were philosophers of religion and that the Golden Age of philosophy of religion in the modern West was primarily an American affair.

This American predominance in philosophy of religion produced profound philosophical breakthroughs. First, major American philosophers, starting with Peirce, radically questioned the subjectivist turn in philosophy. They attacked the notion that philosophical reflection begins within the inner chambers of mental episodes. American pragmatists promoted an intersubjectivist turn which highlighted the communal and social character of acquiring knowledge. American process philosophers accented a primordial form of experience, for example, causal efficacy, which disclosed the often overlooked interpretive and abstract status of sense perception.

These two diverse critiques of the fundamental starting point for European Enlightenment philosophy undermined the relational framework of mind-objects-God. The pragmatists' move led toward a focus on the social practices — from verification procedures to communal values — which produce knowledge about minds, objects, and God. The process strategy yielded a new complicated

vocabulary which rejected lines of demarcation between consciousness, world, and the divine. Furthermore, the legacies of both pragmatic and process thought reclaimed the epistemic and scientific
status of religious beliefs as well as their practical value. In short,
the major movements in the Golden Age of philosophy of religion
undercut the three basic pillars of modern European philosophy.

The distinctive feature of the most influential American philosophies of religion — pragmatism and process thought — is that
they defend religious experience and beliefs under the banners of
radical empiricism, open-ended pragmatism, and ethical activism. Radical empiricism tries to stay in tune with the complex plu-
rality and fluid multiplicity of experience on the individual and
corporate levels. Open-ended pragmatism accentuates the various
problems which motivate logical inquiry and reflective intelligence.
Ethical activism links human responsibility and action to the purposeful solving of problems in the personal, cultural, ideological,
political, economic, and ecological spheres of human and natural
activities. In this sense, the major American philosophers prior to
World War II did not succumb to the secular insularity of their
European counterparts; nor did they cater to the irrational im-
pulses of parochial religious and ideological thinkers. Their plebeian
humanism — more democratic than Matthew Arnold's bourgeois
humanism and more individualistic than Marx's revolutionary
humanism — encouraged them to view sympathetically though critically the lives of common people and hence take religion seriously
in their sophisticated philosophical reflection.

The decline of philosophy of religion

As I noted earlier, the Golden Age of philosophy of religion
is long past. The flowering of American philosophy — with its deep
religious concerns — was cut short. The political and military crisis in Europe resulted in intellectual émigrés to the United States
who changed the academic discipline of philosophy. This change
was inextricably bound to the increasing professionalization of the
discipline of philosophy.

The advent of logical positivism — with its diverse versions of
atomism, reductionism, and narrow empiricism — put an end to
the Golden Age of philosophy of religion. This Viennese-style posi-

tivism, though popularized in America by A. J. Ayer's *Language, Truth, and Logic* (1936), brought with it all the old European Enlightenment baggage pragmatism and process thought had discredited: the subjectivist starting-point, subject/object relations, and the philosophical trashing of religion. As Dewey's long and languishing star faded in New York and Whitehead's legacy courageously persisted in relative isolation at Chicago, the positivism of Rudolf Carnap, Carl Hempel, and others spread like wildfire throughout elite graduate schools in philosophy — especially Harvard, UCLA, and Minnesota. By the death of Whitehead in 1947, few graduate students in philosophy at the influential schools had heard of Hocking and Brightman, had read Wieman, or had grappled with Whitehead (besides maybe his *Principia Mathematica*). James was deemed a cultural critic who lacked philosophical rigor; Dewey, a mere social activist with scientistic sentiments and fuzzy philosophical meditations. Technical argumentation, logical notation, and rigorous analysis — with their concomitant subfields of logic, epistemology, and methodology in the natural sciences — had seized center stage.

To put it crudely, logical positivism was based on three fundamental assumptions. First, it assumed a form of sentential atomism which correlates isolated sentences with either possible empirical confirmation (as in the sciences), logical necessity (as in mathematics and logic), or emotion (as in ethics, religion, and the arts). Second, it emerged with a kind of phenomenalist reductionism which translates sentences about physical objects into sentences about actual and possible sensations. Third, it presupposed a version of analytical empiricism which holds observational evidence to be the criterion for cognitively meaningful sentences and hence the final court of appeal in determining valid theories about the world. These crucial assumptions, which constitute independent yet interrelated doctrines, were held at various times by the leading logical positivists. More importantly, they were guided by fundamental distinctions between the analytic and the synthetic, the linguistic and the empirical, theory and observation.[2]

The immediate consequence of logical positivism on philosophy of religion was the near collapse of the latter as a serious academic discipline, or even a subfield within philosophy. This consequence had a devastating effect: during the early stages of the professionalization of philosophy after World War II, philosophy of religion had little or no academic legitimacy. Therefore most of those interested in philosophy with religious concerns were forced to study in graduate programs of divinity schools or seminaries such as Yale, Chicago, or Union. Furthermore, since American philosophies of religion also were forms of social and cultural criticism, the near collapse of philosophy of religion was a symptom of the narrow mode of philosophizing promoted by logical positivists. Needless to say, as philosophers had less and less to say about religion, politics, ethics, the arts, and the normative role of science in the world, and more and more to say about analytical sentences, methodological operations in physics, and the reducibility of objects to sense data, the literate populace lost interest in the intellectual activity of philosophers. In other words, philosophy in America was losing touch with American philosophy.

The resurgence of American philosophy

The major tragedy of contemporary philosophy of religion is that the resurgence of American philosophy occurred at the time when most American theologians were being seduced either by the antiphilosophical stance of Karl Barth or by the then fashionable logical positivism and linguistic analysis. The great contributions of W. V. Quine, Nelson Goodman, and Wilfred Sellars which undermined Viennese-style positivism and Oxford-inspired linguistic philosophy were made just as A. J. Ayer, J. L. Austin, and Ludwig Wittgenstein or Karl Barth and Emil Brunner were becoming prominent on the American theological scene. The result of this situation is that Quine, Goodman, and Sellars are relatively alien to most contemporary religious thinkers and that either refined forms of German idealism as with Paul Tillich, heuristic mythological versions of Christianity as in Reinhold Niebuhr, and indigenous updates of process philosophy as in Schubert Ogden and John B. Cobb, Jr., constitute the most significant contributions of philosophy of religion in America after World War II.

The resurgence of American philosophy was enacted by the powerful critiques of logical positivism launched by Quine, Goodman, and Sellars. Quine's epistemological holism which heralded systems of sentences (or theories) as opposed to isolated sentences as the basic units of empirical significance discarded sentential atomism. Furthermore, his methodological monism that rejected the analytic-synthetic distinction rendered unacceptable the positivist classificatory criterion for tautological and meaningful sentences.[3] Goodman's post-empiricist antireductionism highlighted the theory-laden character of observation and undercut the narrow empiricist standard for adjudicating between conflicting theories of the world. And his ontological pluralism relegated the idea of truth to that of fitness and promoted diverse true versions of the world instead of a fixed world and unique truth. He thus called into question the monocosmic naturalism of logical positivism (a radical move which even Quine resisted owing to his ontological allegiance to physics — a lingering trace of positivism in the great critic of positivism!).[4]

Lastly, Sellars's epistemic antifoundationalism precluded any "given" elements as acceptable candidates which serve as the final terminating point for chains of epistemic justification — thereby condemning any form of empiricist grounding of knowledge claims.[5] The Quine-Goodman-Sellars contributions, though related in complex and often conflicting ways and still questionable in some philosophical circles, signify the American takeover of analytical philosophy — a takeover which has led to the demise of analytical philosophy.[6]

The Quine-Goodman-Sellars insights bear striking resemblances to the viewpoints of earlier American pragmatists. The resurgence of American philosophy is, in part, the recovery of the spirit and temper of American pragmatism reflected in Charles Peirce's first rule of reason: Do not block the way of inquiry.[7] Yet this resurgence is silent regarding the status and role of religion (and social and cultural criticism) in philosophical reflection. Contemporary American philosophy is post-analytical philosophy with deep debts to pragmatism yet little interest in religious reflection.

This is so principally because post-analytical philosophy has been preoccupied with the secular priesthood, the sacred institution in modern culture: the scientific community and its practices. Thomas Kuhn's influential book, *The Structure of Scientific Revolutions* (1962), can be viewed as the grand post-analytical philosophical text written for the positivist philistines — the great popularization of the implications of the Quine-Goodman-Sellars contributions for the paradigm of rationality in modern culture, that is, the practices of scientists. Paul Feyerabend, who describes himself as a "church historian," deepens these implications (in the political and ideological spheres) regarding the demystification of scientific method and practices in *Against Method* (1975) and *Science in a Free Society* (1978). In short, the philosophy and history of science function in contemporary American philosophy as did the philosophy and history of religion in the Golden Age of American philosophy. The gain is a more sophisticated dialogue concerning the content and character of rationality in modernity; the loss is a less engaged relation with the wider culture and society.

This situation is exemplified in Richard Rorty's masterful manifesto of American post-analytical philosophy, *Philosophy and the Mirror of Nature* (1979), and Richard Bernstein's learned meditations on the role of philosophy after Rorty in *Beyond Objectivism and Relativism* (1983). Despite their Kuhnian perspectives regarding the social character of rationality, both focus their philosophical concerns almost exclusively on philosophy of science and say nothing about philosophy of religion. And this latter silence is accompanied by a glaring absence of sustained social and cultural criticism. The salutary contributions of Rorty and Bernstein are that (like Hegel and Marx at their best) they make historical consciousness central to their philosophical reflections without falling into the transcendentalist trap of making historical consciousness the new candidate for philosophically grounding knowledge claims (as did Hegel and Marx at their worst). Yet Rorty and Bernstein put forward "thin" historical narratives which rarely dip into the complex world of politics and culture. Both remain seduced by a kind of Lovejoy-like history of ideas far removed from concrete historical processes and realities. "Thick" historical narratives, such as those of Karl Marx, Max Weber, Simone de Beauvoir, W. E. B. Du Bois, and Antonio Gramsci, elude them.

In other words, Rorty and Bernstein hold at arm's length serious tools of social theory and cultural criticism. Presently, Rorty's self-styled neopragmatism — much like Jacques Derrida's poststructuralism — is creating waves in the academy. But these waves remain those of departmental internecine struggles between old-style empiricists and new-style pragmatists, argumentative realists and narrativistic historicists, establishmentarian humanists and professional post-humanists. These noteworthy conflicts within the discipline of philosophy in the academy have yet to spill over into serious cultural and political debates regarding the larger issues of public concern.

The theological discovery of history

While professional philosophers lingered under the spell of the grand Quine-Goodman-Sellars breakthroughs and academic theologians nested in Barthian cocoons or emulated logical positivists and linguistic analysts, liberation theologians discovered history. This discovery did not consist of systematic reflections on historicity, which has been long a priority of German-trained theologians and Heideggerian-influenced philosophers, but rather of linking historical processes in society to political praxis. In this sense the theological discovery of history by Gustavo Gutierrez, Mary Daly, and James Cone was qualitatively different from the recovery of historicism by Richard Rorty and Richard Bernstein.[8] The former was philosophically underdeveloped yet politically engaged and culturally enlightening; the latter, politically and culturally underdeveloped and philosophically enlightening. Gutierrez was responding, in part, to the hegemony of Jacques Maritain's integral humanism among liberal Latin American Catholic elites and the "developmentalism" of U.S. foreign policy which masks corporate interests and Latin American social misery. Daly and Cone were recuperating the experiential and activist dimensions of American thought. The early works of Daly are not simply religious critiques of ecclesiastical and cultural patriarchy; they also explore — at the behest of Whitehead and James — primordial forms of female experience which may empower victims of sexist oppression. Even in her post-Christian texts, these experiential and activist dimensions remain. Similarly, the initial works of Cone are not only sustained diatribes against Euro-American racism; they also probe into the degraded and devalued modes of Afro-American experience that promote and encourage resistance against white supremacist practices. Yet, for many of us, Daly's neo-Thomist metaphysics loomed too large and Cone's Barthian Christocentrism was too thick — and their early one-dimensional social analyses were too parochial.

Notwithstanding their philosophical and social analytical limitations, liberation theologians put historical processes, social analyses, and political praxis at the center of theological discourse in seminaries and divinity schools. Their linking of historical consciousness to present-day political struggles — to anti-imperialist, feminist, and black freedom movements — galvanized new intellectual energies throughout the religious academy. This intellectual upsurge caught many neo-orthodox theologians and liberal philosophers of religion unaware and unequipped to respond adequately. Yet it is no accident that the two major theological responses to liberation theology have come from process theologians: Schubert Ogden's *Faith and Freedom* and John B. Cobb, Jr.'s *Process Thought and Political Theology.*

Just as Rorty and Bernstein's historicism is philosophically groundbreaking yet lacking in serious political substance, Gutierrez, Daly, and Cone's liberation perspectives are theologically groundbreaking yet lacking in serious philosophical substance. For example, Gutierrez's conception of Marxist science is quite positivist, Daly's ontological arguments often slide into mere cathartic assertions, and Cone's religious claims reek of a hermetic fideism. Unfortunately, the nonexistent dialogue between academic philosophers and theologians nearly insures an intellectual estrangement which permits the political insouciance of American neopragmatists and promotes the philosophical insularity of liberation theologians. What is needed is a rapprochement of the philosophical historicism of Rorty and Bernstein and the moral vision, social analysis, and political engagement of the liberation perspectives of Gutierrez, Daly, and Cone.

The present need for the philosophy of religion

American philosophy at its best has taken the form of philosophy of religion. This is so not because philosophy of religion possesses some special privilege or wisdom as a discipline, but rather because of the particular character of American philosophical thought. For complex national reasons, when American philosophers turn their backs on religion, they turn their eyes toward science. This usually results in muting their social and political concerns. My point here is not that American philosophers become religious, but rather that they once again take religion seriously, which also means taking culture and society seriously.

The contemporary tasks of a responsible and sophisticated philosophy of religion are threefold. First, it must deepen the historicist turn in philosophy by building upon the Quine-Goodman-Sellars contributions and "thickening" the "thin" historicism of Rorty and Bernstein's neopragmatism by means of undogmatic social analysis and engaged cultural criticism. Second, it should put forward moral visions and ethical norms which regulate the social analysis and cultural criticism drawn from the best of available religious and secular traditions bequeathed to us from the past. Third, it should scrutinize in a rational manner synoptic world views of various religious and secular traditions in light of their comprehensive grasp of the complexity, multiplicity, and specificity of human experiences and their enabling power to motivate human action for the negation and transformation of structures of oppression.

The historicist turn in philosophy of religion must steer clear of the Scylla of transcendental objectivism and the Charybdis of subjectivist nihilism. My particular version of philosophical historicism is neither the neo-Kantian historicism (à la Wilhelm Dilthey) which presupposes a positivist conception of the *Naturwissenschaften* nor the Popperian-defined historicism that possesses magic powers of social prediction and projection. Rather the historicism I promote is one which understands transient social practices, contingent cultural descriptions, and revisable scientific theories as the subject matter for philosophical reflection. Hence, social analysis and cultural criticism are indispensable components of such reflection.

On the one hand, transcendental objectivism is precluded by rejecting all modes of philosophical reflection which invoke ahistorical quests for certainty and transhistorical searches for foundations — including most realist moves in ontology, foundationalist strategies in epistemology, and mentalistic discourses in philosophical psychology. On the other hand, subjectivist nihilism is avoided by condemning all forms of philosophical activity that devalue and disregard possibilities, potentialities, and alternatives to prevailing practices. Wholesale leveling and trashing of standards, criteria, and principles which facilitate dialogue, conversation, and exchange results from subjectivist nihilism. Such nihilism is not simply parasitic on the failures of transcendental objectivism; it also shuns historical consciousness and thereby remains captive to the subjectivist turn. In this way transcendental objectivism is delusory though not necessarily socially pernicious, whereas subjectivist nihilism is inescapably insidious.

My version of historicism flows from the tradition of mitigated skepticism signified by Sebastian Castellio of Basel, William Chillingworth, and Pascal at the birth of modern conceptions of knowledge and science. It is deepened and enriched by the tempered Pyrrhonism of David Hume, the Hegelian-inspired historicisms of Kierkegaard and Marx, the demystifying perspectivalism of Nietzsche, and the enabling pragmatism of James and Dewey. Like Gadamer, my version of historicism acknowledges the unavoidable character and central role of tradition and prejudice, yet it takes seriously the notion of sound human judgment relative to the most rationally acceptable theories and descriptions of the day. In this way, the historicism I promote is akin to that of Rorty and Bernstein — and especially that of Jeffrey Stout.[9]

My philosophical historicism is inextricably bound to undogmatic social analysis and engaged social criticism, because if one is not nihilistic about history, one must be open to new possibilities, potentialities, and alternatives to present practices. In this view the major role of social analysis and cultural criticism is to understand these practices and discern forces for betterment. Therefore philosophical historicism — if logically consistent and theoretically coherent — leads to "thick" historicism, to social and heterogeneous narratives which account for the present and project a future.

Although social analysis and cultural criticism play central roles in my historicist philosophy of religion, some forms of such analyses and criticisms are not acceptable. Adequate social analyses and cultural critiques must be regulated by moral visions and ethical norms which are ensconced in religious or secular traditions — shot through with their own set of presuppositions, prejudgments, and prejudices. A historicist philosophy of religion is not limited in an a priori manner to religious traditions. Yet in its attempts to take seriously the human dimensions of ultimacy, intimacy, and sociality, it usually incorporates elements from religious traditions.

Secular traditions are indispensable, yet they have had neither the time nor the maturity to bequeath to us potent cultural forms of ultimacy, intimacy, and sociality comparable to older and richer religious traditions.

Acceptable modes of social analysis and cultural criticisms are guided by moral visions and ethical norms which flow from synoptic world views, including such crucial matters as the ideal of what it is to be human, the good society, loving relationships, and other precious conceptions. These world views are to be rationally scrutinized in light of their capacity to illuminate the complexity, multiplicity, and specificity of human experiences and their ability to enable oppositional activity against life-denying forces, be they biological, ecological, political, cultural, or economic forces.

Since I believe that the major life-denying forces in our world are economic exploitation (resulting primarily from the social logic of capital accumulation), state repression (linked to the social logic of state augmentation), bureaucratic domination (owing to the social logic of administrative subordination), racial, sexual, and heterosexual subjugation (due to the social logics of white, male, and heterosexual supremacist practices), and ecological subjection (resulting, in part, from modern values of scientistic manipulation), I entertain a variety of social analyses and cultural critiques which yield not merely one grand synthetic social theory but rather a number of local ones which remain international in scope and historical in content. My general social analytical perspective — deeply neo-Gramscian in spirit — is more influenced by the Marxist tradition than by any other secular tradition, but it also acknowledges the severe limitations of the Marxist tradition. By claiming that the Marxist tradition is indispensable yet inadequate, my social analytical perspective is post-Marxist without being anti-Marxist or pre-Marxist; that is, it incorporates elements from Weberian, racial, feminist, gay, lesbian, and ecological modes of social analysis and cultural criticism.

I arrive at these analyses because the moral vision and ethical norms I accept are derived from the prophetic Christian tradition. I follow the biblical injunction to look at the world through the eyes of its victims and the Christocentric perspective which requires that one see the world through the lens of the Cross — and thereby see our relative victimizing and relative victimization. Since we inhabit different locations on the existential, socioeconomic, cultural, and political scales, our victim status differs, though we all, in some way, suffer. Needless to say, the more multilayered the victimization, the more suffering one undergoes. And given the predominant forms of life-denying forces in the world, the majority of humankind experience thick forms of victimization.

The synoptic vision I accept is a particular kind of prophetic Christian perspective which comprehensively grasps and enables opposition to existential anguish, socioeconomic, cultural, and political oppression, and dogmatic modes of thought and action. I do not believe that this specific version of the prophetic Christian tradition has a monopoly on such insights, capacities, and motivations. Yet I have never been persuaded that there are better traditions than the prophetic Christian one.

My acceptance of the prophetic Christian tradition is rational in that it rests upon good reasons. These reasons are good ones not because they result from logical necessity or conform to transcendental criteria. Rather they are good in that they flow from rational deliberation which perennially scrutinizes my particular tradition in relation to specific problems of dogmatic thought, existential anguish, and societal oppresion.

My reasons may become bad ones. For example, I would give up my allegiance to the prophetic Christian tradition if life-denying forces so fully saturated a situation that all possibility, potentiality, and alternatives were exhausted or if I became convinced that another tradition provides a more acceptable and enabling moral vision, set of ethical norms, and synoptic world view. I need neither metaphysical criteria nor transcendental standards to be persuaded, only historically constituted and situated reasons.

Yet, presently, I remain convinced by the prophetic Christian tradition. Its synoptic vision speaks with insight and power to the multiform character of human existence and to the specificity of the historical modes of human existence. Its moral vision and ethical norms propel human intellectual activity to account for and transform existing forms of dogmatism, oppression, and despair. And the historicist turn in philosophy of religion helps us understand that we are forced to choose, in a rational and critical manner, some set of transient social practices, contingent cultural descriptions, and revisable scientific theories by which to live. This historicist stress on human finitude and human agency fits well, though it does not justify, my Christian faith. And, to put it bluntly, I do hope that the historicist turn in philosophy of religion enriches the prophetic Christian tradition and enables us to work more diligently for a better world.

NOTES

1. For intellectual explorations in the American grain for philosophy and theology, see John E. Smith, *The Spirit of American Philosophy* (New York: Oxford University Press, 1963); and Randolph Crump Miller, *The American Spirit in Theology* (Philadelphia: United Church Press, 1974). A more contemporary expression and examination can be found in John Rajchman and Cornel West, eds., *The New Philosophy: Questions of an American Intellectual Tradition* (New York: Columbia University Press, forthcoming).

2. The major essays on the refinement and rejection of these philosophical distinctions are Carl G. Hempel, "Empiricist Criteria of Cognitive Significance: Problems and Changes" and "The Theoretician's Dilemma: A Study in the Logic of Theory Construction," in his *Aspects of Scientific Explanation and Other Essays in the Philosophy of Science* (New York: Free Press, 1965), pp. 101–22; 173–226.

3. For the persuasive arguments for Quine's epistemological holism and methodological monism, see his classic essay, "Two Dogmas of Empiricism," in his *From a Logical Point of View* (New York: Harper & Row, 1963), pp. 20–46; and his less rigorous personal reflections in "The Pragmatists' Place in Empiricism," in *Pragmatism: Its Sources and Prospects*, ed. Robert J. Mulvaney and Philip M. Zeltner, pp. 23–39.

4. Goodman's post-empiricist antireductionism is best illustrated in his powerful essay, "The Test of Simplicity," and his classic piece, "The Way the World Is," in his *Problems and Projects* (New York: Bobbs-Merrill, 1972), pp. 279–94; 24–32. Goodman's full-fledged ontological pluralism is put forward in his *Ways of Worldmaking* (Indianapolis: Hackett, 1978). For Quine's critique of Goodman, see *Theories and Things* (Cambridge: Harvard University Press, 1981), pp. 96–99.

5. Sellars's classic statement is "Empiricism and the Philosophy of Mind," in *Minnesota Studies in the Philosophy of Science*, vol. 1, ed. Herbert Feigl and Michael Scriven (Minneapolis: University of Minnesota Press, 1956), pp. 253–329.

6. For a more detailed account of this takeover, see Cornel West, "Nietzsche's Prefiguration of Postmodern American Philosophy," *Boundary 2: A Journal of Postmodern Literature*, Special Nietzsche Issue, vol. 9, no. 10 (Spring–Fall 1981): 241–70.

7. C. S. Peirce, *The Collected Papers of Charles Sanders Peirce*, 6 vols., ed. Charles Hartshorne, Paul Weiss, and Arthur Burks (Cambridge: Harvard University Press, 1933–58): 1:135.

8. The texts of liberation theology I have in mind are Gustavo Gutierrez, *A Theology of Liberation*, trans. Sister Caridad Inda and John Eagleson (Maryknoll: Orbis Books, 1973); Mary Daly, *Beyond God the Father* (Boston: Beacon Press, 1973); and James H. Cone, *God of the Oppressed* (New York: Seabury Press, 1975).

9. Jeffrey Stout, *The Flight from Authority* (Notre Dame, Ind.: University of Notre Dame Press, 1981). This important book has yet to receive the attention it deserves.

3

Our Knowledge of God
CHARLES HARTSHORNE

KNOWLEDGE IS OF TWO KINDS, empirical and a priori. *Empirical* I define with Karl Popper as knowledge of the truth of propositions that actual experience to some extent supports or corroborates, though not, if the propositions are general, strictly verifies, but that some conceivable experience would falsify. It is knowledge of truths vulnerable to conceivable observational tests. Such truths are contingent, might have been false. Truths of arithmetic are not such truths, nor are those of formal logic. A third class of nonempirical truths are those that metaphysics seeks to find. Mathematical, formal-logical, and metaphysical truths are the three kinds of nonempirical, noncontingent truth. Those who talk of empirical metaphysics are not using words as Popper or I use them. I believe our usage is the one most likely to lead to clarity.

Metaphysical propositions, if true, are not vulnerable to conceivable observational tests, for they claim to harmonize not simply with actual but with conceivable experience. Their testing is in the imagination, not in perception; by intellectual, not by physical, experimentation.

One reason important metaphysicians are few is that not every philosopher has the imagination to do the appropriate testing. Leibniz, Peirce, and Whitehead, like Plato long ago, were highly imaginative persons. Another requirement is knowledge of mathematics and formal logic, for these subjects deal with the other two classes of nonempirical truths beside the metaphysical. Plato, Leibniz, Peirce, and Whitehead meet this second requirement also. By the standards of their time they were mathematicians and logicians as well as philosophers. Aristotle, though less imaginative, was the

52

very founder of formal logic and competent in mathematics. Descartes, a great mathematician, was deficient in formal logic, and his imagination went primarily into prompting and helping to ground empirical natural science. So I do not quite include him.

In nonempirical matters falsity is shown either by contradiction or by lack of any clear and coherent meaning. Truth on this level is the same as making clear sense. The classical formula "truth by coherence" is correct of metaphysics, but not of science or of knowledge in general.

The idea that metaphysical systems may be quite clear and coherent yet mutually incompatible, and that only observation of facts can decide among them, is a myth. My challenge is: Show me two such internally coherent and clear, yet mutually incompatible, systems. Indeed, show me one whose clarity and coherence are undoubted. Clarity and coherence are precisely what are hard to achieve in metaphysics. Did Spinoza have them, or Leibniz? The latter was remarkably clear, but incoherences are not hard to find in his system. Spinoza's terms *substance, attribute,* and *mode* are hardly models of semantic clarity. I have repeatedly said that Spinoza did not really know what he meant by these terms, especially by *mode*. Tschirnhausen said so at the time and Spinoza's reply was weak.

In metaphysics observation merely furnishes illustrations of meanings. It does not test truth. The meanings metaphysics deals with are those whose generality transcends the actual world to take possible world states into account. It follows that observation of the actual world alone cannot establish metaphysical principles. The test is the coherence of these principles among themselves. Because of their generality they must dictate their own interrelations. They all express what is meant by reality, truth, being, becoming or process, value, purpose, or knowledge; not some particular reality, truth, being, becoming, value, purpose, or knowledge.

With these usages of words clarified, how are theological problems to be regarded? Is truth about them empirical or a priori? Clearly such truth is not merely mathematical or formal-logical. Truths about God are neither exclusively empirical nor exclusively metaphysical. There is an empirical aspect and an a priori or metaphysical one. However, the metaphysical aspect has a logical priority. The biblical saying "The heavens declare the glory of God" was written by a believer whose belief was not derived from the heavens. Granted that God exists, then everything must, by the very concept of God, manifest the divine power and goodness. By contrast, from an unbeliever we may have Santayana's grim words: "But morning, with a ray of tenderest joy / Gilding the iron heavens hides the truth." Observation of nature enriches faith but does not create it.

Santayana's sense that a sunrise is not the manifestation of a cosmic, benevolent power was not derived from visual experience of sunrises. It was derived from the conceptual incoherences of traditional theism. These same incoherences have led many believers to attempt a radical revision of that theism. Which way one reacts to metaphysical failures is a matter of personal experience and disposition. Complete consensus seems unlikely in any future we can foresee.

To suppose that belief in God's existence is empirical is to suppose that while actual observations might be at least compatible with the existence of deity, some conceivable observations would not be. The actually experienced world, then, may be such that God could have created it, but some conceivably experienced kinds of world would be such that God could not have created them. An empiricist theologian has attempted to state how such a definitely godless world would look. What he actually does is to describe an incoherent jumble of negative ideas, a pseudo-world of which there could be no experience and in which there could be no thinking. The test of coherence is not met in this instance, and words are being used either without meaning or with inconsistent meanings. A world in which striving is systematically frustrated, love is met only with hatred, creatures achieve no mutual adjustments, nothing goes right — in such a world could there be striving, love, or even hatred? Could there be any organized creatures? In what sense would it be a world? The very existence of an organism is already a harmony of lesser creatures constituting the body of the creature! Even a solar system is an order suggesting a divine orderer. I think the attempted concept of a godless world is a confusion, not a successful intellectual experiment. I challenge anyone to arrive at a plausible way of distinguishing two kinds of possible world systems, those that could be divinely inspired or organized and those that could not be.

If such a necessarily godless world could be conceived, then what would be shown would not be that, by good or bad luck, theism is contingently false. What would be shown is rather that the very idea of God fails to make sense. For, as John Findlay was the first to say clearly, the traditional idea of God as worthy of unqualified devotion, love, or worship implies not merely that divine existence and goodness has made our world possible but that the very meaning of *world* or of *possible* or of *conceivable* implies God's existence and goodness. A possible kind of world is one God could make; the actual kind is the one God has made; nothing less than this suffices to express the religious idea of God. Among the things that require God, possibilities are included. As Findlay put it, "God must be lord over possibility as well as actuality."[1] If God *is* lord over possibility, then there can be no possibility of the nonexistence of God, unless indeed the very idea of God is incoherent and the attitude of worship which produced the idea is subtly absurd. Then of course God does not exist.

Suppose the foregoing is correct, and the existence of God is a matter of concepts and not of observational facts. It still would not follow that there is no empirical component in theology. In all the Western theistic traditions, with very rare exceptions — the most notable being Aristotle and a few of his followers — God has been supposed to have something analogous to what in us is called knowledge, usually also benevolence and love. Assuming this, there must, by logical necessity, or by the test of coherence, be an empirical aspect of the divine reality. For, if God knows your or my existence, then God knows something that is contingent and knowable only empirically, if anything whatever is contingent and so knowable. If you or I might not have been, then knowledge of your or my existence might not have been. To know something as existent is possible only if the known *is* existent; otherwise the supposed knowledge would be error. Medieval theology never quite saw the contradiction in affirming the contingency of the world and the noncontingency of God's knowledge of the world. But Aristotle saw the contradiction clearly and therefore denied that God knows contingent worldly details. Spinoza also saw the point but chose the opposite solution: there are no contingent details, he implies; all is necessary. Serious objections can be made to both positions — conceptual, not observational, objections.

Faustus Socinus took the third way out of the difficulty and attributed contingency to God's knowledge of contingent things, though definitely not to God's existence. Socinianism clearly anticipated the process view of God. Like Berdyaev much later, and a good many others since Kant, Socinus held that not only is God's knowledge partly contingent, it is also partly changing. Each new act of a creature, if the act is free or is determined by that creature, adds something to God's knowledge, something that could not have been there before. Much less could it have been there eternally. The timeless view of divine knowledge magnifies the absurdity; it does not mitigate it. Knowledge of the necessary and eternal can itself be contingent and temporal, as when you or I have such knowledge, but knowledge of the contingent and temporal can only be contingent and temporal. The concepts of knowledge, modality, and temporality together entail this difference between the two modalities. Aristotle knew this but was too much in love with the idea of eternal fixity and the contemplation of abstractions to apply the insight to God. So he made God the contemplator only of abstractions, the pure "thinking of thinking." No religion preaching divine love can accept this limitation of deity.

The Socinians, by implication, made a lucid distinction between the divine essence and the inessential qualities that make God the God of the present actual world, including those that once made and still make God the God of Abraham, Isaac, and Jacob. In principle this is Whitehead's two natures of God, the primordial and the consequent. My doctrine of dual transcendence formally states what these fine thinkers divined, which is that God surpasses all others, not simply by eternally and necessarily existing and insofar being immutable, but also by being, in a uniquely excellent manner, ever able to acquire additional contingent values and enjoy newly created features of a world in which at least some creatures are in part self-determined or self-created. God is supremely free or self-creative, as well as creative of others. These others are, at least some of them, in their lesser ways free or self-creative and thereby add novelty to the divine life, a point that was later expressed more explicitly in France by Lequier and the Russian exile Berdyaev, then in America by Tillich and Whitehead, the last probably not knowing any of these others.

In what follows I take for granted that the term *God* is defined by the dual transcendence principle. For instance, consider the duality of universal/individual. Tillich says that God is "not *a* being" and does not "exist" but is "being itself." Dual transcendence says that God is both individual and universal, or is *the* individual (not simply *an* individual) with uniquely universal functions, self-related to all, concerned with all, to which all are, in their various fashions, related, and with which they are concerned. God is subject for all objects, and object for all subjects; primordial and everlasting as no other being is, and with an immutable identifying or essential character, yet in concrete detailed content an ever-increasing awareness. God's unchanging aspect is the supreme identity; God's changing aspect is the supreme variability or growth. If change means loss, corruption, vacillation, fickleness, then God is unchanging; but if change in the supreme form means greeting with unsurpassable love and appreciation each new display of creaturely freedom, then God is the being with infallible power to change in the ideally right manner. In essence God is absolutely perfect and changeless, but in concrete actuality the divine life is the ideal form of increase with no final maximum possible, an open infinity and not a terminal quantum of value. The divine capacity to assimilate value is absolute, unlimited; but actuality, as Whitehead says, is by its very meaning concrete, and that means definite and somehow limited. What Aquinas called an "indeterminate sea of being" can only be an infinitely indefinite reality, what God *could* be, do, or have, and not what God actually is, does, or has. In capacity or potentiality God, according to dual transcendence, is indeed absolutely infinite, but this is a mere abstraction compared to the divine actuality in which each new creature is a partly new content, ideally taken into the divine life. We should worship God, not absoluteness, infinity, or eternity.

With all this understood, in what sense, if any, can we know that God exists? Human individuals are identified by pointing to them and interacting with them. Since God is ubiquitous one cannot point to God, and although according to dual transcendence we do interact with God we cannot distinctly perceive or intuit this transaction unless we have the intuition some mystics claim. I do not deny their claim but I am not able to make it for myself or, without hesitation, for them either. God must for most of us be identified purely conceptually.

The divine essence, according to Anselm, proclaims its own

existence. Even Aquinas did not deny this. He only objected that it is controversial whether or not we have a clear and coherent idea of the divine essence. Hence though that essence may evidence its own existence (so that for God, as the sanctified theologian said, the ontological argument is valid), for us, who do not surely know the essence, the intrinsic necessity of the divine existence is of no help. Here Aquinas, as in much of what he said, was about half right and half wrong. The intrinsic necessity of divine existence, granted the essence, may not help us, by itself, to be sure of the existence. But it does help us to understand what sort of question the theistic question is, and hence what sort of evidence might be available. Our conception of God may not be clear enough to resolve our doubts about the divine existence, but it may be clear enough to exclude the possibility that that existence could be contingent or that empirical evidence could be the appropriate court of appeal. For if the idea is not coherent, then the answer to the existential question must on a priori grounds be negative, but if it is coherent then the answer must be positive. Empirical evidence is beside the point.

The ontological argument depends on two extralogical premises, not just one: first, that we have a clear and coherent idea of the divine existence; and second, that this idea implies the necessity of its being somehow actualized in concrete existence. The second premise I call Anselm's Principle. I have no doubt that it is sound. Nothing that John Hick and others have said to the contrary seems to me decisive. But the first premise is another matter. Over and over again definitions of deity have been proposed, and over and over it has been shown that these definitions either lack clarity or are glaringly inconsistent. Carneades long ago showed inconsistencies in the Stoic idea of God, and some of his points apply just as well to classical theism as it was almost universally accepted by the scholastics and by most Islamic and some Jewish theologians.

My theism is a radical revision of classical theism, designed to avoid the absurdities mentioned. But what is to show that there are not other absurdities in the revised form? Moreover there are difficulties that I can see in working out the implications of "neoclassical theism," as I call my view. My hope and faith is that the difficulties can be overcome, but this is a faith, not a certainty.

For me it is close to a certainty that a clear and coherent idea of God would settle positively the question of existence, and that a clear understanding that every possible version of theism appropriate to the religious meaning of the idea is incoherent would settle it negatively.

Since the conceivability of the divine existence is the decisive question, and the ontological argument supposes that conceivability to be granted, the argument, as many have said, begs the question of belief. However, what it does not beg but settles, in my judgment, is the nature of the question as nonempirical.

From the foregoing it follows that other reasons for belief are required besides the ontological argument. It also follows that all the arguments must be a priori or purely conceptual. As Duns Scotus said long ago, for a demonstration of God's existence no empirical premise is required, and indeed no empirical premise is as such relevant. For instance, the argument "In empirical fact a world exists; hence God as creator of that world must be inferred" is wrongly put. As a Roman Catholic priest, Father Schorsch, held, the right way to put the cosmological argument is as follows: A priori, either something or nothing exists. Not only is it obviously true that something exists, but it is true a priori. For no possible experience could show that nothing at all existed, and this for two reasons: (1) the experience would exist, and (2) (as Heidegger put it, or should have put it) any experience is experience of being in a world. Even in dreams this holds, as Bergson, more right than he knew, showed in his essay on dreams.

So, "Something exists" is a necessary truth. The declaration "There might have been nothing" is a fine example of what Wittgenstein calls "language idling." To refer to absolutely nothing and not to refer are indistinguishable. Next question: Is the something that exists necessarily contingent or contingently so? If the former, we already have the necessary being and can go on to argue, as even Kant admitted, that our only positive conception of necessary existence is the theistic one. If, on the other hand, the "something" exists contingently (the necessity being only that the sole possible alternative was something else existing contingently), then we can go on and argue that this reduction of the necessity of something to a mere disjunction is unplausible. No empirical premise is needed.

But my favorite arguments for belief are the argument from order and the argument from what Kant called the *summum bonum* and I call the rational aim: what rational beings could reasonably accept as the final purpose of their existence and activity.

The argument from order is often called the argument from design, but this usage has been largely spoiled by the form the argument has traditionally taken. The empirically given cosmos in its detailed patterns is supposed to be sufficient evidence for the existence and essential nature of deity. On that basis Hume's and Kant's objections are cogent. There is no way to show that the actual universe is so perfectly patterned that only a perfect designer could account for it.

The proper question about order is much more radical. Could there be any viable cosmos at all, any conceivable state of affairs, any set of nondivine beings coexisting in a world, unless there were a divine being to set limits to mutual conflicts and frustrations among the nondivine beings, each of which, as Plato said of souls, was self-moved, in some degree self-determined? Generalizing this Platonic principle to eliminate the supposed class of entities entirely lacking in self-motion (a concept that modern physics, even before quantum theory, had shown to be vacuous so far as we are likely ever to know), the question is acute. Can cosmic orderliness result merely from, or consist merely in, nondivine beings adjusting to one another? One cannot adjust to a chaos, hence the explanation begs the question. Without order there is nothing to adjust to.

Orderliness in this argument does not mean absolute order, entirely free from randomness or disharmony, something no amount of observation could ever establish or significantly confirm. Rather, it means a degree of order such that the risks of conflict are justified by the opportunities for harmony. Absolute order makes no sense if it is partly free beings that are to be ordered. But there must be some order, or there is nothing coherently conceivable. Mere chaos is a combination of words, not a coherent idea, in spite of a remark of Strawson's. Risks must be limited and opportunities proportional, or life and intelligible reality are impossible. Sisyphus may inhabit Dante's imagination but not any possible world state or region. And I see no serious rival to the idea of supreme or divine freedom inspiring the lesser forms of freedom by a vision of cosmic order. Thus the nondivine beings adapt not simply to one another but to common directives from God. This is the principle of leadership which is found in all forms of political order. A committee with assigned tasks and an elected or appointed chair may get something done; but with no assigned task and no chair, they will achieve little if anything. Given divinely decreed laws of nature setting limits to what is possible, individuals can to some extent create their own special forms of order and partial disorder.

Physics has given up the idea of laws that fully determine details of what happens, making no allowance for self-determination. But there must be laws setting limits to what creatures can do. Given these conditions, the creatures can, with some freedom, manage their interrelations from moment to moment. What is needed is not a dictated absolute design but stage directions giving outlines, rules of the game. Yet the playing is by the players, not by the director or playwright. Who but God could decide upon rules for the cosmic game? Atheists always leave the regularity of nature a mere brute fact or blind mystery.

The argument from the rational aim takes into account the a priori truth, not merely empirical fact, that any individual other than God must be a fragment of reality, limited both spatially and temporally. What rational aim can such a fragmentary being have? It cannot be merely the creature's own future advantage, for its definitive future state is death. Is there any advantage or disadvantage for the dead? I fail to see any. The dead make no such distinctions, enjoy and suffer nothing. Also, a mere fragment of the world, such as each of us is, loses its sense of humor if it thinks that its final value in the world is what the world gives to it. In the end we are all only contributions to the inclusive value of reality. If the inclusive reality is just the physical cosmos, with no cosmic consciousness to go with the cosmic body, then what rational aim is there for such as we are? But if there is cosmic consciousness, as Plato thought, then our joys and sorrows, and those of any nondivine being, are contributions to that consciousness, somewhat as the health and also the misery of our bodily cells contribute to our happiness.

Most philosophers and theologians have signally failed to see things in this way. Whitehead and Berdyaev could have so viewed the matter without much changing their doctrines, as I understand them. Whitehead's definition of the mind-body relation gives a good basis for analogically extending the idea to God, who as he says physically prehends all creatures. The service of God is the rational aim. But a merely absolute God cannot be served.

I am not saying, Unless God exists life has no meaning or rational aim and the cosmos no order. I am sure life has meaning and the cosmos order. I am saying that I can understand how there is meaning and order only by believing in God as enriched by our experiences. Even Tillich in the third volume of his *Systematic Theology* seems to accept this idea.

I close with some bibliographic remarks. The only one of my writings that really gives my reasons for belief is *Creative Synthesis and Philosophic Method*. Chapter 14 deals with six arguments that, taken together, are for me *the* reason, not any one of them by itself, and certainly not the ontological argument.

There is an excellent book on my ontological argument by Lawrence Goodwin which deals with various objections that have been made to the argument. Like several other writers, Goodwin deals with John Hick's criticisms, and does not accuse me of the equivocation that Hick finds in the notion of *necessity* employed. We have a number of criteria (I give ten in *The Logic of Perfection*) for ideas whose instantiation in actuality is logically contingent. Not one of the ten applies to the idea of God. Hick asserts that we can conceive the divine nonexistence as contingent fact but does not convey to me any way of giving clear meaning to the alleged conception. Would it be a godless world, and what would constitute its godlessness? A world without human beings or without elephants is quite conceivable and once existed, according to the evidence. But I have yet to learn of genuinely conceivable evidence for the nonexistence of God (assuming that the idea makes sense). Would it be the existence of nothing at all?

Various kinds of world would exclude various kinds of thing, but what would exclude God no one has shown. Evils can be explained as springing from the same freedom that makes good things possible; and the notion of God, supreme freedom, creating beings with no freedom, is nonsense in my view. Creatures can only be lesser creators, and nothing could guarantee that their decisions would never cause suffering, or even that they would never be consciously malicious or irresponsible — provided they were to be conscious in the moral sense at all.

I hold that any world would declare the glory of God if any other world would, and that any experience must exhibit the reality of some world or other. God-with-creatures, some creatures or other, is for me the common element of all possibilities — or else the notion of God is only a verbal formula and not a genuine self-consistent idea. But in that case various other ideas that I cannot give up would also lack intelligible significance, at least for my understanding. So for me belief in God is reasonable. Is it knowledge? Yes, if knowledge is defined as reasonably justified belief. Otherwise it is faith. We do not know as God knows.

NOTE

1. J. N. Findlay, "Can God's Existence Be Disproved?" in *New Essays in Philosophical Theology*, ed. Antony Flew and Alasdair MacIntyre (New York: Macmillan Co., 1955), p. 52.

4

The Varieties of Religious Knowing

J. N. FINDLAY

THE TITLE OF MY present paper is not of my own invention. It was proposed to me by Professor Rouner, and it is of course copied from William James's book *The Varieties of Religious Experience*, which all of you must have read, and which I read very long ago. I am not, however, to talk of religious *experience*, in which case I might have cited the most varied and exciting documents, much like those that William James cited from Starbuck's remarkable collection. The bringing in of the term *knowing* means that my paper will be concerned with valid religious assertions and inferences. It will have to be an essay on religious epistemology, not merely on religious psychology and phenomenology. I am, however, happy to take up Professor Rouner's challenge. For I believe religion to be a basic human enterprise, whether in its intellectual, emotional, literary, ritualistic, practical, or social aspects, and fit to be set on a level with the scientific, the aesthetic, the political, and the other rational human enterprises. I believe that religion reveals something important about the world and its human inhabitants, and that while it has many false and bad and hideously perverted forms, it also has other forms, not always easy to isolate and bring to purity, which are profoundly normative and good and true. I shall try to bring out these good, true, and normative aspects of religion, and also dwell on the criteria by which their reasonableness is established.

My view of religion, which I have worked out in some detail in my best book, *Values and Intentions*, is that religion represents the supreme achievement of our axiological or value-consciousness. The objects that religion constructs, and with which it endeavors to have emotional and practical dealings, represent a carrying to the limit of the heads of the worthwhile to which our emotional and practical life inevitably and validly gravitates, and also a carrying to the limit of our distancing and purgation from the heads of the counter worthwhile from which that emotional and practical life shrinks in avoidance. You will see that I believe in something rather like an internal validation of emotional and practical trends which most modern philosophers would regard as utterly empty, nugatory, and non-explanatory. I believe, moreover, that such an emotional, practical validity spills over into the cognitive realm and gives us reason for believing in the real existence of objects that would in some measure fit in with and satisfy the emotional and practical trends in question.

My views on axiological validation must not, however, be misunderstood. I do not believe in the existence of non-natural, Moorean qualities of the Good and the Bad, the Better and the Worse, and so forth, which we simply intuit, and by which we are inevitably attracted or repelled. Nor do I see how the presence of such intuited qualities would explain anything, although we sometimes seem to see the Good and the Beautiful *out there* in a wave or a meadow, precisely as we seem to intuit a height and a color in such cases. And I do not believe in an unanalyzable, inner *Berechtigung* for an emotional, practical stance, such as Brentano postulates in his *Origins of Moral Knowledge*, nor do I see how this inner knowledge of such an unanalyzable *Berechtigung* would validate our axiological orientations and judgments.

What I hold is that axiological validation rests essentially on the fact that we always feel ourselves to be one among others, that our inner life always spills over and informs the acts and gestures of others, and that we can only be conscious of ourselves and our needs and aversions in a context of actual or possible others. In such a context we move inevitably toward an orientation to a set of goals and countergoals that anyone and everyone could pursue or avoid *for* anyone and everyone. We and our emotional-practical orientations become mere values of variables for which any emotional-practical subject could be substituted. This rise to being a mere value of a free variable is built into our self-consciousness, however much there may be other factors which resist it. It strengthens every practical transaction with others, including, of course, those all-important transactions that involve the use of speech. And even when we seek to impose our personal, egoistic aims on others, we are, after a fashion, seeking to universalize ourselves, and to be everyone.

This is apparent in that very strange axiological assertion in which we say that everyone should pursue his or her own maximum satisfaction, where the variable implied by "everyone" ranges freely over all practical agents. The variable implied by "his or her own," however, is dependent in each case on the particular value given to the previous free variable. Universalistic egoism is half-hearted, self-contradictory egoism which tries to universalize an attitude that is essentially non-universalistic, and all intercourse with others must tend toward its invalidation. One cannot persuade others to act exclusively in pursuit of one's own preferences and projects, and one cannot feel that one would oneself be persuaded by such a form of egoistic persuasion. Valid goals and countergoals are goals and countergoals that everyone can without internal contradiction pursue for everyone. They are goals and countergoals that enter into all our intersubjective life, inevitably moving us in virtue of a kind of universalistic spiritual gravitation which is built into our self-consciousness and the consciousness of our common world. Hume regarded the laws of association as a case of universal psychic gravitation. We can with justice speak of a similar gravitation in the case of our intersubjective, emotional-practical tendency toward universalization. And we are not, moreover, unlike Hume, positing a mere empirical law but a tendency necessarily built into human self-consciousness as such.

Trying to discover what everyone could desire for everyone, and should desire for everyone, yields remarkable dividends. It in fact yields nothing less than a transcendental deduction of the heads of the worthwhile and the counter worthwhile. For obviously what one can and must desire everyone to desire *for* everyone, whatever their actual aims, is that, other things being equal, and no intersubjective conflicts involved, everyone's aims should be *satisfied*, and all forms of *dissatisfaction* and frustration avoided. Strange as it may seem, universalistic hedonism permits of an axiological validation, despite the fact that mere satisfaction is the humblest of goods.

Obviously there are higher forms of Good than pursuit of a

precisely similar validation. Thus knowledge and truth are essentially tied up with the transcendence of purely personal pictures of things. They are essentially communicable and intersubjective. They build on the percepts and arguments which everyone can share with everyone, and in our desire for what everyone can desire for everyone they will inevitably be included. Consciousness is nothing if not an interest in what is objective and intersubjective, however much other personal interests may, and at times must, resist this magisterial aim. And our interest in the Beautiful can arguably be shown to be an interest, not in that whose contemplation pleases us *personally*, but in that which so fits our contemplative faculties that *anyone* can be satisfied in its contemplation, and could desire such a satisfaction *for* everyone. Power and efficiency and successful activity are things that everyone can, conflicts of interest excluded, pursue for everyone, and desire that everyone should pursue for everyone.

Lastly we shall, as universalistic pursuers, inevitably be attracted to the practical love which breaks down the barriers to such a universalization of interest, however much such a love may in certain cases be particularistic. We shall also be attracted to the justice which breaks down any arbitrary practical particularization of such love and favor, and likewise be attracted to the personal virtues which consist in the practical observation of such justice. I do not think that there is any head of value or disvalue which cannot be shown to stem from that universalization of interest which subordinates all purely personal interest to goals which can without inner conflict be pursued by everyone for everyone. I am not here maintaining that our universalistic attractions and repulsions are the only ones we should feel. They would be meaningless if there were not contingent personal attractions and repulsions that they could organize and unify, and which represent what we and other actuals happen to want. Nor would I suggest that they could give acceptability to any arbitrarily chosen set of goals, which were only distinguished by the fact that it was not self-contradictory to desire that everyone should pursue them for everyone. To desire that everyone should desire that everyone should be trained to like nothing better than chewing bits of popcorn, or always looking at New York subway graffiti, would acquire no validity thereby.

I am, however, maintaining that the higher-order interest in shareability can provide a setting in which contingent personal interests can be incorporated. It can also lend its sanction to certain higher-order interests in such things as Beauty, Truth, Justice, Freedom, Moral Integrity, Love, Efficiency, and other recognized forms of excellence. I also think that universal sharing can develop its own peculiar zest and can become a value in and for itself. This does not mean that such a higher-order value might not, if divorced from the other values which are its natural complement and foundation, become perverse and senseless. There are everywhere counterfeit possibilities of universality which base themselves on interests which are arbitrary and counterfeit, or even counter-universalizable. In general, we may say that shared values are native to conscious subjectivity. What is an object must be there for everyone and anyone and is essentially shared. Consciousness in fact may be said to have an intuitive disposition not toward attitudes that are narrowly personal but toward attitudes that everyone does or could have. Consciousness therefore has an intrinsic aspiration toward a mind-state that achieves every dimension of omnitude, whether in range of power, of freedom, of vision, of understanding, of love, of sympathetic entry, or what not. As conscious beings, we may say that we are always in a sense trying to reach up to the omnific performances of a God, and this is where religion necessarily enters the picture. But the best omnific performances are also in a sense self-naughting, for they make the person and personal desires only one among other, inalienable right ends with only such a right as must also be accorded to everyone.

Religion is not therefore some alien graft upon our conscious human life, inspired perhaps by the terrifying or marvelous powers of circumambient nature, as many have surmised. It is rather a carrying to the limit of the basic aspirations of conscious life, its search for practical mastery, for deep understanding, for widely ranging vision, for spectacles that please by their harmonious, not-too-easy perspicuity of structure, for penetration of the inner life of others and for finding it deeply understandable and supportive of our own. Inevitably, we form an ideal of pure reason, as Kant styled it, in which all the basic aspirations of consciousness are carried to the limit, of a thought that covers all truths and all possibilities, of a power that can realize anything and everything, of a sympathetic entry that surmounts all personal difference and understands everyone in every situation, of a judgment that can assess the value and disvalue of anything and everything in the light of all facts and all fundamental goals. It is also a consciousness that understands the possibility of all deviations and corruptions, distortions and departures from what is good, and understands the many mitigations which render them well-nigh predictable and certainly forgivable.

There are also negative ways in which the fundamental aspects of consciousness can be realized in which nullity, rather than omnitude, becomes the goal. Thus we find a profound intellectual value in a simple law of nature, in a tautology of logic, or a moral value in virtues which remain within a small compass, or a religious value in a state of mind which values nothing so much as its inner peace. Certainly these negative values are at their highest when they do not exclude positive ones but rather supplement them, when the presence of the positive rather brings out the dignity and integrity of an absence than makes it seem empty. Thus in certain schools of Buddhism emptiness is valued above plenitude, but the crowded stage of this-worldly life is none the less as much a realization of emptiness as the more explicit emptiness of nirvana.

Religion, since it enlists everything in the conception of its object, has an inherent tendency toward an identification of its object, not with the total range of its omnitude, but with any and every individual object that falls within that range. The object of religion is so all-inclusive that there is nothing, however trivial and base, that does not involve its total presence. This means that there is no object, however humble, that cannot assume immense religious significance: a portion of a human or animal body, a piece of fabric, a picture, a garment, an utterance, a gesture, an act or practice, a light, a portion of food or drink, a book, a song, and especially a person who, in virtue of consciousness, embodies the omnitude that is intrinsic to all consciousness as such.

Thus, religion is always open to a particularistic perversion which is traditionally covered by the name of idolatry, that is, an identification of the religious object with a particular something or other included in its range, not extended to cover all the instantiations of value but including only certain specially selected ones among them. A book, a performance, a practice, a person, an artifact, an utterance, become religiously significant in a special degree, while another highly similar book, performance, practice, person, or artifact has no religious significance accorded to it at all. This practice destroys the omnitude and suprapersonality of religion and necessarily gives rise to strife among the worshipers of particular emblems or symbols. And the practice is made doubly evil when religious significance is extended to objects and practices which have an ugly or cruel aspect, as has happened in many of the cults of India. The omnitude of religious significance is rightly extended to what deviates from the highest values in various directions. Sin, in its various forms, is always a distortion of genuine values, and the ability to make short work of enemies is quite understandably attributed to the Lord of Hosts.

In the same way the sex-worship which colors the carvings of Khajurāho, or the worship of animal slaughter which colors the rituals of the Mother Goddess Kali, is directed to distortions and exaggerations of values which have in a purer form a genuine claim to interpersonal validity. Slaughter can be for hunters and fishers a form of communion with the whole of nature and so can, no doubt, the orgiastic sex performances depicted in the statuary of Khajurāho, which to most of us seem so addictive and perverse. The omnitude of religion with its deep tendency to confer its whole meaning on each of its contingent embodiments makes it a fertile field for perversion. There are as many perverse forms of religion as there are perverse forms of sex, and there is nothing, however disgusting or horrific or ridiculous, that cannot receive religious consecration and perhaps be violently imposed on those who can barely stomach it. There can be sacred prostitution, sacred murder, sacred suicide, sacred cannibalism, sacred necrophilism, sacred babbling, sacred flogging, sacred whatever. Nothing escapes the comprehensive lasso of the sacred.

However much this is so, there remain values, positive and negative, which have a more built-in relation to the shareable and the comprehensive, which are essentially geared to rising above the narrow interests of particular persons, or bodies of persons, or the contingencies of special instances, and which involve always a putting of oneself into anyone's and everyone's position and a seeing of what goals and categories survive such a comprehensive projection. The values and disvalues, in fact, which recommend themselves to all who are said to reflect detachedly on what we should choose to pursue or avoid are, not surprisingly, values and disvalues that have a relation to anyone and everyone, whatever his or her contingent circumstances and personal interests may be, and are validated by their unlimited comprehensiveness.

There are of course many dialectical puzzles which surround such processes of validation and many cases where we construct unacceptable alternatives without any clear hope of a universally acceptable decision. The problems of a final decision are never solved. Yet many such problems are solved by the way, or at least solved, like the problems of conscience, in a manner which takes account of the situation and temperament and insight of the particular person, and which represents the person's own highest degree of success in transcending the limitations of his or her personal position. It is wrong to hold that there is not some approach to a consensus, and some necessity of such an approach, in the various values which reflective people have felt to be mandatory, whatever the difficulty of clearly choosing among these in practice or implementing them in detail. Absolute Knowledge, Absolute Satisfaction, Absolute Efficiency, Absolute Harmony, Absolute Love, Absolute Self-discipline, and so on, plainly strike notes to which no one can be deaf.

The religious consciousness is self-validating like all the other basic forms of our conscious life, such as our consciousness of space and time, of number, of natural law, of the structure of our inner life, and of basic values. The position in regard to religion is the same as it is in all these fields: we can only learn by experience, or by reflective argument, if we already know in principle what sorts of things experience or reflective argument can teach us. There is no problem about a priori knowledge, nor does it require a subjective foundation, if it is impossible to learn anything from experience or reflection, if one does not have an advance knowledge of what they can teach us. All justification of the ultimate forms of consciousness is and must be circular, and consists rather in the removal of internal difficulties than in finding a new and secure way to establish them.

Since religion has a relevance to everything in the world or human life, whether factual and scientific, or practical, or political, or aesthetic, or philosophical, or connected with a specific cult-behavior, it is obvious that in speaking of the way or ways in which we are to validate different sorts of religious pronouncements I have undertaken a big task. First of all, however, I shall deal with the philosophical validation of religion: the attempt to construct a satisfactory delineation of the object of religion and to determine its phenomenological and ontological status.

If religion is geared to carrying to an all-comprehensive limit of the heads of our impersonal valuation, we must try to achieve clarity as to what such a comprehensive carrying to the limit must involve, and whether it is capable of fulfillment in some sector of what we ordinarily call the world, perhaps in the world as a whole, or in some sector of being beyond the *ordinary* world. Here we have a question, first of all, as to the category in which we must put the object of religion, which is to incorporate all the highest values. Shall we think of it as an individual instance of all those values, individuated, if not by an individual spatio-temporal position, at least by the mutual exclusiveness of conscious beings, or shall we rather think of it subsistentially, as being more of the nature of a universal, being present, with varying richness of conception and realization, in all instances of any form of being whatsoever? And, if we think of it in the former individualistic manner, we have many theologies, singular or pluralistic, to choose from. If we think of it in the latter manner, we have not only Platonic and Neoplatonic categories of Absolute Goodness itself, and Absolute Unity itself, which in some obscure manner are endowed with a species-forming, instance-forming efficacy, but also Germanic theologies of a self-positing consciousness or a self-specifying and self-instancing *Begriff,* or pure concept or idea, or a self-asserting, suprapersonal will, which views likewise belong much more to subsistential Platonic ontology than to an existential, individualistic one.

There is even room for theologies that move into other categories. Our religious object can be a consummate fact or truth, or an ultimate categorical imperative, or the purest of negations, or the most comprehensive of disjunctions. If we choose this sort of ontology, we shall have to attribute something like a creative efficacy to our chosen category, whatever it is, but I concede that this involves difficulty. What some people call abstract and ideal, other people call concrete and real, and what some people think of as actively causal, others think of as merely modal. I do not myself see why universal values and truths should not be said to effect certain results as much as confessedly existent things. I certainly feel that particular or general, present or past states of affairs force certain acceptances or expectations on me, and can see no reason why I should limit effectiveness to my less active bodily or mental states. Our language is freely chosen, and the motivation for one's choices is widely various and has differing justifications. Even a total absence can be rated an important causal factor for some effect. The object of religion, however, is arguably not a mere absence.

I wish, however, to express a personal preference in regard to the category which it is feasible to attribute to our all-comprehensive, value-consummating religious object. I think it best, myself, to place it beyond all of our ordinary categories, *hors Catégorie*, as they say of very good French hotels. The supreme object of religion is, in my view, universal in the sense that it is active in everything and in every conscious person, and is not separately individual; but it is individual in the sense that it is concrete and active in individuals, and is not a mere abstract or side of their being. It corresponds most closely to the Logos of Saint John's Gospel which is the light that lighteth everyone that cometh into the world, or to the Holy Ghost, which, the Creed says, spake by the prophets. I am sure we all understand and know this unique sort of categorical status.

That the object of religion may have dimensions of its own and its own kind of comprehensiveness that is communicated to us is also a view to be reached. Saint Thomas and Hegel, the two best theologians, teach us that we must speak of this central absolute in a unique manner. God, according to Thomas, *is* essence, being, goodness. God does not merely have them, like you or I. God knows everything by knowing essence directly, and not as we do, through forms which are other than God.

Hegel's absolute idea is similarly the most tirelessly active of essences: after summing up in itself all the categories of possible being, it externalizes itself in nature and achieves self-conscious self-identity in Spirit, being supremely self-conscious in art, religion, and philosophy. Much of his system might suggest that Hegel is a humanist, and Feuerbach and the Hegelian Left read him in this sense; so did I at one time, but a deeper immersion has cured me of this error. I am not, however, going to give you my own theology or my philosophy of religion in detail. It is in some respects rather inchoate since I have patches of Upanishadic and Buddhistic and Neoplatonic influences to weave into it. What I wish to say is that philosophical theology and the philosophy of religion are themselves part of religious knowing. We are looking for concepts that will fit what we know intuitively and enable us to formulate it better. That there are many quite different ways of conceiving the object of religion testifies not to its internal self-contradiction but to its omnitude and plenitude. And I would say, further, that all the deep ethical meditations that engross us at present, and also all our scientific and logico-methodological meditations, have their religious implications. A philosopher like Whitehead obviously contributed to developing the latter, and there are profound religious implications in contemporary discussions of abortion, sexual perversion, or the right to live or die.

Religion also has obvious implications for problems of eschatology, which concern the possibility of a liberated life without the compulsive centrality of the body. I myself see an a priori likelihood in a spectrum of states leading from the *Aussereinander* of sensuous bodily being to the total *Ineinander* or mutual interpenetration of thinking subjects, such as is gorgeously described in Neoplatonic and in Buddhist writings. And I imagine that the reports of sensitives might throw some light on these matters. I intuitively have no sensitivity in these fields. I believe, however, that only when we have transcended the externality of sensuous, material being will we know, or do something better than know, the object of religion as it truly is, and also learn to conceive of it and worship it in a truly appropriate manner. These are commonplace utterances, but I think they express the truth.

I wish, however, to finish by saying something about the merits of transcendental skepticism. We certainly inhabit a Cave, and cannot even conceive of the Cave's internal structure in a single, conceptually firm manner. Even the phenomenology of our experienced life world presents conceptual alternatives between which no clear decision is possible. Much less is a decision possible in regard to matters like the absolute object of religion, which can only be approached by an analogy with ordinary categories and so necessarily with skepticism. We are Cave-dwellers, and Cave-dwellers ought to remain in part skeptics. Some of our best Cave-dwellers, such as Pascal, Mill, and Voltaire, have been skeptics. We must accept the fact that our devotion to religious objects, and the values they incorporate, transcend questions of existence. Even if they are only reflections and shadows on the walls of the Cave, they remain magisterial reflections and shadows, by which we must direct all our living and thinking. The removal of the values which culminate in religion from our Cave does not make the human condition desperate; it only devalues the world, to which *we* remain superior.

Meditations of this sort may have passed in his last months even through the mind of Christ. He had believed with implicit faith that he would be called upon to inaugurate a new heaven and a new earth, and that this inauguration would be surrounded with a plethora of celestial phenomena. It was in the fulness of this faith that he had ridden through the streets of Jerusalem, evoking a messianic ovation. Now, however, as the days passed, and as fundamentalist and political forces gathered against him, he began to feel that perhaps the divine Kingdom was not of this world at all, but lay in a paradise beyond this world and its evil Prince, or in the many mansions of a heavenly house where a place would be prepared for his disciples. Jesus himself in his last hours arguably became a skeptic, but he also reached a point when he saw and felt that skepticism did not matter. It was the Way, the Truth, and the Life that alone mattered, and this would be a living message to all people unto the end of the world.

5

On Knowing What Is Uncertain

NINIAN SMART

THERE IS A PARADOX abroad today — a paradox which indeed was secretly with us in older, more closed, less cosmopolitan days. I want to explore it, for it bears directly upon our religious, political, and social condition.

The paradox is this: on the one hand nothing seems more certain than faith or more compelling than religious experience. On the other hand, nothing seems less certain than any one particular belief system, for to any one system there are so many vital and serious alternatives. One might, of course, if one has little faith or exiguous experience of the right sort, see the plural character of the world's religions as a good ground for skepticism about the whole lot. But even here the worm of relativity can eat into certitude, since not only do differing nonreligious world views present themselves, such as scientific humanism, various Marxisms, and so forth, but also the question remains as to why we should dismiss in this way all the long and rich history of the transcendent as it presents itself in human history and affairs.

Initially I shall discuss primary religious claims and only later comment on the effect of our conclusions upon world views in general, both secular and religious. So to return to our paradox: the person of faith is certain, but necessarily what she or he believes in is uncertain.

One reason why the issue of religious knowledge is important for political and social conditions is that if we should come to adopt what may be described as a "soft epistemology" in matters of religion, then this will reinforce the case for pluralism and a kind of federal approach toward religious relations. It helps to

76

create what may be called a higher-order criticism to judge religions themselves and to set the tone of a more embracing world view.

But first it is useful to glance at some usages of religious language. It is indeed a common claim that in religion there is knowledge. Thus Clement of Alexandria writes of the gnostic who worships God "who was manifested indeed by the Lord so far as it was possible for the learners to understand, but apprehended by those whom the Lord has elected for knowledge. . . ."[1] The notion of *gnosis* reflects the idea of a cognitive direct experience, which in this case is conveyed through Christ and requires grace. On the other hand, in some religious traditions knowledge or insight (for example, *vidyā/vijjā, prajñā/paññā*) may be, as in Theravāda Buddhism and certain other forms of yoga practice, a do-it-yourself matter. Very often this knowledge is associated with the mystical, that is to say, the contemplative, path. Indeed there is greater naturalness in speaking of knowledge in this context, because mysticism very often contains features which give it a cognitive air. There are procedures for gaining insight (even in religions where the dominant accent is on God's power and grace and human incapacity to attain to a control over divine self-disclosure). There is often rather abstract language used to delineate the object of knowledge, often thus far removed from the more colorful language of the mythic ambience of worship of the gods and God. There is a sense that a kind of intuition is involved. But there are differences of course from ordinary knowledge — for the highest experience is often depicted as nondual. Its emptiness of ordinary experience drives the mystic toward the negative way, which subtracts from any kind of content to the knowledge.

In the *bhakti* faiths, from the world of early Christianity to the faith of the Lotus Sutra, and in *dharma*-projecting traditions, from the Judaism of the Torah to the Islam of the *sharī'a*, and from the customary deliverances of the tribal path to the oracles of priests and shamans, there is a powerful sense that revelation gives knowledge. Knowledge rooted in revelation is contrasted with what is known by ordinary perception and inference, but it is knowledge nevertheless. Especially in the Hindu tradition was there insistence on *śabda* or transcendental testimony as a *pramāṇa* or source of knowledge.

Indeed the classical Indian schema of three main *pramāṇas* is a convenient framework for analyzing the developing crisis in the concept of religious knowledge. As well as transcendental testimony, there is perception, which incorporates yogic perception or what we in the West would recognize as at least one form of religious experience, and inference or more generally reasoning. In the religious context we are in effect speaking of revelation, religious experience, and reason.

The last reminds us that some religious traditions have tried to put religious knowledge on a scientific basis by the standards of that day. But though there may still be some life left in both the cosmological and teleological arguments, as I have argued, as also Swinburne and others in various ways, I do not think the arguments are very vigorous, and they surely must remain controversial, not probative. Thus we may think that the existence of the cosmos requires explanation, and suggest an X which is its source; but that X has to be clothed in at least a wispy attribute or two before the explanation is anything more than empty. But why these attributes rather than others? Different gods so to say could be candidates for Prime Mover. In any event the agnostic option remains powerful. The wispily clothed Prime Mover needs to be hooked to some living God of revelation, and this too becomes problematic — for why hook to Viṣṇu rather than Yahweh?

It looks then as if the *pramāṇa* of inference can do little more than supply us with a little assurance that our faith in the transcendent is not absurd. Or it itself may serve as a kind of meditative discipline. Thus Mahāyāna emptiness philosophy is in effect a dialectic in the service of insight and enlightenment, a way of bringing the intellect to bear in a way which is itself a mode of concentration. It has, so to speak, an engineering function; engineering, that is, a higher intuition or experience of emptiness. But again the Madhyamika arguments are, like the so-called proofs, controversial. Typically, such arguments present grounds for a kind of metaphysical vision, a world view, but alternative visions and world views are known to be available.

And the reason for the decay of natural theology and its Eastern cousins is fairly clear, aside from problems of argumentation. It is the consequence of a breakup of the intellectual world and an increasingly clearly perceived autonomy of scientific inquiry. That autonomy can be interpreted aggressively, as by positivism: *extra scientiam nulla salus.* Or it can be seen more pluralistically. Science then becomes, in its substance, an ingredient in a possible metaphysical world view whose ultimate bases lie beyond science. Whereas science, for all its softening up by Kuhn and Feyerabend, has procedures which yield widely accepted and useful results, metaphysics and world-view construction yield up options, opinions, visions, and therefore, of course, also debates.

But what of the other *pramāṇas?* Matters are somewhat different with them. If you have an argument which is shown to be defective you then no longer have it. But even if your interpretation of your experience is called into doubt, you still have the experience. This relates somewhat to revelation too. Revelation can be treated up to a point as a record of human experiences and their effects. But before I get on to this, let me just sketch some of the moves that can be made in the modern era during which revelations, as embodied in scriptures, have come under a double challenge — from the perception of the plural world of religions and from critical historical probing.

Criticism, which is the leading edge as it were of a different epistemology and cosmology from that which had previously dominated the faith tradition, stimulates differing moves. One is to evolve a form of liberal Christianity which takes an inductivist view of revelation. The texts are, as it were, a screen through which you penetrate to historical events and experiences which themselves are the self-revelation of God. The Bible (or the Vedas) thus becomes testimony to revelation, but fallible testimony. Typically liberal Christianity has involved a synthesis of prevailing liberal-scientific values and the Christian — or the Hindu — message. This may be criticized by traditionalists and others as conceding too much to the fallible spirit of the age. Thus another move is to try to maintain a traditionalist synthesis — most notably the Catholic attempt to ward off the critical challenge by a combination of ecclesiastical discipline and Thomist ideas (but ideas which had to be themselves modernly interpreted and so had to become neo-Thomist). That move largely went out with Vatican II, which opened up the possibility of a Catholic variant on liberal Protestantism. It also allowed for a synthesis critical of this, namely between Marxism and Christianity, which reinterpreted the New

Testament in a radical way but again abandoned in effect the old *Spiritu Sancto dictante*. Another possible move is a strongly transcendental inductivism. You take the scriptures as a record of a vertical self-revelation which owes nothing to human ideas and can stand as a place from which we may criticize human values. In the West this is Barth. In the East there are analogies arising out of the two-level theory of truth, as in Śaṁkara and in forms of Mahāyāna Buddhism.

This indeed is the problem for Barth and for other unique transcendentalists. The argument can be put as follows:

> The ultimate transcends all human creations including religions. The ultimate is _____. Therefore _____ is not challenged by alternative religious positions; on the contrary they are challenged by _____.

But the problem is that if we fill up the blanks with some determinate characterization of the ultimate, say Christ, then the others can fill in with their own determinate ultimate, say Brahman-*ātman*, as the criterion for judging religions. So we now have the alternatives laid out once again, but now at a higher level. And how do we judge between *them*? Well, we can have a meta-transcendent X, but it is an X which genuinely has to be utterly characterless. And is even the goal and focus of the mystical path, in the cloud of unknowing, utterly characterless?

Another path is to say indeed, somewhat in line with this, that all revelations point to the same truth (ineffable again it has to be). That is a possible position, not in my view too realistic from the standpoint of the history of religions, but attractive nonetheless. The latest version of this position is that of John Hick. The logic of it is to say that all embodied, lower-level religions have much truth, and so have to be accepted as equals in a kind of federation of faiths. This again is attractive in today's world. But it has problems because many actual believers will react against this irenic synthesis bought at the cost of underplaying important practical differences over peace and war, or the place of women, or the relative importance of various ritual activities.

The reactions of actual believers often go far beyond this in criticizing criticism and stressing uniqueness. Such a neoconservative reaction can be seen in a number of religious contexts. In the modern world it is typically a synthesis between traditional religion and nationalism of one kind or another. Typically too it tends to use the substance rather than the methodology of modernity, so that it becomes in this degree cognitively distant from the modern mainstream.

But in practice, whatever the intellectual position which is reached, traditions do tend to take the scriptures, together with certain elements of ritual activity, institutional organization, and so forth, as given; and I shall later return to consider whether anything of this givenness can be taken to yield knowledge. But also in rationalizing the given believers are liable to look on the scriptures as a record of religious experience and places of history and the cosmos as experientially interpreted. And so already the *pramāṇa* of testimony includes and points to experience.

There are of course differing kinds of religious experience — numinous visions, inner mystical states, shamanistic ecstasies, moral conversions, panenhenic apprehensions, and so forth — but some recent discussions of mysticism help to illuminate some main issues which apply across the whole field. Debate primarily has touched on the relation of experience and interpretation, and this question highlights our starting paradox.

One way into the question is to consider whether there is a single sort of mystical experience, clothed differently so to speak by the differences of cultural and creedal interpretation. On this view there is an essential similarity between the experiences of the Sufi, the Hindu yogi, the Buddhist contemplative, the Christian mystic, the Taoist sage, and so on. If so, then how do we account for the very different things they say? Well, it is because their hindsight view of their experience, and their preconditioning too, have helped to color and embroider their accounts of what happened. But we can detect from a core of similar things said about the experience itself that it is alike. There is naturally a host of questions and methodological problems which arise wormlike out of this can. Personally, however, I am favorable to the likeness of mystical experience thesis, and favorable also to the thesis of the diversity of types of religious experience.

For all that, it is clear that the meaning of an experience, as of other events in the life of a religious person, will depend upon concepts and attitudes which he or she already holds, and, for the most part, these will not be epistemologically dependent upon the type of experience. But experiences nevertheless can be *suggestive* of differing kinds of theology and doctrine, of ethics and ritual practice, and so forth. Numinous experiences suggest dualism, dependence, and grace, while mystical experiences suggest nonduality, questing, self-discovery, emptiness, and the negative path. The numinous suggests authority, commandment, mercy, dynamism; the mystical suggests illumination, self-discipline, compassion, quietude. But though there is this suggestive relationship (and it helps to explain differing patterns of religious development), the converse effects are typically even more powerful. My numinous is Yahweh, not Kṛṣṇa; or Allah, not Śiva; my cloud of unknowing is Christ, the birth of Christ in the soul, not the luminous realization of the Buddha-nature. One person treads the path to nirvana; another seeks the inner meaning of the Torah.

So I think there is a gap that can be opened up between a relatively homogeneous experience and varieties of interpretation. Some say: All experience is interpreted. However, there are still differences between highly ramified and minimally ramified descriptions of experience.

The interpretative gap is an epistemological one. If the degree of interpretation is great then the experience guarantees less. The less ramified the description the more it guarantees. Thus if I have a certain experience of a white-colored figure, I can say with fair confidence, "There is a white-clothed person"; but if I see no more details, it is more of a gamble claiming that I see the Pope. If I say, "In that dazzling obscurity I saw the Timeless One," it is less of a distance from experience than saying, "I saw the Timeless One who is Christ himself." Christ ties us among other things to a sequence of historical events and a rather complicated doctrine of incarnation and the godhead.

As we would expect, each religion and each subreligion is unique, because of its differing past and special combination of motifs. Each has elements echoed in other traditions, either by similarity or by borrowing. We find uniquenesses and typology. It is like our own case: my nose is like others' noses, but it is also unique in its configuration and history (even identical twins have tiny differences, as well as the divergences of location and experience).

We would expect, then, some typological likenesses in other traditions than our own. Such echoes have themselves a paradoxical effect. They reduce the epistemological weight which the experiences give to particular doctrines and practices, but they increase the epistemological weight of the more minimal claims to have contact with the transcendent. The relative universality of experiences of a given type is ground for taking them seriously, but that itself weakens the particularist claims.

A community, then, which nourishes its members in a certain kind of religion and thereby helps its members to have what they see as contact with the transcendent can make some claim to a sort of wisdom and knowledge. (I leave on one side the question: But what if all this supposition of the transcendent is a grand illusion? I shall, however, return to it.)

Moreover, it is not just that there is knowledge of the ultimate. There are other claims to knowledge which could be made — that the experiences in question have certain fruitful effects on life, perhaps on the community as a whole, and so on. There is knowledge — if true — that the sacraments "work" in terms of creating appropriate fruits. The person whose life is changed can well say, "I know that my redeemer liveth." Viewed phenomenologically, religion has whatever power it has, and Christ or Viṣṇu or whatever experiential or ritual focus of faith has the power it has, and this cannot be taken away by the mere disproof that there is a Viṣṇu as such (not that any proof of the sort exists, or could exist). So we might say: On the one hand communities may make claim to some contact with the ultimate, and this they can naturally speak of as knowledge. And in a harder sense of *know* they can be said to know what the effects of the focus are. This is a sort of phenomenological positivism.

But the claim about the transcendent cannot be to knowledge of the details. Near the edges of the ramification of beliefs which form part of the organism of a community's tradition the epistemological weight of experience becomes slight, and the thought of prophets and mystics elsewhere should remind a community of the plausibility of an inductivist position on revelation and the given. That in turn points to a less ramified knowledge.

I may still, as an adherent of a tradition, feel that the collage of ideas and practices which constitute the world view through which I live my life is good and highly persuasive and makes better sense than alternatives. I can have reasons for my world view. But I can hardly disprove alternative world views any more than I can prove my own. It is true that if a world view includes very rigidly deductive material, then I can in a sense say that, as a total package, it is false because of one or more wrong items in it. But it is usually possible for the other community to modify its package, so my critique merely changes the shape of the other collage slightly.

The thought that we can have reasons to believe in one world view rather than another, and that though we may have fragmentary knowledge of the ultimate and an awareness of the actual power of our focus of faith upon ourselves, leads me to reject relativism (there are of course other reasons as well). But it implies too the rejection of absolutism, if by this is meant the claim that we can or could be absolutely sure about one world view being exclusively or most comprehensively true. We can have faith in what the world view delineates, and belief that the world view is as true a one as can be found and better than all others. But these are epistemologically soft claims, and so I use the expression "soft nonrelativism" to characterize the reality of our situation.

The same by the way applies when we stretch our concerns to secular as well as transcendent-related systems of belief and practice. There cannot be proof of a Marxism or of scientific humanism or of some form of religion. The world views have their plausibilities, and evidences and arguments can be adduced. But think of the alternative evidences.

So we cannot seriously be absolutists, and yet we cannot say either that all world views are equally persuasive or valuable. To whom, you may ask? It seems to me that soft nonrelativism suggests that world views are like aesthetic objects in a sense. Whether Manet is a great artist is gradually determined as humanity sifts its experience of art and of Manet. I rather like the idea propounded by Duncan Howlett of a Council of Human Judgment to which we in the long term appeal. Truth will out, but gradually and probably always plurally and defectively. But there are reasons, as I have said. One of the criteria turns out to be dogmatism itself. Given that soft nonrelativism is right, then absolutistic religious movements cannot be all good, and are likely to be greatly misguided. Likewise, it is unlikely that a world view which is accepted uncritically can make much sense of scientific knowledge, since criticism is part of the process by which the latter is arrived at. So there are some higher-order criteria for evaluating world views.

There are some consequences of this. The first is that the only real basis for the state to propound an ideology is if there is unanimity about it. Otherwise, there should be separation of world view (party, church) and state. Since, moreover, there are no proofs of world view, toleration of world-view divergences is the only rational position to adopt. It may be that some world views themselves are not tolerant. Should they be tolerated? It seems reasonable that we should reduce intolerance, and that may mean some restraints ultimately upon nontolerant groups. But the intention should be to allow as many world views to live together as possible, in order to maximize toleration.

Another apparent consequence of soft nonrelativism is that the pursuit of truth, so far as it can be achieved, and of practical fruits which are good for life, implies that the delineation of various world views should be part of education. This is an aspect of education severely neglected. We turn out young people from high schools and colleges most often ignorant of the varieties of Christianity, Judaism, Eastern faiths, Southern cultures, Marxisms, and humanisms. Why do we teach the world's physical geography but not its spiritual or mental geography? Underlying this thought are twin aims. First, we should understand other world views than our own simply from the point of view of their actual power in history and in the present. Second, an educated person should be capable of attempting sensitively to evaluate alternatives.

Soft nonrelativism as I have expounded it implies also a greater space for trust or faith. Often traditional faiths teach their traditions as if their truth were known. But what can be known is rather limited, on my argument, and is largely confined to what immediately concerns religious encounter and various fruits and effects. But subjectively a person can be not only committed to the gamble that one's world view represents, but also sure that it "works." And one can be convinced of the essential, though unprovable, correctness of one's world view.

There is no reason why affirming one's world view should not be a matter of passion. It may be that soft nonrelativism increases the room for passion, but it reduces the room for fanaticism.

Lastly, I would like to make the following observation. In a plural world and in a pluralistic society the possibilities of individual choice of religion have, of course, multiplied. This is part of the decline of authority and therefore dogma (the rise of rhetoric in the religious preacher may itself reflect this). For both epistemological and social reasons the old role of religious doctrine has changed, for it is hard to enforce any conformity. Thus authoritative figures, such as the Pope, themselves become the objects of choice. One elects to be a Catholic, since walking out of the Church is so easy, and excommunication holds few terrors. Now all this does not imply that the doctrinal dimension of religion is unimportant, for a very good reason: it is one of the major means of keeping religious attitudes pointing toward the transcendent. And the importance of this lies partly in the way it allows the religious person or community to stand above or beside the world, and to have a position from which to criticize our institutions and values. In other words, the transcendent supplies a place from which to criticize, not to dogmatize. It is a partly precarious place, for it is only found through commitment and experience. But it enables religion itself to take up a fresh, incisive role.

Thus there is a sort of solidarity, in a strange new way, between a plural religious world and the heritage of the Enlightenment. For the free and scientific society is critical and imaginative, and the life of religion can offer both a transcendent place of criticism and a path to liberating the imagination. But such criticism needs not only the transcendent reference point but also the nourishment of spiritual values through that kind of religious knowledge which still remains to us.

NOTE

1. J. E. L. Oulton and Henry Chadwick, trans., *Alexandrian Christianity* (London: SCM Press, 1954), p. 94.

PART II

Religious Truth Claims Reconsidered

6

God and Coherence:
On the Epistemological Foundations
of Religious Belief
KAI NIELSEN

I

THERE IS LITTLE INTEREST now in so-called proofs for the existence
of God. The salvos fired against these classical arguments by Hume
and Kant have been, though sometimes in rather rationally recon-
structed forms, convincing to philosophers. There are those who
would claim that some of these attempted proofs are useful in giving us a sense of deity but, a few scholastic philosophers apart,
few would claim they give us a proof of, or even good evidence
for, the existence of God.[1] The arguments for God's existence can,
of course, given certain *prima facie* plausible assumptions about
their intelligibility, be so stated that they are formally valid arguments, but a sound argument must in addition have reliable premises, and there is little inclination to take the premises in these
arguments either as self-evident and substantive or as empirically
confirmable or disconfirmable.[2]

The appeal to religious experience is not quite so dead, but
even here, where the appeal is used to establish the existence of
God as an objective supernatural fact, there is a shying away from
it. "A felt utterly dependent or B had intimations of the numinous
but there is no God" is not self-contradictory or even logically
odd. The assumption that such feelings result from crucial childhood experiences and make no transcendent reference is a sim-
pler hypothesis that does not seem to be at cross-purposes with
the facts.

89

Many believers acknowledge both these points. Religious experience does not confirm divinity and God's existence cannot be demonstrated. Yet they remain believers and are not led down the primrose path to agnosticism or that fate worse than death, atheism. To understand that such rationalistic devices as we have been discussing will not work only makes room for the proper instrument of religious belief: faith. And Judaism and Christianity being what they are, this is just as it should be.

Alasdair MacIntyre, when he wrote *Difficulties in Christian Belief* and "The Logical Status of Religious Belief," was writing as a fideistic Christian.[3] In these two works he sets forth an argument of this general sort with considerable clarity and force. He points out that it is a theological requirement of Christianity that human beings be free to accept or reject God. If there were a proof for the existence of God that had geometrical rigor, it would be coercive for rational and informed people. If this were so, however, God's existence would *not* be something they could freely accept on trust and thus the belief in God available to us would not be the sort that was religiously appropriate. Such people could not freely accept or reject God. God, MacIntyre argues, "reveals himself in a way that depends on a response of trust which human beings are free to withhold."[4] The belief that there might be a rational demonstration of substantive religious claims, culminating in unquestionable conclusions following from unquestionable premises, clear to the light of reason, is a hangover from a thoroughly discredited rationalist metaphysics. It assumes, as Richard Rorty might put it, the worst sort of foundationalism.[5] Explicitly or implicitly, it models the structure of all reasoning on logico-mathematical reasoning, but while reasoning is often a form of calculation, a drawing of inferences, and a weighting of various considerations, it is not characteristically deductive in form. There is no undeniable evidence for the existence of God, "but both in the works of nature and in that history of revelation which is the Bible," God "offers us opportunities for accepting or rejecting him."[6] But "to ask for proof," MacIntyre concludes, "is to put oneself outside the only attitude in which it is possible to confront God; and therefore to refuse to believe because one cannot have proofs is a simple missing of the point."[7] A God vindicated by geometrical demonstrations, MacIntyre claims, "just would not be the God of the Bible,"[8] for no such validation of credentials is attempted in the Gospels or even envisaged as a possibility. (Here MacIntyre echoes what Karl Barth put more profoundly.) MacIntyre repeats Kant's claim that to defend religion by such rationalistic arguments as we find in traditional philosophical theology is in effect to prepare the ground for unbelief. We should not look for such epistemological foundations for religious belief. Belief is achieved by conversion rather than by argument or investigation. We can only know God, fideists claim, "by trusting in what are taken to be the signs of his being in the world. And where we are unwilling to trust, no argument will take the place of trust. Belief cannot argue with unbelief, it can only preach to it."[9]

What we know about God, fideists claim, we do not and cannot learn from philosophy. All that the philosophers can hope to achieve is to clear up misconceptions about the nature of religious concepts and by so doing partly neutralize the acids of skepticism. Argument about whether or not to be a Jew or a Christian or to have any religious commitment at all is always finally *ad hominem*. When push comes to shove, all we can do in wrestling with such a question is to take a leap unto faith — a leap that we must take without any rational guarantee that our faith or any faith is or could be *the* true faith. Above all, we must recognize that philosophy itself cannot provide any adequate substitute for faith and it cannot, fideists claim, finally criticize, on logically relevant grounds, a religion accepted (as all religion should be accepted) solely on faith.

For Jews, Christians, or Moslems who so reason, belief in God does not and cannot rest on empirical or intellectual discoveries; "God created the heavens and the earth" is not a hypothesis that believers have confirmed and it is not a statement that is open to test and objective refutation. There are, these fideists claim, no proofs one way or another. We no more have a cosmological disproof of God's existence than we have a cosmological proof of God's existence. There may be signs, but they remain unalterably ambiguous; they are never rationally compelling. Belief and unbelief remain, some fideists claim, intellectually speaking, equally compelling. One must finally decide, finally wager, finally will, to believe or not to believe. The Jew or Christian is a person who in the last analysis must simply resolve to live his or her life as a person of faith. It is in this rather peculiar way that one can will to believe.[10]

Even after such an affirmation of faith, believers still do not come to know God with any certainty. In faith they find disclosed *Deus revelatus*, a God who has disclosed the divine self but who is not identical with that disclosure. *Deus absconditus*, God as God actually is, must remain beyond anyone's ken. Faith at best understands through darkened glass. The mystery of God remains, and even *Deus revelatus* can be known only through faith. With such a revelation we are provided with a sure foundation for life, but even so, we remain without any intellectual assurance, for our feeling of certainty in our faith springs from our very trust. Our certainty here is in feeling; it is not that at last we have grasped the truth of our faith after an arduous intellectual voyage of discovery.

It is this very pervasive view, most evident in non-neanderthal Protestant Christianity, that I call *fideism*. It is the claim that religious belief cannot be based upon demonstrative knowledge, empirical investigation, or some set of rational principles uncovered by philosophical reflection, but rests solely on faith. There are neither metaphysical foundations nor epistemological foundations for religious belief. Religious knowledge is completely beyond the limits of finite human understanding. But all that notwithstanding, a fideist would argue, we are hounded by heaven; our very human condition drives us to faith if our lives are to have any meaning at all. Our wills are indeed free and we can, in our pride, turn from God, but if we do, we will in effect destroy ourselves by destroying all hope for a meaningful existence. Without faith, sensitive and nonevasive persons will be caught in the spite and self-laceration of a Dostoyevskian underground person, but out of despair they will finally come to realize true helplessness. Despair will finally drive them to a leap of faith. Even though they are in the position of utter skepticism about the very possibility of religious knowledge, they will, to make some sense of their fragmented lives, be driven to a religious affirmation. An utterly secular world vision is just too bleak to be humanly acceptable. Reflective and passionate people who care about their own lives and the lives of others will be driven to a Kierkegaardian leap of faith even while in the grip of a sense that there is something absurd about believing in God. Scandal to the intellect or not, the believer will stick with it.

II

There is no doubt that this is a psychosocial reality for a not inconsiderable number of people. I want here to ask the normative and justificatory question — the epistemological question if you will — whether this need be or even should be so for any reflective and sensitive person of strong commitments who can also think clearly and live nonevasively.

I think a careful and dispassionate look at the facts, and a taking to heart of those facts, will give us good grounds for believing that this is not so. Our lives need not be without sense if we are not knights of faith committed to a belief in God. God or no God, there are things we can enjoy and find intrinsically good: the warmth of the summer sun coming down on me now as I write this, the rustle of the poplars in the clear northern air, a good meal with good companions, a life with people I love, and so on. There are many things of intrinsic or at least inherent value which are not at all dependent on the existence of God or belief in God or any kind of spiritual beings as Tylor might put it. To find these things of value we do not have to have any religious commitments or religious beliefs. And to prove, if that can be done, that what we reflectively value under conditions of undistorted communication is really of value is as much, or as little, of a problem for the believer as it is for the person without any religious belief at all.

But why commit yourself to moral ends, why care about the fate of others, particularly if they do not happen to be people who are close to you? It is natural enough to respond that we must do so because that is the right thing to do. Indifference to human suffering or human weal and woe is just evil. Anyone who is capable of moral response must recognize that, and whether you are capable of moral response or not does not depend, either causally or logically, on whether or not you were brought up in a God-fearing culture. Plenty of people who are utter atheists so respond with as much resoluteness as any believer.

To say that they must unwittingly be living off the cultural capital of their religious heritage is a claim that is without foundation. Even if those ideas originally got into the stream of their lives from a cultural endowment which was in origin religious, this would not establish their personal rationale or show why these people remained committed to them. The validity of our beliefs, and what justifies our holding them, does not depend on their origin.

There are deep puzzles about the foundations of moral belief. Indeed even foundationalist claims over questions of empirical knowledge seem to be in shambles.[11] To make foundationalist claims in moral epistemology is very chancy indeed. I am inclined to agree with Isaac Levi that to be an antifoundationalist is a virtue in a philosopher.[12] But, be that as it may, questions about the foundations of moral belief are equally problems, if indeed they are problems, for the believer as for the skeptic. To try to take a foundationalist turn with a divine command ethic runs into all the usual difficulties. Suppose fideists claim that they know with certainty what they ought to do, at least in many circumstances, for they know they ought always to do whatever God commands and usually God commands them what to do. But, for a starter, how does the fideist know, or how *can* she know, as Martin Buber once asked, that it is God telling her these things and not the devil? How can she know that it is God and not the promptings of her own objectivized id or superego?

Even suppose a person could in some way ascertain that there is a God and that it is God who is telling him to do these things, why does that make it something that he ought to do? That someone tells you to do something is not at all a sufficient reason for doing it. But in God's case, the fideist responds, we can know that we should do what God tells us to do because God is all-powerful and all-knowing. But an all-powerful being could still be evil and so could even a perfectly intelligent being who knew everything that could be known. And adding the two things together doesn't necessarily produce goodness either. Surely, if we know anything about the world at all, we know that evil can go with power and intelligence. And while it is plainly prudent to do what an all-powerful and all-knowing evil being commands, it does not establish that those commands are the *right* thing to do. Indeed we can have rather good grounds for believing that they are not, for such a being is the author of evil. We may, feeling the strains of commitment, have to make what Brecht would call our little adjustments, but this hardly makes that being's commands morally obligatory.

The believer will respond that this line of argument is silly because God is the Supreme Good. Asked, in turn, how she knows that, one can respond in a number of ways, none of which are satisfactory. One might say that we don't know that God is the Supreme Good but, as a fideist, one takes it as a given on trust. That is where one starts. But then the foundationalist quest has been given up. And, more importantly, since following God's commands is what she claims she ought to be doing, she has given us no reason to follow her there. People, particularly if we look at the matter cross-culturally and with different historical epochs in mind, can and do start from many places; there are innumerable givens. She has not shown, or even given the slightest inkling for believing, that her starting point is preferable to any other starting point. She has not justified her belief, either for herself or for others, or shown that it is not arbitrary.

Alternatively, a person might say that he knows that God is the Supreme Good or at least has good reason to believe that is so because it says so in the Bible and/or that this is a central teaching of the Christian tradition. But, it will in turn be asked, why take the Bible or any Scripture as the supreme guide or even as a guide for your life? If we consider the various cultures and subcultures around there are many alternative guides and alternative holy writs about. Why give the Christian one or indeed why give any one such pride of place, such deep authority over your moral life? If the answer is, in turn, because that is the way I was brought up, the reply should be: Why give such weight to that, why assume that gives you the true morality? People over cultural and historical time and space have been socialized in a not inconsiderable number of ways, ways that often conflict. Just to do, in such a circumstance, what you have been taught to do is ethnocentric and arbitrary.

To say, instead, that you accept Christian writ and tradition because it is really divinely inspired immediately prompts the question: But how do you know, or *do* you know that? The faithful of every religion believe that about their religion and tradition. To claim, in trying to escape relativisim here, that you have some sort of philosophical or rational grounding that will prove that your particular holy scripture is so inspired, or that your tradition is the embodiment of religious truth, is to go beyond anything that fideists believe they have available to them and requires us to re-

turn to the very shaky territory of rational or philosophical theology: the territory the fideist, not without good reason, puts aside
as rationalistic foolishness or hubris.

The last tack of the believer that I shall consider in this context is the response that it is true by definition that God is the Supreme Good. She would not call anything God that she also did
not take to be supremely good. If there is a God then God is the
Supreme Good. But, it needs to be asked, how does she know that
there is a God or a Supreme Good? She cannot rightly respond
that she must take that on faith, on pain of life being revealed as
senseless or morality as being absurd. For even if we do not know
that there is a Supreme Good we can still know many things about
what we ought to do and ought not to do. We can know, for example, that kindness is good, that integrity is good, that a life without agony is good, that cruelty and exploitation are evil, and the
like. Here we can perfectly well have knowledge without foundations.[13] To the skeptical question, How do we know these things
are good? we can and should reply that this, if it is a problem,
is a common problem for believer and skeptic alike. And if we cannot rely on such deeply considered judgments, judgments held on
reflection by both atheists and believers, we could not even begin
to know what the Supreme Good is. But the point that is most
germane here is that for these judgments to be available to us, for
these convictions to be our considered convictions, and for there
to be convictions on which we can act, we need not know, or even
have the faintest inkling of, what the Supreme Good is. Morality
does not crumble and life does not become senseless if we are
without an understanding of the Supreme Good.

The believer might concede that and still say, But wouldn't
it be a very good thing indeed if we could have such knowledge?
Yet here the skeptical question returns. What is the Supreme Good?
And why think the religious believer has any better grip than anyone else? If the fideist responds: "If you really know God you will
know what the Supreme Good is," we should in turn respond that,
given his claim that God by definition is good, his deep-sounding
remark must turn out to be a dressed-up and thinly-disguised plati-
tude logically on a par with "If you really know what a bachelor
is you will know what an unmarried male is." The substantial questions are what, if anything, is denoted by *God*, and what, if

anything, is the Supreme Good; and why should we believe that there is either a God or a Supreme Good to be discovered? To be told that "God is the Supreme Good" is analytic or true by definition does not help us at all in dealing with the substantive questions that grip us in any quest for the Supreme Good. But, even more fundamentally, we can have a robust sense of what morality requires of us, how we ought to live, even if we have no understanding at all of what the Supreme Good is or what God is. And Camus and Sartre to the contrary notwithstanding, we need not think our lives are without meaning even if we have no understanding at all of what the Supreme Good is or what God is. Indeed such things could be perfectly available to us, even if we denied that there is a Supreme Good or that God exists.

What has been neglected in the above discussion, for more important fish, is the claim that one might coherently claim to know that there is a Supreme Good and still deny that God exists. And this, also note, is perfectly compatible with "If God exists then God is the Supreme Good," though it is not, of course, compatible with "If there is a Supreme Good then God exists." But, compatibility aside, there is no good reason to believe that last proposition is true unless we mean "God is the Supreme Good" to be an identity statement. A believer, however, who takes "God is the Supreme Good" to be true by definition need not so read it, and indeed he shouldn't so read it on pain of making other things he wants to say about God nonsense. Remember that neither are all analytic propositions identity statements, nor all identity statements analytic.

III

So we have seen, if so far my arguments have been near to the mark, that we have no good reason to believe that God exists or that God is the Supreme Good, or even that there is a Supreme Good. We have also seen that there is no reason to conclude from this that morality crumbles or that life is meaningless.[14]

A fideist might respond that even if all of this were established there still would be another feature of our lives that would drive a reflective person to faith. Our lives are in myriads of ways unsatisfying and disillusioning. We often experience a defeat of our deepest hopes, the loss of people we very much love, horrible conflicts with those we love, debilitating illness, and the like. Moreover, sometimes we are people of extensive self-deception and of uncontrollable self-destructiveness or destructiveness. And the world we live in is a world of horrible conditions of degradation and exploitation, a world in which starvation and poverty are both rife and unnecessary and a world in which many people, again quite unnecessarily, are sunk in conditions of ignorance and without a reasonable control of the conditions of their own lives. Perhaps the world and our condition in the world is not as bleak as Pascal, Dostoyevsky, Sartre, and Beckett have portrayed it, but it is very bleak indeed.

Against such a background the fideist could remark that a person with a good awareness of the above, who wishes to be a humane person, will hold out for herself and for others the Christian hope for immortality and eternal community with God. Like Kierkegaard, one might very well regard such a belief a scandal to the intellect and as something that has the worst sort of probability weight, but still, given the options, something for which we can rationally hope.

It isn't, as Pascal would put it, that we have everything to gain and nothing to lose. For perhaps we may lose our intellectual integrity by believing in something which at best seems plainly false and at worst is plainly incoherent, simply because we want or need to believe such things. Isn't it irrational to entertain such wishes for ourselves and for humankind generally? But need we, if we entertain such hopes, subvert our intellectual integrity if we continue to have such hopes in the face of an utterly unblinking awareness of the fact that a belief in immortality is such a scandal to the intellect? In what way must such a person be kidding herself? She sees the belief has no good warrant, indeed that it is an utterly fantastic, perhaps even an incoherent, belief. If she sees this clearly and still wishes or even hopes for immortality, how has she kidded herself? She doesn't somehow believe that after all it is really true or a little more likely than what the skeptic believes. Indeed, she agrees with the skeptic fully about the probabilities but continues to hope that in spite of everything she will survive the death of her present body and find eternal communion with God and other human beings. How is she being irrational or unreasonable in entertaining such a hope, if she has it under the conditions described above and does not let that hope divert her from making the life she has as meaningful as possible and from struggling to bring a world into being which is not as nasty as the world I have described? If this is her pattern of behavior and her mindset, it does not seem fair to me to describe her as evasive, double-minded, or in any way irrational or even diminished in her reasonableness.

Shouldn't we all then hope or at least wish for immortality? Wouldn't we all, if we could behave decently, be with those we really care about, remain in good health, and continue to have good mental faculties, wish to live forever? Isn't it to be a spoilsport and indeed to be a little bit irrational *not* to have such wishes?

Here it is best to speak personally. Wishes are one thing, hopes another. Hopes involve some conception of the possibility of what is hoped for. Wishes do not require anything that strong. When I think about it and articulate it to myself, I recognize that I do wish I could live forever under the conditions I have described above. However, this is not something I think about very often; nor do I think it should have any priority in my life. Such wishes do not count for much with me and do not translate into hopes. Why do they not count very much with me? Because they seem to me so plainly fanciful and, as well, very prone to produce self-deception. Moreover, they have a way of directing one's thoughts away from what is, humanly speaking, more important. There are so many other things to be wished for, hoped for, and indeed struggled for, that are vital and have some reasonable possibility of being achieved.

An analogy might help. I am a socialist living in a capitalist society which is not on the immediate threshold of a socialist transformation. I hope, I hope reasonably, for a socialist transformation in the next fifty to a hundred years — and indeed for one whose birth pangs will not be hellishly hard, though as a bettor I wouldn't bet on an easy birth. I think that such a transition is a reasonable possibility in the next fifty to a hundred years or perhaps even sooner. I often wonder if it is something I will see in my life and have sadly concluded that the chances are not very good; but I often hope, and I think not unreasonably, that after all I will be part of it and do my part in building it and making it flourish.

That hope is frequently with me, given its importance to me and the likelihood of its achievement. But a hope that weighs much more with me is the hope, which I also judge to be a reasonable expectation, that in fifty to a hundred years' time we will not have blown ourselves to smithereens and we will have firmly made the transition to socialism. That, I judge, is not a quixotic ideal and is worth really struggling for, worth making a central part of my life. But I could understand a cultural pessimist who might, with a very different assessment of the possibilities, think of my hopes here as mere fanciful wishes. In the extreme case, he might see them, if he was very deeply pessimistic indeed, on a par with the Christian's wish for immortality. What we hope for, if we are reasonable and caring, is tied to what we think is really important and to what we think the empirical possibilities are.

Let me extend the parallel a little further. As I would fancifully wish to live forever, I would fancifully wish to wake up in the morning and miraculously find that a socialist transformation had bloodlessly and effortlessly taken place. We, the fancy goes, now live in a world free of war, in which capitalism and the authoritarian control of people no longer exists. People — everyone, everywhere — are at last free. They control their own lives in a world where there are no bosses and bossed, no exploitation or degradation, no sexism, no racism, no intolerance of human peculiarities, in a world of social equality in which we are all comrades together. The ideal, of course, means a lot to me. But the wish, the idle dream, that I might wake up tomorrow and find myself in that world means very little to me because it is so fanciful. It is like, in that respect, the wish for immortality. It is idle, utterly idle, and, if dwelt on, a distraction from the social realities of our lives, including the day-to-day concrete struggle to try to make something approximating that idle dream a social reality.

The wish to wake up tomorrow and find a dream of your life or world in place and the wish for immortality are rather parallel, except that the wish for immortality is perhaps incoherent or even a logical impossibility. For me neither wish counts for much — though I do not attempt to drive either out of my mind or reject either — for they are not tied to the real world where your fate and mine is indeed tied up. And it is to that world that an overriding importance should be attached, and where we will achieve our liberation, our human and moral majority, and our emancipation.

Late at night, perhaps after many drinks, we can wax sentimental about what it would be like if tomorrow the world were very different and immortality were really possible. I suspect it is all rather maudlin. Yet, I suppose, we could rather idly entertain all these things. But if we care about ourselves and care about our fellows there are things which are far more important that should engage our attention instead. Such idle wishes are not rejected; they are not to be driven out of our minds; they will just wither away as the demystification of the world gradually gains ascendancy and people gain greater social wealth, are better educated, and come to have more secure lives.

Fideists are bad psychologists if they think that all reflective atheists are tortured souls despairingly longing for the absolute or stoically fighting off Pascalian urges. The wish to live forever for many of us is idle, something we are concerned neither to accept nor to reject. It is not true that if we no longer entertain these wishes our lives will become meaningless, fragmented, emotionally crippled; it is not true that, given our atheistic intellectual convictions, our lives are something to be stoically endured with nihilism at the door. Fideists should not take their own personalities as humankind writ large, and they should not flatter themselves with the conceit that their response is the deepest, most human response to nonevasive reflection about our condition.

NOTES

1. Austen Farrar, *Finite and Infinite* (Westminster: Dacre Press, 1943); and Austen Farrar, *Faith and Speculation* (New York: New York University Press, 1967), pp. 131–55.

2. Kai Nielsen, "Arguing about the Rationality of Religion," *Sophia* 12, no. 3 (October 1973): 7–10; and Kai Nielsen, "A False Move in Reasoning about God," *Understanding* 4 (Autumn 1975): 10–16.

3. Alasdair MacIntyre, *Difficulties in Christian Belief* (London: SCM Press, 1956); and Alasdair MacIntyre, "The Logical Status of Religious Belief," in *Metaphysical Beliefs*, ed. Ronald W. Hepburn (London: SCM Press, 1957), pp. 168–205.

4. MacIntyre, "Logical Status of Religious Belief," p. 175.

5. Richard Rorty, *Philosophy and the Mirror of Nature* (Princeton, N.J.: Princeton University Press, 1979). For how much of the positivist attack on metaphysics he would accept, see p. 384.

6. MacIntyre, "Logical Status of Religious Belief," p. 180.

7. Ibid.

8. Ibid., p. 182.

9. Ibid.

10. Kai Nielsen, *Reason and Practice* (New York: Harper & Row, 1971), pp. 204–25.

11. Richard Rorty, *Consequences of Pragmatism* (Minneapolis, Minn.: University of Minnesota Press, 1982); and *Philosophy and the Mirror of Nature*.

12. Isaac Levi, "Escape from Boredom: Edification according to Rorty," *Canadian Journal of Philosophy* 11, no. 4 (December 1981): 589–601.

13. Kai Nielsen, "Grounding Rights and a Method of Reflective Equilibrium," *Inquiry: An Interdisciplinary Journal of Philosophy and the Social Sciences* 25 (September 1982): 277–306; Kai Nielsen, "On Needing a Moral Theory: Rationality, Considered Judgments, and the Grounding of Morality," *Metaphilosophy* 13, no. 2 (April 1982): 97–116; and Kai Nielsen, "Considered Judgments Again," *Human Studies* 5 (1982): 109–18.

14. Kai Nielsen, *Ethics without God* (Buffalo, N.Y.: Prometheus Books, 1973); Kai Nielsen, "Linguistic Philosophy and 'The Meaning of Life'" in *The Meaning of Life*, ed. E. D. Klemke (New York: Oxford University Press, 1981), pp. 177–204.

7

The Burden of Proof

ANTONY FLEW

I

MODERN PHILOSOPHY BEGAN in 1637 with the publication of the *Discourse on the Method*. In Part 4 Descartes suddenly opens up with the most shattering single-sentence salvo in the entire literature: "So, because our senses sometimes play us false, I decided to suppose that there was nothing at all which was such as they cause us to imagine it; and, because there are men who make mistakes in reasoning, even with the simplest geometrical matters, and construct paralogisms, judging that I was as liable to error as anyone else, I rejected as unsound all the reasonings I had hitherto accepted as proofs" (Descartes, *Discourse on the Method*, Pt. 4).

Many objections have been deployed against what is thus presented as a program for doubting systematically everything which conceivably could be doubted. C. S. Peirce, for instance, urged that all our individual inquiries have to start from wherever we individually happen to be. Peirce's charge is nowadays usually brought in a more conceptual-analytic form: all doubt presupposes some knowledge, or at least some belief sufficiently plausible to constitute a reason. It would, that is to say, be a solecism to profess to be doubting, as opposed to confessing plain nescience concerning, any proposition in an area in which one was totally ignorant.

But Descartes has a complete answer to the main charge here. He has offered reasons for doubting: both the truth of all his previous beliefs about the universe around him; and the validity of all his previous reasonings. In all his doubting, however, Descartes

103

scarcely even pretends to doubt any of his previous beliefs about one particular subject. In Part 1 of the Discourse, while reviewing his own education, Descartes contrasts philosophy with theology rather sharply: "Theology teaches how to gain heaven . . . philosophy gives the means by which one can speak plausibly on all matters and win the admiration of the less learned." He then affirms his own commitment: "I revered our theology, and aspired as much as anyone else to gain heaven; but . . . the revealed truths which lead to it are beyond our understanding . . . to undertake the examination of them, and succeed, one would need some special grace from heaven, and to be more than a man" (Descartes, *Discourse on the Method*, Pt. 1).

Considered by itself this may be all very well. Yet what it certainly does not do is consist with one very pertinent remark made later in the same Part 1. "For it seemed to me that I might find much more truth in the reasonings which someone makes in matters that affect him closely, the results of which must be detrimental to him if his judgment is faulty, than from the speculations of a man of letters in his study; which produce no concrete effect, and which are of no other consequence to him except perhaps that the further they are away from common sense, the more vanity he will derive from them, because he will have had to use that much more skill and subtlety in order to make them seem dialectically probable" (Descartes, *Discourse on the Method*, Pt. 1).

We may expect everyday and practically oriented perceptual judgments to be, typically, correct. But, at least initially, speculations either about another world or about the operations of unobservables in this world must be reasonably suspect and doubtful. The reason is this. Whereas the price of your failing to perceive, say, advancing traffic will likely be immediate injury or death, the incomparably more appalling penalty of eternal damnation is by you felt to be — understandably even if falsely — both remote and unsure.

In Part 2 Descartes goes on to provide a second and more decisive general reason for doubting all theological claims. The crucial statement in Part 2 is this: "Having learned from the time I was at school that there is nothing one can imagine so strange or so unbelievable that it has not been said by one or other of the philosophers; and since then, while traveling, having recognized that all those who hold opinions quite opposed to ours are not on that account barbarians or savages, but that many exercise as much reason as we do, or more; and, having considered how a given man, with his given mind, being brought up from childhood among the French or Germans becomes different from what he would be if he had always lived among the Chinese or among cannibals . . . I was convinced that our beliefs are based much more on custom and example than on any certain knowledge" (Descartes, *Discourse on the Method*, Pt. 2).

II

The outcome of our Part I is that Descartes indicated a compelling case for challenging every current theological belief. To meet such a challenge successfully would require two things: first, adequate reasons for holding all the theological beliefs which those directly challenged do hold; and, second, a convincing account of how it is that other no less rational and truth-concerned persons have different and often contradictory beliefs.

An adequate religious apologetic must therefore meet and defeat what in another place I have christened "the presumption of atheism."[1] That is about where the burden of proof must lie. It is, in that respect, like the presumption of innocence in the Common Law of England.

The word *atheism*, however, has in this contention to be construed unusually. I want the originally Greek prefix *a* to be read in the same way in *atheist* as it customarily is read in such other Greco-English words as *amoral*, *atypical*, and *asymmetrical*. In this interpretation an atheist becomes, not someone who positively asserts the nonexistence of God, but someone who is, simply, just not a theist. Let us, for future ready reference, introduce two labels: *positive atheist* for the former and *negative atheist* for the latter.

Such negative atheism is to be distinguished from agnosticism. The agnostic is one who, having entertained the proposition that God exists, now professes not to know whether that proposition is true or whether it is false. But the atheist in my peculiar interpretation, unlike the atheist in the usual sense, has not as yet and as such conceded even the legitimacy of the concept of God. The point is crucial. The protagonist of my presumption of atheism wants to show that it is up to the theist to do two essentially successive things: first, to explain and defend whatever theological concepts it is proposed to introduce; and, second, to provide some sort of sufficient reason for believing that this concept, or these concepts, do in fact have application.

Once the need to proceed through these two successive stages has been thus spelled out, it becomes obvious that the successful completion of the first must be a presupposition of the achievement of the second. It has nevertheless been normal practice either altogether to neglect, or at best to skimp, that necessary preliminary. It is, for example, notorious that Descartes abandons his much-trumpeted skeptical principles the moment he steps onto theologically sensitive ground. Thus he first takes it absolutely for granted that he is providentially possessed of the one and only indisputably correct and coherent concept of God. Then he proceeds to take this putative concept, and the supposed fact that he is possessed of it, as the premises for two allegedly knockdown demonstrations that it has, and indeed must have, true application.

III

The outcome of our Part II is, therefore, that the burden of proof must lie upon anyone holding any positive theological beliefs. Part III will now attend to some objections which have been or might be launched against this conclusion. Then, finally, I shall in Part IV try to suggest how difficult it is going to be to compass what I have been urging must be the indispensable first stage in any project for meeting and defeating the presumption of atheism. The main payoff of this whole essay is, indeed, to put emphasis upon that normally neglected preliminary.

1. The first and least sophisticated objection consists in merely ignoring the challenge, or else dismissing it as irrelevant, on the grounds that we are here in the province not of reason but of faith. Notwithstanding that this is precisely what today appears most often to be done, it will not do. If the venture of faith is to be

anything but wholly arbitrary, then there have to be reasons: both for venturing at all; and for venturing in one particular sense. To refuse such reasons, especially in matters which you yourself are insisting to be of supreme importance, is — to borrow the properly offensive term which Thomas Aquinas chose to employ in his own discussion —"frivolous" (Thomas Aquinas, *Summa contra gentiles* 1.6).[2]

2. The second objection is to argue that many believers have, in effect, already met and defeated the presumption of atheism; and, second, that they have done this in ways similar to those in which all of us satisfy ourselves that our everyday and practically oriented perceptual judgments are, typically, correct. Professor John Hick puts this second objection in the following way: "The right question is whether it is rational for the religious man himself, given that his religious experience is coherent, persistent, and compelling, to affirm the reality of God. . . . What is in question is the rationality of the one who has the religious experiences. If we regard him as a rational person we must acknowledge that he is rational in believing what, given his experience, he cannot help believing."[3]

It is clear that, in talking about the believer's experience of God, Hick wants to construe the word *experience* in its ordinary, everyday, public sense. In another, peculiarly philosophical sense of *experience*, the claim to have had experience of something has reference only to the logically private. It carries no implications of cognitive contact with, or even of the public and external-world real existence of, that something.[4]

Now the existence of objects of experience, in the first sense of *experience*, neither is nor could be inferred either from the occurrence or from claims about the occurrence of experience, in the second sense of *experience*. Yet just this, surely, is what Hick's own believers are trying to do when they claim to be in their experience as it were perceiving their God? For they all know, just as well as everyone else knows, that, whenever and wherever they themselves claim to be enjoying their brand of supposedly cognitive religious experience, there is nothing available to be perceived, other than what is perceptible equally by all the rest of us; and, hence, that they are to all appearance engaged in nothing more or other than exercises of the imagination.

They know too, presumably, that adherents of other and often incompatible systems of religion are also persuaded that they too have had experience, in the everyday sense of *experience*, of the very different objects of their religious devotions — experience, that is, of Apollo and Athena, of Śiva and Ganesh, just as much as of Jesus bar Joseph and of his supposedly virgin mother. So how can it be reasonable of Hick's cobelievers to rest so confidently upon their conviction that they alone have been privileged to enjoy genuinely informative religious experience? How can it be reasonable, that is, until and unless they have, by first meeting and defeating the presumption of atheism, maneuvered themselves into a position to maintain that it is through some prior knowledge of the existence and normal activities of its ostensible objects that they have become qualified to pick out their own brand of religious experience as uniquely revelatory?

3. The third and two later objections are drawn from a long and extremely sympathetic review by my sometime colleague Professor Kai Nielsen. He starts by quoting a previous critic, who asserted that my own insistence upon the presumption of atheism itself depends on the unargued assumption that "the only reasonable position for anyone is to be 'completely noncommittal' concerning God unless and until good enough reasons are produced."[5] This in turn, according to the same earlier critic, depends on the further assumption "that an uncommitted stance on matters of grave import where there is a paucity of universally acceptable reasons/evidence is always morally superior."[6] Nielsen comments: "At the very least we need further argument from Flew on this point."[7]

But no moral assumption is required in order to justify my contention about the burden of proof. For the word *proof* is being employed in an appropriately liberal sense. It embraces any and every variety of sufficient reason: motivating reasons are not ruled out a priori. Reasons of this kind are, however, precisely not evidencing reasons for believing that propositions are true. Instead they are, as their descriptive label suggests, motivating reasons for persuading ourselves that propositions are (known to be) true whether or not they truly are. To accept and to act upon such reasons may on occasion be the course of rationality. It may be the best available means for securing your particular chosen ends. Where it is not rational is where the objective is truth.

4. Nielsen's next objection is a drastic demand: "He must give us . . . good reasons for believing that we have a common concept of rationality with strong enough criteria to give us grounds for assessing the comparative rationality of the commitments of believers and skeptics. Without such an articulation and defense there will be a large question mark before Flew's presumption of atheism."[8]

I cannot see that it is incumbent on me to do anything of the sort. Surely our presumption should be that all terms are univocal until and unless we find some reason for distinguishing? It is only if and when someone suggests that all my reasons are either irrelevant or not reasons at all that there begins to be any question of different conceptions of rationality. But suppose that such a deep and extensive gulf has opened up, and that all efforts to build bridges fail. Then what will it be which the two sides have in common sufficient to warrant talk about two rival conceptions of rationality?[9]

A parallel question about delusions is even more difficult to answer. Nielsen refers to my hostility to "the false and dangerous contention that 'which beliefs count as delusions is a matter of the standards of a given time and place.'" He also cites my response: "What truly is determined by such relativistic standards is: not what really is a delusion; but which delusions are recognized as such."[10] I see no reason to retreat from that straightforward and decisive rebuttal. For what room is there here for two or more different sets of criteria, both of which or all of which are equally correct; and neither of which or none of which determine different meanings for the word *delusion*?

5. Nielsen concludes that "if [Flew's] presumption of atheism is to have any force he needs to show how groundless religious beliefs are different and require justification before they can be reasonably accepted."[11] Finally Nielsen says that he "would make much" of a point, which he falsely attributes to Peirce rather than to me, "that 'one positive reason for being especially leery towards religious opinions is that these vary so much from society to society; being, it seems, mainly determined, as Descartes has

it, "by custom and example."' But more of that on another occasion."[12]

Yes, indeed. I entirely agree. And on this occasion I have taken up and developed that suggestion and hence, hopefully, met Nielsen's third and final objection.

IV

All my previous publications, it is elsewhere alleged, have relied upon a now utterly discredited verificationist theory. So in any future contributions I must first repent and then, perhaps after doing penance, expound and defend some superior alternative. But the charge is false, arising from a misreading of my much reprinted Note on "Theology and Falsification."[13] Nor is it necessary, in order to be in a position to make individual judgments about meaningfulness and meaninglessness, to cleave to any comprehensive theory of meaning.

The Note was not in any case concerned with judgments of that kind, whether particular or general. Nor was it either urging or employing falsification as a criterion of significance — any more than Sir Karl Popper was in his *Logik der Forschung*, or before, or after.[14] What I was doing there was developing a challenge to believers, and especially to those believers whose beliefs appeared to have a "human interest." It was a challenge to them to begin to make clear, not least to themselves, what it was which they were asserting. Its conclusion ran, it may be recalled, as follows: "I therefore put to the succeeding symposiasts the simple central questions, 'What would have to occur or to have occurred to constitute for you a disproof of the love of, or of the existence of, God?'"[15]

What I recognized there is that the particular meanings being attributed to these utterances by particular utterers must depend upon what several answers these several persons took to be appropriate. This contention is itself an immediate consequence of that Note's sole general thesis about meaning: the tautology that any proposition must be equivalent to the negation of its own negation.

So, if anyone now chooses to respond to that challenge by saying that, in their own usage, these claims carry no implications about any sorts of matters of fact, then I shall be more inclined to accuse them of uttering heresy than of talking nonsense. Suppose next they complain that some later work of mine "confines its considerations to the same narrow range of alternatives with respect to questions of religious belief, to which Flew has long seen fit to restrict his attention,"[16] which "narrow range" does not embrace their own preferred and surely somewhat esoteric doctrines. Then why is it incumbent upon me to provide any excuses other than two questions: Why shouldn't it? and Why should it? Certainly I was, even in that brief Note, at pains to indicate that my main interest here was, as it continues to be, in religious doctrines which might either explain Humean matters of fact and real existence or have some bearing upon equally Humean questions of human conduct. But again, why not?

As for the alleged need to develop and defend a general theory of meaning before attacking any particular questions of significance, this is, surely, a classic case of putting the cart before the horse. For, were we truly unable to answer questions of this sort without reliance on such a theory, we could never test whether any theory was adequate to the facts which it was supposed to explain.

It is not only Descartes but also Aquinas who assumes that the development of a radical and systematic apologetic can begin with what I have been distinguishing as the second rather than the first stage. For, although he elsewhere devotes a lot of attention to the question of how it can be possible to say things about the infinite in language intelligible to finite human beings, in answer to the crunch question "Whether the existence of God can be demonstrated?" he proceeds at once to deploy his five putative proofs, more than one of which concludes with the triumphant phrase "which all men call God" (Thomas Aquinas, *Summa theologiae* 1.2.3). It is as if we all know that everyone is equipped with the same concept of God, a concept which we all know could have — even if, unlike that vouchsafed to Descartes, it does not have to have — actual application.

More remarkable is the fact that the latest book by a leading philosopher to develop and defend a positive atheism, J. L. Mackie, has an equally short way of dispatching the whole business: "There is really no problem."[17] Mackie has begun by quoting the working definition of God given by Richard Swinburne. Swinburne explains that he is talking about "a God who is 'a person without a body (i.e., a spirit), present everywhere, the creator and sustainer of the universe, able to do everything (i.e., omnipotent), knowing all things, perfectly good, a source of moral obligation, immutable, eternal, a necessary being, holy, and worthy of worship.'"[18]

At first Mackie sees the problem as "whether such descriptions can be literally meaningful."[19] But, as Austin once so characteristically remarked, "You've got to have something on your plate before you can start messing it around."[20] Yet that has not been provided for. The expression offered, "person without a body," is flatly self-contradictory. For persons in our ordinary everyday understanding just are a kind of creatures of flesh and blood — a very special kind, of course, possessed of many attributes not attributable to any other sort of material thing, yet no less essentially creatures of flesh and blood for all that.[21] So, if sense is to be given to the expression "person without a body," then we shall need to be provided with some appropriate means of identifying and re-identifying a person, in the corresponding new sense of *person*.

Neither Mackie nor Swinburne make such provision. However, whereas Swinburne argues extensively for his conclusions, Mackie has a very much shorter way with dissent: "Although all the persons we are acquainted with have bodies, there is no great difficulty in conceiving what it would be for there to be a person without a body: for example, one can imagine oneself surviving without a body, and while at present one can act and produce results only by using one's limbs or one's speech organs, one can *imagine* having one's intentions fulfilled directly, without such physical means."[22]

But, whether or not I can coherently conceive of myself witnessing (what is not just falsely pretended but truly will be) my own funeral, I certainly cannot imagine (image) myself witnessing that perhaps to some sad yet to many joyous scene; and hence I cannot argue, as Mackie does and so many others have done, from what is imaginable, a fortiori, to what must be conceivable. For how is my mental picture of my witnessing my own funeral supposed to differ from my mental picture of my own funeral, unwitnessed by me?[23]

Swinburne, by contrast, does see a problem. In a chapter on

"An Omnipresent Spirit," Swinburne attends more closely to it. On the reidentification issue, arguing against Terence Penelhum, Swinburne takes it that the objection to analyzing the identity of disembodied persons in terms of memory claims is that such claims could not be checked — which he contends that they could be. But the decisive objection, put first and perfectly by Bishop Butler, is that true memory presupposes, and therefore cannot constitute, personal identity. When I truly remember doing that, what I remember is that I am the same person who did it.[24]

From here Swinburne proceeds to argue "that the identity of a person over time is something ultimate, not analysable in terms of bodily continuity or continuity of memory or character."[25] The surely fatal step in Swinburne's argument here is to assume that, in our dealings with the ordinary flesh-and-blood persons whom we all are, "we may use bodily continuity to reach conclusions about personal identity."[26] For what we use bodily criteria for is to establish bodily continuity. And this is not just a usually reliable criterion for, but a large part if not the whole of what is meant by, personal identity.

Swinburne goes wrong, I think, mainly because, like so many others, he employs an unsound method. He insists on introducing imaginary puzzle cases, challenging us to decide what we would say were we ever in real life actually confronted by something of the sort. He then construes responses to such challenges as indications of the present meaning of "same person." But, to the extent that such puzzle cases are completely outside the scope of our ordinary experience, there may be no unequivocally correct answers to possible new questions about personal identity.[27] So Swinburne cannot be allowed to have established, by these unsound procedures, the conclusion that we do already have, and therefore could have, a concept of "the identity of a person over time [as] something ultimate, not analysable in terms of bodily continuity. . . ."[28]

Finally, in order to end not with a whimper but with a bang, I will quote from that most incorrigible of metaphysical materialists, Thomas Hobbes: "All other words are but insignificant sounds: and those of two sorts. One when they are new, and yet their meaning not explained. . . . Another, when men make a name of two names, whose significations are contradictory and insignificant; as this name, an *incorporeal body*, or, which is all one, an *incor-*

poreal substance, and a great number more" (Thomas Hobbes, *Leviathan*, chap. 4).

NOTES

1. Antony Flew, "The Presumption of Atheism," *Canadian Journal of Philosophy* 3 (September 1972), revised and reprinted in *The Presumption of Atheism* (London: Pamberton/Elek, 1976); reissued as *God, Freedom and Immortality* (Buffalo, N.Y.: Prometheus, 1984).

2. Aquinas uses the Latin word *levis*.

3. John Hick, review of *God and Philosophy* by Antony Flew, *Theology Today* 24 (April 1967): 85–87.

4. For a fuller explanation of this distinction in its present application see Antony Flew, *God and Philosophy* (London: Hutchinson, 1966), chap. 6; reissued as *God: A Critical Enquiry* (LaSalle, Ill.: Open Court, 1984).

5. Quoted in Kai Nielsen, review of *The Presumption of Atheism* by Antony Flew, *Religous Studies Review* 3 (July 1977): 144–50.

6. Ibid., p. 146.

7. Ibid.

8. Ibid., p. 147.

9. As Nielsen notices I raised this question earlier, in an article on "Anthropology and Rationality," revised and reprinted in my *Sociology, Equality, and Education* (London and New York: Macmillan & Co., and Barnes & Noble, 1976).

10. Nielsen's review of Flew's *Presumption of Atheism*, p. 146.

11. Ibid., p. 149.

12. Ibid., p. 150.

13. Antony Flew, "Theology and Falsification," in *New Essays in Philosophical Theology*, ed. Antony Flew and Alasdair MacIntyre (New York: Macmillan Co., 1955), pp. 96–99. This essay has been reprinted twenty-nine times at the last certainly incomplete count, including translations into Italian, German, Danish, and Welsh. Ought I perhaps to urge my friend and Freedom Association colleague Norris McWhirter to admit this as a (first?) philosophical item for the *Guinness Book of World Records*?

14. For his most emphatic denials see Karl Popper, *Conjectures and Refutations* (London: Routledge & Kegan Paul, 1963), chap. 1. For mine see Antony Flew, "'Theology and Falsification' in Retrospect," in *The Logic of God*, ed. Malcolm L. Diamond and Thomas V. Litzenburg (Indianapo-

lis, Ind.: Bobbs-Merrill, 1975); also reprinted, in a revised form, in Flew, *The Presumption of Atheism*.

15. Flew, "Theology and Falsification," p. 99.

16. See Schubert Ogden, review of *The Presumption of Atheism* by Antony Flew, *Religious Studies Review* 3 (July 1977): 142–44, and compare his contribution in Diamond and Litzenburg, *The Logic of God*.

17. J. L. Mackie, *The Miracle of Theism* (Oxford: Clarendon, 1982), p. 1.

18. Ibid.

19. Ibid.

20. J. L. Austin, *Sense and Sensibilia* (Oxford: Clarendon, 1962), p. 142.

21. It is now all of thirty-two years since I first began to insist upon this point, and to draw out its consequences for discussions of human survival and immortality, but the point has become no less crucial and fundamental with the passing of time. See, for instance, the Note on "Death" reprinted in Flew and MacIntyre, *New Essays in Philosophical Theology*, a Note which, unlike "Theology and Falsification," has never been reprinted elsewhere.

22. Mackie, *The Miracle of Theism*, pp. 1–2.

23. See Antony Flew, "Can a Man Witness His Own Funeral?" *Hilbert Journal* (1956); reprinted in *Meaning and Existence*, ed. W. J. Blackstone (New York: Holt Rinehart & Winston, 1972); in *The Art of Philosophy*, ed. F. A. Westphal (Englewood Cliffs, N.J.: Prentice Hall, 1972); in *Exploring Philosophy*, ed. P. A. French (Morristown, N.J.: General Learning Press, 1975); and, in a slightly revised version, in Flew, *The Presumption of Atheism*.

24. See, for instance, Antony Flew, "Locke and the Problem of Personal Identity," *Philosophy* 26 (1951): 53; reprinted, in variously revised versions, in *Locke and Berkeley*, ed. Charles B. Martin and David M. Armstrong (New York: Doubleday, 1968); in *Readings in the Philosophy of Religion*, ed. Boruch Brody (Englewood Cliffs, N.J.: Prentice-Hall, 1974); and in Flew, *The Presumption of Atheism*.

25. Richard Swinburne, *The Coherence of Theism* (Oxford: Clarendon, 1977), p. 110.

26. Ibid., p. 109.

27. It was a main, disturbing contention of my article in "Locke and the Problem of Personal Identity," that there may be no antecedently correct answers to such decision questions about personal identity; and hence that the persons themselves might be no better qualified than anyone else to give true answers.

28. Swinburne, *The Coherence of Theism*, p. 110.

8

The Body of Knowledge: "Religious" Notions in the Convergence of Psychoanalysis and Feminism

NAOMI R. GOLDENBERG

PEOPLE HAVE BEEN progressively dehumanizing themselves by taking their human senses, human functions, human parts, and abstracting them from their human bodies. We then create machines to do our seeing, listening, touching, talking, or thinking for us in a more perfect form. I see nothing wrong with this when we use machines to support and enhance life — such as in the case of artificial limbs or with the use of labor-saving technology. The problem arises when we begin to envy the machines — when we try to imitate them and thus model ourselves on inanimate objects. We then lose touch with what it is to be human. For example, Susan Sontag wrote in her essays *On Photography*[1] that there are ways in which the photographic image has now become more real for us than what we actually see. The camera, she argues, has altered our sense of sight and perhaps has even begun to define reality for us.

But it isn't just with machines that we dissociate ourselves from our humanness. There are ways of thinking that encourage us to flee from what is human and to despise ourselves. We fall into these habits whenever we imagine ourselves as controlled by purposeful entities outside of ourselves. Religions usually call these things gods. But, in philosophy, Plato called them forms, and in psychology, Jung called them archetypes. By treating these things as real we distort our world and dehumanize ourselves.

116

I suggest that much of our Western religious tradition can now offer little help in formulating strategies for living. The concept of a God who is outside the context of human contingency is itself a machine fantasy, *Deus ex machina*. By imagining any rules or laws, any propensity toward good or evil, any knowledge or wisdom as coming from outside a human sphere, we fuel the modern contempt for what is human. A transcendent godhead is an idea we can no longer afford.

But what then? What sort of theory can now carry a salvific, "religious" message? I suggest that such theory lies in a place theology has shunned — the human flesh. Instead of theology, I want to recommend two bodies of theory that appreciate human physicality: psychoanalysis and feminism.

Theology vs. Psychoanalysis

The idea of finding grounds for an optimistic view of human possibility within the corpus of psychoanalytic theory is ridiculous from the standpoint of traditional theology. It is generally concluded among theologians who discuss Freud that, if one stays with the psychoanalytic perspective, the world will look quite bleak and that life will be emptied of hope. This was certainly Oskar Pfister's feeling which he expressed by titling his critique of Freud's *Future of an Illusion*, *The Illusion of a Future*. More recently, Hans Küng has expressed the hopelessness he sees in accepting Freudianism. "Religious belief," Küng writes,

> would be in a bad way if there were no genuine grounds for it or if no grounds remained after a psychoanalytic treatment of the subject; however devout its appearance, such a faith would be immature, infantile, perhaps even neurotic. . . . Why should I not be allowed to wish that the sweat, blood, and tears, all the sufferings of millennia, may not have been in vain, that definitive happiness may finally be possible for all human beings — especially the despised and the downtrodden? And why should I not, on the other hand, feel an aversion to being required to be satisfied with rare moments of happiness and — for the rest — to come to terms with "normal unhappiness"? . . . May I not feel an aversion also in regard

to the idea that the life of the individual and of mankind is governed only by the pitiless laws of nature, by the play of chance, and by the survival of the fittest, and that all dying is a dying into nothingness?[2]

Note how insufficient and unsatisfying Küng finds the physical world. Because this world appears dismal and harsh, another world becomes necessary — a world of God which he sees as "unconditioned." For Küng this unconditioned reality that is "independent of our thinking, willing, and feeling, of psyche and society"[3] is where hope resides.

The work of Paul Ricoeur strikes a similar theme. Although Ricoeur greatly admires Freud, he is ultimately dissatisfied with the materialism of psychoanalytic theory. "In our day," he writes,

reductive hermeneutics is no longer a private affair; it has become a public process, a cultural phenomenon; whether we call it demythologization, when it occurs in a given religion, or demystification, when it proceeds from without, the aim is the same: the death of the metaphysical and religious object. Freudianism is one of the roads to this death.[4]

Ricoeur wants to use Freudian theory in the work of restoring a more authentic faith. Psychoanalysis, he thinks, can help us see through the idolatry clinging to cultural religious symbols. It can then lead us to glimpse something he calls the "Wholly Other"— something which he contrasts to the human world of culture. Thus, for Ricoeur just as for Küng, that which is truly meaningful is positioned outside of the physical, human universe with which psychoanalysis is concerned.

The same uneasiness with the Freudian perspective can also be glimpsed in the work of Peter Homans, who is nevertheless careful not to side with either psychoanalysis or religion. Yet, in *Theology after Freud*, he refers to "the grim and comfortless conclusion of Freud's 'analytic' of religion, his 'antitheology.'"[5] Homans proposes no easy answer to the grimness he sees in Freud. He suggests that theorists maintain "an active, real tension in which both identification with Freud and aloof, rebellious, active dismissal of his theories are avoided."[6]

Homans might well be right. Perhaps it is inappropriate to

abandon an objective perspective on the dispute between psychoanalysis and religion and to advocate one view over another. But such is the folly in which I am engaged.

I suggest that the conflict between psychoanalysis and religion can be usefully seen as a conflict about the body and what the body knows. Religion, on the one hand, sees the source of some kinds of knowledge — namely "religious" knowledge — as lying outside the body. It maintains that there is a purposeful reality external to human beings which can affect, direct, or instruct human existence. Psychoanalysis, on the other hand, refuses to accept an external source for any human knowledge. Psychoanalysis sees human knowledge as growing out of wholly human experience. For psychoanalysis the word *knowledge* is similar to the words *thought* or *idea*. All ideas, all thought, all knowledge come from somatic sources. To put it very simply, and, I think, not too simply, in psychoanalysis all knowledge is carnal knowledge.

Now what if we hold the analytic view to be true? What if we take the Freudian and post-Freudian perspectives seriously? What if we abandon all musings about transcendence and resolve to stay with psychoanalysis in its relentless insistence on the physical nature of human beings and all that they know? Do we, as theologians maintain, wind up in a bleak, grim physical world? Just how hopeless is the body?

'Body' in religion and psychoanalysis

Body certainly is hopeless if we conceive of it in terms of the major tradition of Western philosophy. The dominant theme in Western thought since Plato has been that the body is a vehicle for a higher entity — mind or soul. General knowledge, it is believed, develops in the mind. Religious knowledge, however, is thought of as emanating from something even higher than mind or soul. Various terms are used to refer to the thing outside of mind — the thing which informs the mind. *God* is the most common term in religions. Platonists used the word *forms*; Jungians use the word *archetypes*.

I am simplifying these distinctions in order to point out a basic difference between a "religious" notion of the person and a psychoanalytic one. In religions, such as Judaism and Christianity; in philosophies that are religious, such as Platonism; and in psychologies that are religious, such as Jungian psychology, there is always a duality about the human being. Something—usually mind or soul—is contrasted with body, and is then seen as better, nobler, cleaner, and ultimately of a different character or substance than the body. In such religious views of the person, the higher part is seen as being closer to whatever is accorded divine, directive status. The soul is closer to the forms. The psyche is linked with the archetypes. And mind or reason is joined with God.

If we accept this familiar dualistic view of the person, the body becomes unimportant. This happens because all the truly fine things about human beings are seen as coming from the mind or soul which, in turn, is believed to have gotten the good things from something wholly transcendent to anything physical. I would argue that this view of the person as having two parts, one of which is better in the sense of being closer to God, holds true in general terms for both Christianity and Judaism. In both religions the flesh is seen as needing salvation. In Christianity the flesh is redeemed by Jesus' sacrifice; in Judaism it is saved by adherence to God's rules for living. In both religions the body is slighted because something other than body—indeed, something other than human—is placed in charge. The body then becomes dumb. It can only be "mere" body, the "apparatus for life,"[7] as D. H. Lawrence once said.

In contrast to what I am labeling the religious conception of body as something opposed to a higher mind or soul, there is the psychoanalytic view. In psychoanalysis the body becomes more complex because the mind is never separated from it. All of the fine things about human beings—their intellects, their morality, their aesthetic sensibilities—arise from bodily sources. Many have seen this analytic view as reductive because mind and soul are reduced to body. I would put it another way. Instead of reducing the mind, psychoanalysis elevates the body by granting it all the qualities which most of Western philosophy reserves for the mind.

The respect of psychoanalysis for the complexity of body began in its origins as a mode of treatment for addressing the bodily ailments of women in the nineteenth century. Josef Breuer and Sigmund Freud used their "talking cure" as a way of interpreting and influencing the human body. "Hysterics," Freud wrote, "suffer mainly from reminiscences."[8] It was the conversation between doctor and patient which touched these reminiscences and thus eased bodily sufferings. According to early analytic theory, hysterics had translated or "converted" their memories into physical agonies. They had written their sufferings in flesh. By bringing the memories to conscious attention, Freud believed that their power could be worn away. Recent scholarship has described this early formulation of analytic theory as a technique for interpreting the body language of women.[9]

Certainly psychoanalysis has progressed far beyond the initial, somewhat simple, theory of the influence of memory on the body. But, no matter how complex Freud's theory became, it never lost its original focus. It never departed from the notion that the flesh was cognizant of its history. In his later works, Freud often expressed the hope that scientific progress would one day enable psychoanalysis to express psychological statements in physiological terms. "We must recollect," he said in 1914, "that all our provisional ideas in psychology will presumably some day be based on an organic substructure."[10] And later, in 1939, he explained that psychoanalysis identified "what is truly psychical" with somatic phenomena. The concept of the *unconscious*, he suggested, was the term analysis used to refer to the somatic processes which future research might name more precisely.[11]

The early discovery that the body remembers means that, in psychoanalysis, every physical experience is metaphoric. For example, in psychoanalysis, sex can never be a simple activity of the genitals. Instead, analysis sees sex as involved with earlier experiences of nutrition, excretion, muscular excitation, and sensory activity. Genital sexuality, just as any other physical experience, reverberates with echoes of childhood and infancy. For psychoanalysis, the flesh can never be literal since, as long as it lives, it teems with past memories and future wishes. Body is forever imaging its desires and forever elaborating its past.

Thus, in a Freudian perspective, the body becomes the complex context of all experience. The body is seen as charged with an intellect or, more accurately, with an energy, that is constantly expressing physical history. Thought is one form of this expression; action is another. And for psychoanalysis, thought, like action, is itself an activity of the body. It is this notion of body as the matrix of human cognition that, I suggest, must animate modern philosophy, if that philosophy is to foster respect for life.

Thoughts, words, and physical history

The relationship between thought as expressed in words and bodily life is necessarily stressed in psychoanalysis since treatment aims to alter physical conditions via language. British psychoanalyst Charles Rycroft put it like this: "It is the fact that words can symbolize instinctive acts and objects and carry cathexes derived from them that makes psychoanalytical treatment possible."[12] For analysis, then, mental phenomena like words, thoughts, or ideas are never disembodied. Rather, they are conditioned both by somatic drives and by the past physical context in which those drives were experienced.

Freud believed that for thought to be healthy it must always retain a felt connection to the experiential context from which it arose. For example, he described schizophrenia as a condition in which the link between words and what they represented was severed. This stress on seeking the origin of thought in past physical experience explains Freud's attitude toward words as phenomena which lead backwards and which carry meaning because they are conditioned by memories, by sense perceptions, and by bodily history.

I find it significant that Paul Ricoeur, who tries very hard to make Freudian psychoanalysis compatible with a spiritual view of humankind, finds Freud's ideas of linguistic meaning insupportable. Ricoeur's discomfort with Freud's view of language as a condensation of various sense perceptions is important because it is a basic criticism of how analysis searches for meaning.

Ricoeur sees the psychoanalytic activity of connecting words to past feelings, past sensations, and past impressions as incapable of providing a meaning for the future — a meaning that is "higher." He is right about this. Analysis can support no "epigenesis" of meaning when that meaning is seen as lying beyond or outside the body and the textured intimacy of its past. Ricoeur's desire for a meaning to supplement psychoanalytic method is a desire for transcendence. It is a form of the wish for an escape from the conditioning of body.

Motives for and consequences of the separation of mind and body

Why is the transcendence of mind so attractive? There are some interesting approaches to an answer in post-Freudian analytic thought. These later theories are useful in uncovering possible motives behind philosophical systems which strive for distance from human flesh and blood.

Freud realized that the separation of mind and body was a fact of human experience. In *The Question of Lay Analysis*, he wrote: "However much philosophy may ignore the gulf between the physical and the mental, it still exists for our practical endeavors."[13]

Freud considered the mind's tendency to feel separate from the body as common-sense reality. Further, it is clear that he recognized this feeling of separateness as a blessing in age and infirmity. But it was left to later theorists to explore why the mind distances itself from body and to speculate on how this tendency becomes pathological.

Ernest Jones began the theorizing with his statements questioning whether mind existed at all. "Speaking for myself only," Jones once said, ". . . . I will say freely that I know of no reason for believing that mental phenomena can occur anywhere apart from bodily ones, and furthermore I see no reason to believe that such an entity as mind exists at all, whether attached to the body or not."[14] At another time, he put it like this:

> I venture to predict that . . . the antithesis (between mind and body) which has baffled all the philosophers will be found to be based on an illusion. . . . When we talk of the mind influencing the body or the body influencing the mind we are merely using a convenient shorthand for a more cumbrous phrase. . . .[15]

Jones's invitation to explore mind's illusion that it is separate from the body was taken up by D. W. Winnicott in an essay titled "Mind and Its Relation to the Psyche-Soma."[16] Winnicott began his essay with a definition of *psyche* as "the imaginative elaboration of somatic parts, feelings, and functions. . . ."[17]

Note that this idea of the psyche includes no notions of transcendent, out-of-body forces influencing human imagination. Instead it presents a concept of psyche as an activity of body. This activity extends to every product of human feeling and cognition. All our thoughts, all our images, all our dreams, all our emotions are, according to Winnicott, elaborations of body or, to use his terms, of "physical aliveness." The psyche, Winnicott maintains, is not felt to be located in any particular physical place. It is instead felt to be animating the entire organism. This notion of psyche captures the pervasive "alive" qualities imputed to soul in mystical literature. Yet it has the advantage of being more precise and more somatic.

It is out of psyche or out of "psyche-soma," as Winnicott extends the term, that he believes the idea of *mind* develops. He agrees with Jones that the mind does not exist as an entity, but mind imagines itself to exist and this image varies in intensity from individual to individual.

For optimum development of the psyche-soma, Winnicott thinks that a perfect environment is necessary. At the beginning of an infant's life this need is absolute. However, in the normal development of an infant the environment will, of course, fail to be perfect. This is when mind evolves.

Winnicott believes that mental functioning begins as a compensation for environmental failure. Through cognitive understanding and self-control, the infant transforms the imperfect environment into the perfect one. Mind thus has its origins in the attempt to gain control of the environment.

In the healthy individual the development of mind proceeds gradually. If the environment is not too unreliable, mind will be felt to be not too distinct from body. However, if the infant's environment is unpredictable, or if the care that the child receives is erratic, then mind will develop as a thing in itself which is felt to be very much outside the problematic body and the physical environment. The most common way for this distancing to be imaged, Winnicott believes, is the false localization of the mind in the head.

Thus, Winnicott gives us a possible psychological motive behind the construction of theories which disparage the body in favor of something beyond body—something imagined to be greater than body. Theories of transcendent entities outside and above the head might well be attempts to carry the dissociation of mind even further. Theories of forms, archetypes, gods, and goddesses which direct things from an out-of-body vantage point might be symptomatic of the tendency to escape from the psyche-soma as Winnicott terms it, and to imagine mind in a location totally separate from the person.

I return to those ideas of Winnicott over and over again as I think about the mind-body split. The theory may be helpful in indicating why it is that anti-body philosophies are so often anti-woman. If he is right that an intense opposition between mind and body develops when the early environment of an infant fails, then it would be most likely that, in deep memory, a woman is held responsible since women have been the most important factors in the environment of most babies. In cases in which the mind develops as an enemy to the early environment, it might be developing as an enemy to women. This phenomenon could be what is expressed in anti-body philosophy which is often also misogynist.[18]

Another consequence of the estrangement of what we have called *mind* from what we have called *body* might well be the suppression of affective, emotional content in much of scientific and philosophic tradition. Charles Rycroft refers to "the pathology of the Western intellectual tradition" as being the dissociation of wishful, fantasy thought, from adaptive 'objective' thought."[19] In an essay called "Beyond the Reality Principle," Rycroft suggests that fantasy underlies any healthy individual's sense of reality.[20] He hypothesizes that for the adequately mothered infant, wish and reality will not be felt to be too disparate. In such cases what the body wants and wishes for will generally be what appears. Objective reality will then be experienced as coinciding with the internal bodily world of wishes — wishes for food, for warmth, for physical affection. Rycroft believes that classical analytic theory has been too ready to separate wishful or "primary process" thinking from adaptive or "secondary process" thinking. This attitude, he says, comes from the modern scientific prejudice in which humankind is supposed to view the world "from two unconnected and incompatible standpoints, one scientific and objective, the other imaginative and subjective."[21]

Although Western scientific rationalism has exploited the capacity of human thought to be objective — that is, to view the world "without interference from emotional bias and animistic think-ing,"[22] Rycroft suggests that perhaps the dissociation has become compulsive. When we suppress the emotional, wishful facets of our human ideation and cognition, our lives lose their luster, and our reason is severed from sources of spontaneous life. That spon-taneous life, that wishful, emotional desire for the world arises from our bodies. Thus the trick to maintaining the sparkle is within the body. It lies, according to Rycroft, in never forgetting that "spiritual or cultural functions are equally and simultaneously bio-logical functions."[23] It lies, in the words of feminist poet Adrienne Rich, in never forgetting that "all our high-toned questions breed in a lively animal."[24]

Feminism, psychoanalysis and the body

Psychoanalysis has too small an audience and is too esoteric to influence intellectual life very much. The movement which has a much better chance of bringing Western thought back to the body is feminism. Feminism is much more pervasive in society than psychoanalysis. It reaches beyond therapeutic consulting rooms and academic journals into the very fabric of daily life. Although psy-choanalysis can become part of feminism and thus share its im-pact, it has no chance of equaling the influence of the woman's movement.

Feminism can become a vehicle for psychoanalytic insight because psychoanalysis and feminism share the theme of sexual-ity. As Shulamith Firestone noted in *The Dialectic of Sex*, the fo-cus on sexuality means that Freudianism and feminism "are made of the same stuff."[25] Feminists uncover the sexist directions in re-spected philosophical, moral, and religious systems, just as Freudi-ans reveal instinctual motives in great art and culture. Both theo-ries are continually pointing to the sexual ideas concealed in the products and behavior of "higher" civilization.

Of course, for feminists, as for psychoanalysts, the topic of sexuality includes much more than genitalia. The subject of sex-uality concerns everything that society does to indicate gender. For feminists, the study of sexuality entails detailed analysis of all the rewards and punishments — of all the codes of symbol and language which function in society to proscribe sexual behavior.

The work of feminist scholars seeks to reveal the complex cultural context in which sexuality is experienced.

It is their mutual insistence on the importance and complexity of sexuality that causes both psychoanalytic theory and feminist theory to lead back to the body. Certainly, there are important differences between the two outlooks. Psychoanalysis predates feminism and has so far failed to examine itself in the light of feminist argument. Reading Freud and many other psychoanalytic thinkers from a feminist perspective is as disturbing as it is revealing. Psychoanalytic literature is rife with male bias — bias toward male anatomy, toward traditional male roles, and toward ubiquitous male privilege. Sometimes Freud's sexism is merely funny, such as his warning to Wilhelm Fliess to keep his early drafts about the sexual aetiology of the neuroses away from his friend's "young wife."[26] And sometimes Freud's sexism is maddening such as his insistence on the moral inferiority of women.[27] These sexist beginnings make it imperative for psychoanalysis to reconsider its appraisal of the female body and, concomitantly, to reevaluate its view of the female psyche.

By combining the perspectives of feminism and psychoanalysis on the topic of sexuality, gaps in the outlooks of both can be filled in. It is well known, especially among the British psychoanalysts, that Freud failed to observe and appreciate the importance of infancy and early childhood in structuring personality and character. This pre-Oedipal period is, of course, the time when women dominate the infant and young child's world. It took a female analyst, Melanie Klein, to focus psychoanalytic theory on this phase of human development. Klein, the mother of three children, was herself not a feminist. Nevertheless, she brought a woman's perspective to psychoanalysis. Male theorists like Fairbairn and Winnicott were influenced by Klein, and analytic thinking in Britain began to turn to women in their role as mothers.

Although Kleinian theory is a long way from doing justice to women in roles other than that of mother, at least it has begun to look at the importance of women in civilization. Male anatomy is no longer the dominant theme in analytic discussions about the human body. In Kleinian work, the breast has eclipsed the phallus.

Klein's focus on maternity can enlarge perspective on how the perception of body develops and, accordingly, on how all perception is related to infancy. Her work points out that each sex becomes aware of itself in relation to a *woman's* body. The first experiences of flesh, and, if Klein is right, the most formative experiences of flesh take place exclusively within a female physical context. Thus our first subject of study — our first "body of knowledge"— is a female body. It is no wonder that in Greek mythology the nine muses, who instruct all the arts and sciences, are pictured as female. In a Kleinian view every effort to know anything has its origin in the initial human project of knowing the mother's body as the source of all nutrition and all comfort. The physical interplay of mother and child forms the matrix of all knowing.

Klein's ideas shed light on why it is that women represent the body in so much Western philosophy and iconography. Feminists have pointed to this as a great inequity in our perception of gender. Women are the body in the sense that they have come to stand for body. Simone de Beauvoir has criticized this equation of women and body as being illogical. "As a matter of fact," she writes, "man, like woman, is flesh. . . . "[28] De Beauvoir imputes the identification of woman with body and nature to the fact that "her animality is more manifest."[29] But this is wrong. By thinking that woman's "animality" is more manifest, de Beauvoir has succumbed to the same illusion that she is criticizing. Women are identified with body simply because we all learn about our own flesh next to a woman's flesh. Thus when philosophers, poets, artists, and theologians either idealize or denigrate human physicality and mortality, they will most often come to the female body as their subject or quickly get around to the topic of women. An obvious example is the subject of the mortality of Jesus. Christ is said to have acquired his physical nature and his temporality from his mother, Mary.

It is remarkable how often the equation of woman with body goes unnoticed even by psychoanalytic writers. Adrian Stokes, in a famous essay titled "Reflections on the Nude," mentions only the female nude as a subject for painting. His general discussion of the feeling of sanity which viewing the human body in its entirety can give, quickly becomes specific in what he says about painting a woman's body. Stokes's use of the possessive pronoun *his* to refer to the human body in general becomes *her* when he mentions the model's body in particular.[30]

The deep psychic association of women with body could be responsible for bringing the consciousness of body to all academic disciplines in the decades ahead. The spread of feminism *must* heighten our sensitivity to our own physical nature, since the spread of feminism means that the body will be talking. And what will the body say? "The symptom is there," says French feminist Julia Kristeva, "women are writing, and the air is heavy with expectation: What will they write that is new?"[31]

It is most likely that women will actually write things that are very old. One of the most valuable contributions feminism could make to discourse is that of fostering a writing style, a speaking style that reveals its own subjective origins in the personal and collective past. Feminist writing at its best, I think, could shatter the illusion of objectivity which turns so much modern scholarship into mechanized jargon. It could aim to return rationality to its roots in emotion.

I have been thinking about this goal for feminism in terms of an image from Greek history. At certain times in the long history of the Delphic oracle, the female priestess known as the pythia would prophesy in ecstatic gibberish. A male priest would then interpret her utterances and give the petitioner the oracle's reply. It was the priest's job to make sense of the priestess's babble.

This relationship between pythia and priest typifies the stereotyped roles played by men and women throughout history. Women play the role of the fecund but inarticulate body — full of magic and mysterious wisdom. Men, in contrast, play the role of the Word — full of meaning and objective definitions. One could say that women, playing the pythias of civilization, have spoken in the language of primary process — immediate, emotional, and physical. Men, in contrast, have spoken in secondary process with a style more distant, cool, and seemingly detached. It occurs to me that the role of the pythia was played by all the female hysterics whose ramblings and bodily postures were then interpreted by Freud and Breuer, who became the high priests of psychoanalysis. Analysis itself thus became an activity which interprets primary process thinking in terms of secondary process language. Its power derives from a melding of gender-specific modes of expression.

The widespread illusion that primary and secondary process thought are separate — or, to put it another way, the perception that fantasy is separate from objective thought — is sustained by the separation of men and women into rigid roles such as priest and pythia. Women are seen as the inarticulate body because women formed the human universe when babbling was the only human speech possible. The gibberish of primary process and the overwhelming physical desires of infancy are, at present, exclusively linked with women. When men share in the care of infants, the symbols of this early time will change. It will be possible to imagine men as body as well.

It is even just possible that shared childcare will not be necessary to alter our imagination. The symbolism of body and mind might well change from the direction of adulthood as women become more articulate, more obvious in every aspect of public culture.

In any case, the possibility of imagining body as male is not the most significant change that feminism could effect. As women speak more and more, the human body could become increasingly coherent and increasingly influential. It could become more difficult to advocate philosophical systems in which words are far abstracted from their relationships to things. Hermeneutics might discover the original text, that is, the human body. In the beginning was definitely not the word. The biblical statement reverses the order. It is flesh that made the word.

A new hermeneutics will have to recognize the perpetual subversion of the body. All of our systems of thought, all of our disciplines of knowledge are perpetually, continually changing and thus perpetually and continually inaccurate. Our systems can only be approximations of our always desiring, always alive, very much human bodies. Thus, paradoxically, when our systems become more approximate, and less sacred, they become truer and closer to life.

Because our bodies never cease echoing the past in new ways, with new variations, there is always more to say and always more to want. The body cannot be literal as long as it is alive, and thus it can never be contained in philosophies that lack contact with somatic imagination. Disembodied theories cannot really describe life; instead they can only encourage us to limit life.

For all my talk against traditional religion, I have actually preached quite a bit. This could be a warning that the materialist philosophy I am advocating could be as full of pious rhetoric as any religion. I think this is probably impossible to avoid. I only hope that a feminist rhetoric based in the body inspires theories that value life more than has a patriarchal rhetoric based in the spirit.

NOTES

1. Susan Sontag, *On Photography* (New York: Farrar, Straus & Giroux, 1973).

2. Hans Küng, *Does God Exist?* trans. Edward Quinn (Garden City, N.Y.: Doubleday & Co., 1980), p. 301.

3. Ibid., p. 329.

4. Paul Ricoeur, *Freud and Philosophy: An Essay on Interpretation*, trans. Denis Savage (New Haven, Conn.: Yale University Press, 1970), p. 530.

5. Peter Homans, *Theology after Freud* (New York: Bobbs-Merrill Co., 1970), p. 222.

6. Peter Homans, "Understanding Thy Neighbor as Thyself: Freud's Criticism of the Love Commandment," *Journal of Religious Ethics* 10, no. 2 (Fall 1982): 326.

7. D. H. Lawrence, *Fantasia of the Unconscious* (Middlesex, England: Penguin Books, 1971), p. 12.

8. Sigmund Freud, SE 2:7.

9. Dianne Hunter, "Hysteria, Pychoanalysis, and Feminism: The Case of Anna O.," *Feminist Studies* (Fall 1983): 486.

10. Freud, SE 14:78.

11. Ibid., 23:158.

12. Charles Rycroft, *Imagination and Reality* (New York: International Universities Press, 1968), p. 58.

13. Ibid., 20:247.

14. Ernest Jones, *Psycho-Myth, Psycho-History*, 2 vols. (New York: Stonehill Pub. Co., 1974), 2:237.

15. Ernest Jones, quoted in D. W. Winnicott, "Mind and Its Relation to the Psyche-Soma," *Through Pediatrics to Psychoanalysis* (London: Hogarth Press and the Institute of Psychoanalysis, 1978), p. 243.

16. Ibid.

17. Ibid., p. 244.

18. Elizabeth V. Spelman, "Woman as Body: Ancient and Contemporary Views," *Feminist Studies* 8, no. 1 (Spring 1982), pp. 109–32.

19. Rycroft, *Imagination and Reality*, p. 109.

20. Ibid., p. 111.

21. Ibid., p. 108.

22. Ibid., p. 105.

23. Ibid., p. 113.

24. Adrienne Rich, "Two Songs," as quoted in Spelman, "Woman as Body," p. 109.

25. Shulamith Firestone, *The Dialectic of Sex* (New York: Bantam Books, 1971), p. 44.

26. Freud, SE 1: 179.

27. Ibid., 19: 257–58.

28. Simone de Beauvoir, *The Second Sex*, trans. and ed. H. M. Parshley (New York: Alfred A. Knopf, 1952), p. 685.

29. Ibid., p. 239.

30. Adrian Stokes, *Reflections on the Nude* (London: Tavistock Publications, 1967), p. 6.

31. Julia Kristeva, "Women's Time," trans. Alice Jardine and Harry Blake, *Signs* 7, no. 1 (Autumn 1981), p. 32.

9

Reconceiving God for a Nuclear Age

GORDON D. KAUFMAN

TWO PRESUPPOSITIONS ARE taken for granted in this essay and are indispensable to its argument. The first is that the availability of nuclear power and the building up of massive stockpiles of nuclear weapons has brought humankind into a radically new historical situation, quite unexpected in our religious and philosophical traditions. We now possess the power to obliterate human life, and there is a real possibility that we may do just that if a nuclear war breaks out.

The second presupposition has to do with the nature of theology. I do not regard the theologian's task as being essentially one of handing on past traditions about God and humanity. I take it, rather, to be a task of "imaginatively constructing," as I like to put it, an understanding of God, the world, and humanity which will provide significant orientation for contemporary life. This conception of theology will not be argued here but can be found in two recent books of mine, *An Essay on Theological Method* and *The Theological Imagination.*

*   *   *   *   *

New ways of thinking are desperately needed in our time. We now realize, for example, as earlier generations apparently did not, that the earth has quite limited resources, and if we do not move quickly toward conservation of energy, water, minerals, arable land, and so forth, human life as we know it can no longer be sustained. We are poisoning ourselves in many ways, some known to us, many unknown: the atmosphere, especially surrounding our cities, has become polluted and is dangerous to breathe; fish can

133

no longer live in many of our rivers and lakes; the food that we eat apparently contains cancer-causing agents; "acid rain" falls on our forests and kills the trees. If we do not take account of the long-range consequences of our activities, the ecological crisis in which we now live will deepen beyond repair.

New thinking is also required politically. Defense, protection, and enhancement of the way of life of their own people has always been the first duty of politics, and the doctrine of national sovereignty has been its modern expression. According to this conception, national strength shows itself most fully in the capacity to destroy a threatening enemy, in this way protecting oneself. We are now in a situation, however, in which destruction of the enemy can no longer be the ultimate method of defense. We continue, nevertheless, to be engaged in a spiraling nuclear arms race. With our enormous technological power we may be bringing human history to its close. Before it is too late, we must learn to develop a politics of peacemaking and of interdependence rather than one of self-protection and national sovereignty.

In all this our Western religious symbolism has been more a hindrance than a help. It has been partially responsible for our ecological blindness, and it too easily lends itself to the reinforcement and legitimation of our parochial political objectives. In the struggle between the USSR and the Euro-American allies, for example, we are regularly told — and half believe — that because this is God's battle we are justified in doing whatever is required to protect ourselves and destroy the enemy. This gives us strength and courage because of our confidence in God's omnipotent power. God is ultimately in control in this world and will surely bring victory, no matter how demonic or powerful are the forces in opposition. So we can be assured that all will come out well. For "we know," as Paul put it, "that all things work together for good to them that love God, to them who are the called according to his purpose" (Rom. 8:28 KJV). Religious convictions of this sort have their origins in the Bible, and they have given courage and confidence to many generations of Christians and Jews who found themselves engaged in desperate struggles to maintain their way of life against the threat of powerful enemies. The power, faithfulness, and majesty of God, if it can be invoked in support of one's cause, is among the strongest motivations known to humankind.

Belief in it has been a principal grounding for faith, at least the faith nourished by the Psalms.

> God is our refuge and strength,
>   a very present help in trouble.
> Therefore we will not fear though
>   the earth should change,
> though the mountains shake in the
>   heart of the sea. . . .
> The nations rage, the kingdoms totter;
>   he utters his voice, the earth melts.
> The Lord of hosts is with us;
>   the God of Jacob is our refuge. (Ps. 46:1-2, 6-7)

There may have been justification for such symbolism in the past, but it has now become too risky to use. Such symbolism has nourished massive historical evils: Western imperialism and colonialism, slavery, unrestricted exploitation of the earth's resources, racism and sexism, persecution of those thought of as heretics or infidels, even attempts at genocide. We have come to a turn in human affairs in which such "misunderstandings" or "mistakes" are no longer tolerable. We must critically examine our religious symbolism and attempt to reconstruct it in ways that will more likely assure that it will function to good effect in human affairs. If we are to continue to employ the symbol *God* at all, it will have to be in a much more carefully restricted form than most Christians have thus far acknowledged.

I

How shall we proceed with our reconstruction? If we may no longer simply appeal to traditional images and concepts in developing our understanding of God, what moves are open to us? I would like to outline how a conception of theology as primarily an activity of imaginative construction enables us to address these issues.

Our notion of God needs to be kept as formal as possible as we begin our constructive theological work. The symbol *God* is given its specific content and meaning, and thus enabled to provide actual guidance and orientation in the decisions and actions of everyday life, by the concrete metaphors and images which we use in constructing it. We will need, therefore, to select these with care. For example, thinking of God as "our father in heaven" or as "lord of hosts" or "king of kings" suggests that the proper relation to God is one of subordination, respect, and obedience to a dominant male figure of great authority and power. "He" has intentions and purposes which he is carrying out. He issues commands we are to obey. To cross him or attempt to thwart him would be disastrous. Nevertheless, he loves and cares for us like a father. The concrete stories in the Bible which depict God acting in some particular way, or which say what the "kingdom of God is like," all contribute specific content and meaning to the symbol; more abstract notions like holiness and glory, infinitude and absoluteness, also add special qualities and meanings to the understanding of God. It is not, then, some merely formal "ultimate point of reference" on which the believer meditates and to which he or she prays. It is a concretely conceived God who acts in fairly distinct and definite ways and who requires particular attitudes and modes of life and action from devotees. Obviously if God is conceived as a dominating kingly being, who is working in the world in a domineering all-powerful fashion, and who demands of worshipers that they "subdue" the earth and all its creatures (Gen. 1:28) and that they destroy without remainder all their enemies and God's (Deut. 25:19; 1 Sam. 15:1–33; Rev. 17–18, and so forth), a very powerful motivation toward a disciplined and authoritarian pattern of life will be engendered in the minds and hearts of believers. Corresponding character structures, social institutions, and styles of life will be shaped, as believers seek to respond obediently to the almighty God and King who is their ruler and lord. These particular metaphors, images, and concepts, which give concreteness to the ultimate point of reference, will determine how God is understood. They will also determine the sort of human relationship to God that is fitting and right. For this reason, as we seek to construct an image/concept of God suitable for orienting contemporary human existence with its unique problems, we must choose our metaphors and images with care. What sort of criteria can be invoked to guide such choices?

An ultimate point of reference for human existence and the

world performs two indispensable functions for human life. They are a "relativizing" function and a "humanizing" function.[1] The notion of an *ultimate* point of reference is connected with and articulates a sense of the deep mystery in everything. In relation to the ultimate point of reference, everything in us and about us is relativized and called into question. Its true being and proper significance are not in itself but only in its relationship to God. The mythic notions of God as creator, as sovereign lord of life and history, as judge of all the earth, were often used in the tradition to express this relativizing motif. God as the supreme relativizer is the mystery before whom we can only bow in awe and fear.

But in Western religious traditions God has never been apprehended simply as awe-inspiring or terrifying; God has also been seen as the giver of all good gifts, including life and health and well-being. God has been worshiped as the savior of humankind, the one who could and does bring human life to salvation and fulfillment. Thus, along with the relativizing dimension to the symbol *God*, there is also a profoundly humanizing dimension. God is seen as ultimately a *humane* being, a "father" who loves and care for "his" children, who grieves over their failures and their distresses, and who willingly sacrifices everything—even "his only son"—for their salvation and well-being.

It is the special "genius" of the image/concept *God* that it unites the relativizing motif and the humanizing motif and holds them together in one religious symbol.

> Thus that which serves to call into question everything we do and are and experience is at the same time apprehended as ultimately humane and beneficent, that which fulfills and completes our humanity; and that in which we can put our full confidence and trust and to which we can properly give ourselves in devotion is also that which requires a continuous criticism of ourselves, our values and ideas, our activities and customs and institutions.[2]

In our attempt to formulate an understanding of God for today, our principal concern should be to construct a symbol which can function both thoroughly to relativize and thoroughly to humanize our contemporary existence, institutions, and activities. The principal criteria, thus, in terms of which we will undertake our constructive work, are "relativization"and "humanization"— not, as has usually been the case in theology, images and concepts more or less directly extracted from the Bible and other authoritative traditions.

We men and women today, as the women and men of any other time and place, experience ourselves as in many ways restricted, limited, relativized; and we also, all of us, receive our lives and our humanity as a gift from beyond ourselves. We know ourselves to be nourished and sustained and granted such well-being and human fulfillment as comes our way by life-giving powers which we have not made and by circumstances largely out of our control. In many respects, thus, we still experience our human existence as both relativized and humanized by forces and powers impinging from beyond us, from the context or matrix which has given birth to human life and which continues to sustain and transform it. It is through reflection on this contemporary experience and understanding of our relativization and humanization, and on that which unifies and holds these together in one, that we will begin to discern the outlines of a contemporary conception of God, of that ultimate point of reference to which we today can freely and wholeheartedly give ourselves in devotion and work.

II

Let us begin with the sources and sustaining powers from whence we come. Human life today is generally understood to be an expression of, and to be continually sustained by, the great web of life which has gradually emerged and evolved on planet earth. Human existence, as we understand it today, could never have come into being apart from this long process of differentiation and development. We humans must understand ourselves in the first place, therefore, as one strand in the very ancient and complex web of life, a strand, moreover, which would not exist apart from this context which has brought it forth and which continues to sustain it at every point.

However, these physical, chemical, and biological conditions and developments were not all that was necessary to produce human existence as we know it. Once an animal had evolved with a sufficiently complex nervous system to sustain linguistic and other symbolic activity, thus making possible primitive consciousness, memory, and imagination, a long and complicated *historical* development was required before anything that we would recognize as a truly human mode of existence could appear on earth. As increasingly complex forms of language developed over hundreds of generations, and experience, memory, and imagination all became highly differentiated, humans began to experience their lives as transpiring within a wide context of memories and stories of the past as well as imagined possibilities and hopes for the future. Human creativity was born, together with intention and action, as humans found they could themselves actualize some of these possibilities and hopes. Thus, human existence gradually developed qualities and capacities not found in any other form of life.

This all occurred over hundreds of generations, and it did not occur simply as an activity of mental development. Increasing physical dexterity, upright posture, the development of the opposed thumb, and other changes making possible the invention and practice of new physical skills were occurring at the same time. An increasingly complex brain and nervous system made it possible to coordinate these physical changes with a rapidly growing symbolic capacity. Humans invented simple, and then more complex, tools to facilitate their hunting for food and their protection of themselves against dangerous animals or against other tribes. They mastered the use of fire, and they learned how to make simple skin clothes, so they were able to move into colder climates and survive. As human life gradually became diversified with the development of new skills and activities, human societies became increasingly differentiated, since it was not possible for everyone to develop expertise in every area. So some became warriors and others gardeners, some hunters and others weavers, and some became chiefs — that is, those who coordinated and maintained and protected the orderly practice and interrelations of all these specializations, so they would serve the well-being of the whole community.

Increasing specialization made possible a high development of particular skills and crafts, and this in turn transformed human life in decisive ways, producing further new dimensions of experience and activity. The fine arts, politics, religious meditation, and reflection on the meaning of life, all began to appear, later to be followed by philosophy, mathematics, and the sciences. Thus, in the patterns played out in human activities, in the quantity and quality of what men and women perceived to be needs that must be met, in the interests that increasingly occupied their attention and time, human life moved further and further from its animal origins. Though founded on and indissolubly interconnected with its biological foundations, it had become decisively historical and cultural in all its distinctive characteristics.

If we today are to speak of how we humans are created and sustained, it must be in terms of biological evolution and the ecosystem, on the one hand, and the long process of human history and the diverse sociocultural systems which it has produced, on the other. It is these complex conditions and developments that have made human life possible, and it is the continued working of these which presently sustain it. It is these conditions and developments that have both humanized and relativized us, and it is in connection with them, therefore, and the metaphors and images that they make available to us, that we today must come to understand God if we are to speak of God at all in ways connected with our contemporary experience and knowledge.

III

The boundary line between the historical and the biological is not a sharp or clear one, and it would be a mistake to make too much of it. From their first appearance humans have been engaged in modifying the so-called givens of nature; and in thus creating the world of culture, which is now the immediate context of human life everywhere, they have produced an environment more hospitable to human existence as we know it. We have warm houses in winter and many have air-conditioning in the summer. We have hospitals to treat our diseases and mechanized agriculture to provide us with an enormous quantity and variety of foodstuffs. We are able to communicate instantaneously with any part of the globe, and we can fly to its most distant points in a matter of hours. We have literally transformed the face of the earth — as can easily be seen by anyone approaching one of our great cities by air, or, for that matter, by anyone walking down a city street. Moreover, we are rapidly approaching the time when we will be able intentionally to alter the genetic basis of human life, thus changing the actual physiological constitution of future generations. And it is no longer just a wild dream to imagine human beings leaving earth forever to make some other place in the universe their permanent home. The physical, chemical, and biological conditions of human life are thus all malleable in many ways, and it would be a mistake to regard them as unalterable "givens" which we must simply accept. One of the differences between the modern outlook on life and all ancient or classical viewpoints is this awareness that we are not simply at the disposal of mysterious cosmic powers that impinge upon us unilaterally from beyond — whether these are understood as fate or karma or the will of God — but that many, perhaps all, of the conditions which affect our existence and well-being are subject in certain respects to human modification and adjustment.

This picture of human life in its cosmic context differs sharply from the traditional theological portrait of humanity related to God. Two points in particular should be noted, both deriving from the fundamental image/concept of the divine father-lord-creator, out of which the traditional conception of God was constructed. (1) In the traditional view all that happened in the universe was in its most significant respects the consequence of the sovereign will and action of God. God had set down the basic lines along which the history of the world would unfold, and God, as its omnipotent creator and lord, was sufficiently powerful and sufficiently constant in purpose to assure that cosmic and human history would reach their intended goals. (2) God's purposes for all of creation are beneficent and loving. God is a merciful parent who rules the universe with perfect justice and love, and who desires nothing more than the ultimate well-being and fulfillment of each creature. The overarching context of human life, thus, the purposive activity of the loving creator God, of which believers were assured in faith, gave a kind of security and confidence and hope that every conceivable evil which one might face in this life would be overcome. As the wonderful old Negro spiritual so movingly put it, "He's got the whole wide world in his hands."

The fundamental structure of this picture of human existence and its context is dualistic and asymmetrical. The omnipotent power and love of the divine creator-king determines absolutely and irrevocably the ultimate course and outcome of cosmic and human history. It is this which gives faith the assurance out of which it lives. But the modern world-picture which we have been considering is not structured in this way by an asymmetrical dualism, with a divine intentionality from on high determining unilaterally the course of cosmic evolution and human history. On the contrary, it is a picture of a unified and interdependent order in which deliberate intentionality appears only toward the end of a long evolutionary process on earth, as self-conscious beings emerge and gradually begin to take charge of their lives.

Although it is certainly possible to affirm an understanding of God still rooted fundamentally in the traditional mythic picture, it is clear that the asymmetrical dualism which gives that picture its force cannot illuminate many features of our situation today. In some respects the tables suggested by the old dualistic mythology appear to have almost completely turned. The cosmic order suddenly seems to have no way to protect itself from the onslaught with which we humans now threaten it. We have developed the capacity to destroy ourselves and possibly all life on earth. Our human intentionality and technological power have become portentous of calamity. In this situation we must find a conception of God more in accord with the modern notion of a fundamentally unified ecological order if *God* is to continue to be a viable symbol for orienting human life.

We might, then, attempt to think of God in terms defined largely by the natural processes of cosmic and biological evolution. This would result in a God largely mute, one who, though active and moving with creativity and vitality, was essentially devoid of the kind of intentionality and care which characterized the heavenly Father of tradition. Such a God could certainly evoke a piety of profound awe and respect, and even, in its own way, of love and trust. But it is not a God who could provide much guidance with respect to the great crises we today face: crises which are largely historical in character, not biological; crises of human motivation, policy, action, and institutions.

Further, a God conceived in this narrowly naturalistic way does not do justice to all the forces and conditions that have actually created our human existence. Biological evolution by itself did not bring forth humanity as we know it. A long *historical* process of human cultural creativity was also required before self-conscious and self-directing life could appear. In consequence, human existence has become shaped by the institutions and language, the customs and skills, which women and men themselves created, and human purposes and meaning have come to permeate every dimension of life. If we are to think of God as that reality which actually humanizes us, as well as relativizes us, these matters will have to be taken into account.

The fact that human existence has, in part, created itself in creating a whole array of unfolding histories complicates enormously our attempt to construct a contemporary understanding of God. The divine activity which has given us our human being must apparently be conceived now as inseparable from, and as working in and through, the activity of the human spirit itself, as it creatively produces the cultures which make human life human. It is, of course, not the case that men and women have, by taking thought and deliberate action, directly created themselves. For the most part human cultures were not the direct consequences of anyone's deliberate intention or planning. Consider some examples: Modern science has certainly been a human creation, but no individual or group at the time of its origins in the seventeenth century had any notion of the complex institutional structures, modes of education and discipline, moral and communal commitments, financial and physical resources, not to say ways of thinking and patterns of theoretical explanation, which constitute science today. Though innumerable decisions and actions were certainly involved in the gradual evolution of modern democratic parliamentary institutions, no one simply thought out this mode of political organization and then directly produced it. Every building to be found in any modern city is the product of human planning and intention, but no one simply decided modern London or New York or Tokyo would be a fine thing to build, worked out the plans, and then brought it into being. The English language — or Chinese, or Sanskrit — is certainly a human creation, but who could be said to have taken thought and decided deliberately to create it?

We must say, then, that although every element of culture

appears to be a product of human creativity, none of the great structures of history and culture was anticipated in human prevision or was the product of deliberate human intention. There is a hidden creativity at work in the historico-cultural process, and it is this which has given us the basic social and cultural structures which have actually created and continue to sustain human existence, as well as those qualities of life which we most deeply cherish. The consequences of our decisions and actions always far outrun our most ambitious purposes and our wildest dreams. It is the creativity working in and through history that has made human life distinctively human, and it is only in hope of continuing positive effects of this creativity — this unpredictable grace at work in our decisions and actions — that we today can take up the heavy responsibilities thrust upon us by the prodigious growth of technology and symbolized so dramatically by our stockpiles of nuclear weapons.

We are attempting to find a contemporary way to think of God, to conceive that reality which grounds our existence, and devotion to which can provide us with significant orientation as we face the frightening pass to which human history has today come. We have seen that human existence was produced by and has emerged from an enormously complex configuration of physical, biological, and historical processes, and these continue to sustain and nourish us both in body and in spirit. They both relativize and continue to humanize us. Looking back through this long history of contingency and coincidence, it seems surprising that self-consciously cultivated human life was ever born on earth at all. But here we are, the product of creative cosmic processes we are far from understanding. If human life is to go on, all of the factors which make it possible must remain in place, each making its indispensable contribution.

Devotion to God in our religious heritage has meant attention and gratitude to our creator and sustainer. Devotion and service to God seemed both natural and important to our forebears: natural, as an expression of the wonder and awe evoked by the awareness of having received the gift of life; important, in that consciousness of and response to the creator's will was indispensable if human life was to reach its intended fulfillment. This piety was focused by a mythic conception of God as a quasi-person, a conception fashioned with the aid of anthropomorphic images of lordship, parenthood, and the making of artifacts. In many respects the paternalistic and authoritarian overtones of this mythic notion have now become seriously misleading and dangerous. This does not mean, however, that devotion to and service of that reality which has brought us into being, which continues to sustain us, and which draws us onward toward a fuller and more profound humanity, is any the less natural or important than before. What it does mean is that we must now conceive God in terms appropriate to our modern understanding of ourselves and the world, just as those earlier generations conceived of God in terms drawn from and appropriate to their understanding of human life and those powers with which it had to come to terms. God should today be conceived in terms of the complex of physical, biological, and historico-cultural conditions which have made human existence possible, which continue to sustain it, and which may draw it out to a fuller humanity and humaneness. Devotion to a God conceived in terms other than these will not be devotion to *God*, that is, to that reality which has in fact created us, and a living connection with which is in fact needed if our lives are to be sustained and nourished. It will be, in short, devotion to an idol, a pretender to divinity, and as such will be debilitating and destructive, and may in the end be disastrous.

IV

But if it is true that we have in fact been brought into being by a complex configuration of physical, vital, and historico-cultural factors, powers, and processes, as I have suggested, why introduce talk about God at all? Does not a naturalistic and historicistic perspective of this sort render all such talk superfluous? To deal adequately with this question we must first remind ourselves of an important function performed by our concepts and symbols. They gather together for us, and hold together, those patterns and unities to which we need regularly attend if life is to have an order and meaning within which we can live and act appropriately and fruitfully. Thus, concepts like house or tree or even sandpile enable us, for certain purposes important to us, to grasp as unified and single what is, from other points of view, complex and diverse. The symbol *God*, as no other name or concept in our Western languages, holds together in a unity that complex reality which grounds and sustains our human existence, that which both relativizes and humanizes us, that of which above all else we must be aware and that to which above all else we must attend if in our conscious reflection and in our action we are to be properly oriented in life and in the world. Only such a symbol or concept, which holds all this together in one, can enable us to focus effectively our meditation and activity.

Were we unable to consider the ground of our human existence to be significantly unified and unifying in the way the symbol *God* suggests, our awareness of the oneness and integrity of our individual selfhood, as well as our solidarity as humanity, would not be well supported; and we could easily fall into destructive patterns of language and thought and action. Such patterns have appeared all too often in our tradition; for example, the tendency to divide human beings into parts like "soul" and "body," seeking our "essential nature" in only one dimension of our being and sacrificing other dimensions to that one; or the classification of humanity into categories such as "male" and "female" or "black" and "white," supposing that what is of real importance is more fully realized in one of these groups, which is thus deemed superior, more fully or paradigmatically human. But it is clearly a mistake to reify matter, life, and spirit, and the different genders and races, into distinct and independent realities in their own right, instead of treating them as abstractions from that more fundamental unity which constitutes our existence as human. Similarly, it is important to conceive the ultimate source and ground of this our integrated existence not as some merely composite or accidental aggregation: it must itself be significantly unified. Our symbol *God*, more fully and powerfully than any other in the language, directs attention to this ultimate unity behind and working through all dimensions of human life.

The symbol *God* suggests a reality, an ultimate tendency or power, which is working itself out in an evolutionary process that has produced not only myriads of living species but at least one living form able to shape and transform itself, through a cumulating history, into spirit, i.e., a being self-conscious and free, living in a cultural world which it has itself created. The symbol *God* enables us to hold this whole grand evolutionary-historical sweep together as the cosmic movement which has both given us our humanity and which continues to call us to a deeper humanization. It relativizes us at every point even while it continues to humanize us. This is a movement which we must understand as best we can and within which we must live as responsibly and creatively as possible, if human life is to go on.

V

I conclude this brief sketch with a word about its implications for a theological understanding of the nuclear crisis. We have become aware in recent decades that "life" is not a quality or power possessed by individual organisms. It is a pervasive web of complex interconnections of which individual organisms and, indeed, entire species, are expressions, and apart from which they could not exist. We humans have been rupturing and poisoning that web, and polluting the natural environment which sustains it. We have, that is to say, been living and acting "against God"; and despite the continuing activity of God (that is, of the forces that make for life and well-being) to overcome this evil, the damage we are producing is extensive, and it could end ultimately in the serious debilitation, or even the destruction, of human existence and of many other species as well.

As a strictly biological event, such an occurrence would probably be no calamity. Many species have appeared on earth, thrived for a time, and then become extinct. But in the course of time the cosmic and divine order has brought forth a mode of being, a dimension of itself, that transcends in a significant way even the luxuriant fecundity of life. That mode of being is history — the symbolical order, the realm of spirit — within which consciousness and meaning, self-conscious subjectivity and purposiveness and freedom have reality. We humans are the only creatures we know who are the living incarnations of that distinctive mode of being. In this respect we are "the point farthest out" of the cosmic evolutionary-historical process, the point at which that movement of creativity has brought forth self-conscious selves, with the power

to take some measure of direct responsibility for the further unfolding of that very creativity. God is giving birth, after many mil-
lennia, to finite freedom and self-consciousness in and through our
human history, in *us*. A new and glorious vista — a hope — is gradually, over many generations, coming into view: a vision of life and
community characterized by freedom, love, justice, meaning, and
creativity. This new age (if and as it comes) celebrated mythically
in our religious traditions as the coming of the kingdom of God,
will be a significant fulfillment and enhancement, a realization,
of God's own being. It is a realization, of course, that will come
about, so far as humans can know, only as and if genuine community and full human personhood are actualized here on earth.
In this respect God's own being and destiny with respect to earth
are intimately tied up with the course of human history. Thus the
central Christian claim that God has irrevocably bound Godself
to humanity by becoming incarnate in contingent human history receives momentous new meaning. Our fate on earth has become God's.

Although we can and certainly should hope that the creativity working in history will bring forth possibilities we cannot now
foresee or intend, a pathway through the innumerable potential
disasters that lie before us, this is not something on which we may
rely with easy confidence. Rather, our fate today is very much in
our own hands, and we must take full responsibility for it. Moreover, the disaster we may bring forth upon the earth will not be
one of merely human consequence, the obliteration of our species, and thus of our hopes and dreams. It will be, rather, a disaster for the long, slow, painful evolution through which life has
proceeded here on earth, finally reaching new dimensions of meaning and value with the appearance of love and truth and self-
consciousness and freedom, as human history has unfolded. It will
be, in short, a disaster for God. And we humans in this generation
will have been responsible. It is this kind of historical and cosmic
moment, a moment not even imaginable before our time, which
we today must confront with open eyes and within which we must
find a way to act responsibly and creatively and redemptively.

Obviously, a dramatic and full transformation — a *metanoia*
— of our major social, political, and economic institutions, of our
ways of thinking and acting, of the very structures of our selves,

is required. Devotion to God, loyalty to God — conceived along the lines I have sketched here, which brings this powerfully evocative ancient symbol into connection with and support of our contemporary awareness of the interdependence of all life, indeed all reality — cannot be contented with any sort of private pietism or parochial concern for particular traditions and communities. It demands reflection on and action to bring about a metanoia in human life as a whole, for God is here understood as that ecological reality behind and in and working through all of life and history, and the service of God can consist thus only in universally oriented vision and work. Devotion to God should help to break our loyalties to the less inclusive wholes and the more parochial centers of value to which we so often idolatrously give them in our ideological and patriotic and religious commitments. In this way it can, perhaps, help to open our eyes to some of the factors producing our furious rush toward race-suicide, and can inspire us to bring it to a halt. Awareness of God still means today, as it always has, that at the most fundamental level "we are not our own" (cf. 1 Cor. 6: 19), and what we do with our lives has significance of cosmic dimensions. But it also means, in a way that has not been so clearly visible in the traditional mythic imagery which gave birth to the idea of God, that since we humans now have the power to destroy human life on earth completely, what we do can have disastrous consequences for the divine life itself. Devotion to God today means, thus, that we resolve to make ourselves fully accountable for the continuance of life on earth.

NOTES

1. For elaboration of this claim see Gordon D. Kaufman, *An Essay on Theological Method*, rev. ed. (Chico, Calif.: Scholars Press, 1979), chap. 3; and *The Theological Imagination* (Philadelphia: Westminster Press, 1981), chaps. 1 and 10.

2. Kaufman, *An Essay on Theological Method*, p. 56.

PART III

Philosophy of Religion and Contemporary Culture

10

Meaning, Religion,
and the Question of God
WOLFHART PANNENBERG

A MEANINGFUL LIFE is no longer taken for granted in the modern
world. A concern with emptiness and loss of meaning, together
with a questioning about and searching after meaning, has become a predominant theme in our time. As early as 1925, Paul
Tillich suggested that the question of meaning has attained as fundamental a significance for modern folk as the question of overcoming transitoriness for people of antiquity and the striving for
forgiveness from sin in the medieval world. For Tillich, all individual meaning is dependent on an unconditioned "ground of
meaning," which both surpasses and serves as foundation for the
totality of all individual semantic contents.[1] In a largely similar
manner, Viktor Frankl has spoken of an "unconditional meaning"
(*Über-Sinn*) which grounds that meaning of existence without
which humans could not exist.[2] Frankl, like Tillich, perceives clearly
that one is concerned here in the final analysis with the religious
quest. In the experience of the "lack of meaning," on the other
hand, that malady of our times is visible which stems from our
secular society's disregard for God and which according to Frankl
provides the explanation for the dramatic rise in the number of
neurotic illnesses and especially of suicides.

All such inquiries into meaning are concerned with what it
is to possess meaning, that is, with the possibility of a life that
even in suffering could be experienced and affirmed as meaningful. The meaning-filled life cannot be presupposed or taken for
granted, as the experiences of emptiness and meaninglessness dem-

onstrate clearly enough. From this observation many assume that we must create our own meaning and thus impart meaning to a reality that appears meaningless. Indeed, this view is dominant in contemporary sociology of knowledge under the influence of Husserl, Alfred Schütz, and Theodor Lessing. Thus, for Peter Berger the human formation of culture is fundamentally a matter of the creation of meaning; similarly, Niklas Luhmann views "the overcoming of contingence" as the most foundational accomplishment of a social system. From here it is only a short step to view the overcoming of experienced meaninglessness also for the *individual* as a task which involves a human creation of meaning. Solving the problem would then only depend on finding the power to give meaning to one's own life, in order to extricate oneself from the crippling influence of the Medusan countenance of meaninglessness.

But is the discovery of meaning a matter of creating meaning or of discovering an already given meaning? In order to pursue this question, it is necessary to distinguish a formal concept of meaning from that of the meaning-filled life. The formal concept is more comprehensive than the actually meaningful. The experience of the *absence* of meaning, for example, is semantically structured and thus not devoid of meaning; the same pertains as well to the nihilistic denial of a meaningful world. Indeed, it is only because of the meaning-related structure of language that one can even articulate the conviction of the meaninglessness of life.

The distinction of a formal notion of what it is to be meaningful from actual meaning-filled content (Sauter) is suggested to us also by a study of that meaning which is contained in the sentences of a discourse or text and which is grasped linguistically. This type of meaning is concerned with the meaning of the words in a sentence and of the sentences in the context of a discourse. The individual words have their meaning not only as designations for objects and states of affairs, but also through their positions in the sentence.

Now thinkers have attempted to draw a neat distinction between the two concepts "meaning" (*Bedeutung*) and "sense"(*Sinn*). Frege spoke, for instance, of the *meaning* of the words as names for objects, and opposed this concept to the *sense* of the sentence as a whole. In his view *sense* has to do with the whole within which the words are arranged as components of the sentence. Now it may as a matter of fact be the case that the concept of *sense* does belong primarily to sentences and that of *meaning* to words. However, the words have their meanings initially within sentences, and this meaning is not completely separable from the context of the individual sentence. A sentence is not merely a mechanical construction of words whose meanings are already set. Rather, the individual word, taken alone, always bears a certain degree of indeterminacy. It is no coincidence that dictionaries offer various nuances of meaning for each word, nuances which are abstracted from the word's actual use in sentences.

In a sentence the individual word wins a higher degree of semantic determinacy. This is because the word bears meaning in a sentence in a second sense, namely, as a constituent of the sentence. Here we normally speak of the *sense* of the word within the context of the sentence. It is not only the sentence as a whole that has a sense, but also its individual constituents, the individual words: in the words the sense of the sentence is articulated. Thus, sense and meaning belong together; they resist a neat assignment to sentence and words. It is especially important, though, to differentiate two aspects within the notion of the word *meaning* itself: the reference to an object, and the position of the individual word in the sentence. Since *meaning* has to do with the position of particulars within the context of the whole, it is therefore possible to speak as well of the meaning of the particular sentence within the broader context of a discourse or text.

Linguistic meaning has therefore to do with the relationships between parts and a whole within the context of a discourse. At the same time, however, we are concerned with the subject which is being spoken about and which is "represented" through the mediation of the meanings of the words which make up the sentence. Now of course language has not only a representational function but expressive and communicative functions as well. There are forms of linguistic expression in which these other functions occupy the foreground. Nonetheless, the representational function always plays a part and may in turn occupy the foreground, namely, in the case of assertorial sentences. Assertions claim to be true in the sense that the meaning of such sentences attempts to represent an objectively existing meaning, a state of affairs. It is this truth claim which constitutes the sense or import of such sentences *qua* assertions.

Does the sense which linguistic utterances have owe its existence to a human bestowal of meaning? At first glance, this appears indeed to be the case. Sentences are, for example, spoken *by us*, leading us to think that their meaning is the result of our efforts. Given that meaning can only be grasped linguistically, the view of language as the product of a human activity suggests to us that we view all meaning as the product of a human bestowal of meaning. However, if we do so, two factors which are crucial to the semantic structure of linguistic utterances disappear from sight.

In the first place, this view fails to consider that it is part of the nature of language itself to represent a reality which is already given, as we saw in our examination of the assertion. Even if only a few assertions are "true," it cannot be the case that all asserted meaning is only the expression of a human bestowal of meaning. True assertions are true precisely insofar as their content corresponds to the state of affairs that is being asserted. Now the spoken or written sentence may be the product of a human activity as well; nonetheless, *true* sentences and *true* assertions are related to the reality of the asserted state of affairs in the sense of a discovery of meaning, rather than in the sense of a bestowal of meaning.

A second important factor is the many-layeredness of the meaning of linguistic utterances. A spoken sentence always brings to expression something above and beyond the meaning that the speaker supposed or intended. It often occurs to us that we say in reality something different from what we wanted to say. This is only possible insofar as the meaning of a sentence, once it has been spoken, proceeds from the combination of the words themselves, independently of the intentions which the speaker had in speaking it. A sentence can say more than the speaker actually wanted to say. It can also fall short of the thought which the speaker wanted to express and which can be independently inferred from the context of the speech. Finally, a sentence can convey something completely different from what he or she intended. All of these things are matters of the interpretation of what was said.

Moreover, every linguistic expression stands in need of interpretation by the listener or reader.

Interpretations can, on the other hand, miss the meaning which the author intended the utterances to have, as well as the meaning which actually should have been derived from what was said. This possibility of error weighs heavily against the view which sees in interpretations only a bestowal of meaning. If the interpretation can miss the meaning of its object, then the meaning of a sentence, a discourse, or a text is obviously not merely dependent on the interpreter. On the other hand, as we saw, it does not depend only on the speaker or author of the text. For these reasons, the semantic structure of the texts which we interpret appears to be an independent entity, and the appropriateness or inappropriateness of interpretations must be judged in relation to it.

In a similar manner assertions also presuppose rather than produce the meaning of the corresponding state of affairs. Assertorial sentences rely unavoidably upon the semantic structures of states of affairs themselves, which are prior to human perception and its articulation in language. Meaning can be approached through language but is not the product of language. Otherwise, all speaking with assertorial sentences would be misguided. If the use of assertions is meaningful then reality must be somehow meaningfully structured prior to its being grasped in language, even if language is the only way to articulate this meaning-structure. Language can either grasp or miss the semantic structure of reality. In either case, this semantic structure is not first created through language. To reduce meaning to language is to take the first step along a path which culminates in the position that all meaning is merely created through human action. Yet this position stands the actual state of affairs on its head since human action itself is dependent on perceptions of meaning.

This criticism of the reduction of linguistically grasped meaning to acts of human meaning-bestowal is of fundamental significance for our theme. The connection of religion and the experience of meaning can only be conceptualized appropriately if experienced meaning is seen to precede its comprehension by humans, rather than being understood solely as the product of a human bestowal of meaning. If the latter were the case, religion would be merely a human projection, lacking any truth content that surpasses the human consciousness. But we have seen that the reduction of the perception and comprehension of meaning to a bestowal of meaning pulls the ground out from under the very notion of the truth of assertions itself, not only from the truth claims of religious statements.

We owe the first foundational analyses of religion and the experience of meaning to Wilhelm Dilthey, who dealt with the semantic structures of experiencing in his late notes and sketches, which in turn formed the starting point for Heidegger's analyses of *Dasein*. Dilthey moved the discussion of words in context to an inquiry into the structure of experiencing. He did not explicitly discuss this transition, since he presupposed that the meaning-structures found in language themselves were only the expression of the meaning-relatedness of the psychic life. For this reason Dilthey believed that it was only possible to speak about meaning and meaning-relationships in the realm of the *psyche*.

Although I have already argued for a wider context, Dilthey's special case of the human life-context does carry particular significance for the perception of meaning, since for humans the whole of their lives is present at every moment with the particulars of their own experiencing. Dilthey, at any rate, expressed it in this way with his concept of experiencing. An individual event becomes an experience to the extent that it is grasped as one specific articulation of a whole life. Perhaps Dilthey limited the notion of experience too narrowly by relating it only to the whole of the individual life. Heidegger's analysis of *Dasein* in *Being and Time* suffers from the same shortcoming. We have no specific consciousness of the whole of our own life (in contradistinction to all else) at the moment of immediate experiencing. Much more, it is the whole of reality itself that is present to us in feeling, not only the whole of our own life. In such a vague presence of reality itself, world, self, and God are as yet undifferentiated. The whole has definiteness only in the particular experiencing. The individual occasion of experiencing, though, is not *just* something particular; in it, the whole of reality appears, just as the meaning-context of a discourse appears in the individual words and sentences. In experiencing, the whole of reality is not fully contained in the individual experience; there remains a vague element of "above and beyond," which at the same time forms the framework in which the individual experience can first become that which it is. There is — as modern philosophy since Descartes has seen, and as medieval scholastic thought already knew — a vague awareness of an undetermined infinite which always precedes all comprehension of anything finite or determined. As Descartes said, the finite can only be comprehended as a limitation of this infinite.

This, then, is the background of Dilthey's concept of experiencing. Dilthey narrowed the horizon of the undetermined infinite and whole, which is present to us in our affections as the horizon of our individual experiences, to the totality of life — indeed, of the individual's *own* life. He gained thereby the basis for his life-philosophy (*Lebensphilosophie*) and for his descriptions of the ontological structure of experiencing, as well as for his view of the human experience of the self as a process of self-interpretation. Under this view, as a life-history progresses the meaning-structures of earlier experiencing shift, because the whole of life appears again and again under new perspectives, that is, from the viewpoint of new experiences. What was earlier experienced as important becomes unimportant, and other scarcely noticed moments of earlier experiencing can increase in significance. Thus Dilthey writes: "Not until the last moment of a life can the final estimate of its meaning be made. . . ."[3] We possess the whole, the total meaning of life, only in the manner in which it is represented in the respective individual experience.

It is amazing to note how closely this description of the semantic structure of experiencing in Dilthey's thought is connected with Schleiermacher's description of religious experience in the second of his *Speeches on Religion* of 1799. In that work religious experience is a view of the infinite and whole in one individual, finite content. We come to such a view of the universe when we become cognizant that what is individual and finite does not exist for itself but rather is "cut out," together with its boundaries which constitute its particularity, of the infinite and whole. In point of fact, this is the same conception which we can find already in Descartes, that we can only comprehend finite objects through a circumscription of the infinite. We are, however — as Schleiermacher further points out — normally not aware of this fact in our everyday lives, interacting as we do with finite objects and states of affairs as if they had their existence from and in themselves.

It is only in the higher awareness of religious experience that we become aware of the actual, deeper reality of things, namely, that they are constituted by and through the "universe," that is, the infinite and the whole. Yet even this higher awareness can grasp the universe only through the viewing of finite things and states of affairs.

It is here that the point of contact with Dilthey lies. We "have" the whole of life, its total meaning, only in the individual and the specific, in which the whole manifests itself. But even such an integrating intuition still remains bound to a particular viewpoint, in a manner similar to Dilthey's position concerning the experience of the meaning or significance of one's own life.

Perhaps Dilthey highlighted the historicity of this process more strongly than Schleiermacher. He speaks, for example, of the possibility of a final knowledge of the meaning of our existence at the end of our life. While he had much in common with Schleiermacher, Dilthey no longer spoke in an explicitly religious manner of the presence of the whole in experiencing but only related this state of affairs to the theme of the experience of the self.

I have dealt with Dilthey in such detail because of the incisive nature of his analyses of the semantic structure of human experiencing, analyses which are fundamental for the contemporary discussion. This is especially true of his position on the significance of individual moments in the context of the whole, a whole which always remains incomplete for the experiencing individuals themselves during the process of their history. Wherever the question of meaning is related to the whole of life and of experienced reality — as, for example, in Tillich's work — such that each individual meaning possesses its significance only from an all-encompassing context of meaning, there Dilthey's analyses can be detected in the background. In Frankl's psychology we also meet up with this understanding of meaning, which is occupied with the relationship of the parts of life to the whole and with the presence of this whole in the individual experience. In contrast to Dilthey, Frankl seeks in this way to do more than merely describe the meaning-structure of experiencing. Whereas such a description would leave open the question whether life is actually experienced as meaningful or as meaningless, Frankl also desires to encourage trust in life's meaningfulness through a total meaning

(*Gesamtsinn*) which encompasses life as a whole, though for him such a total meaning can only be grasped indirectly through the mediation of, and in, concrete life situations. Once again the semantic structure of experiencing, viewed formally, proves to be linked with the religious theme.

Before we pursue the question of the particularity of the religious awareness of meaning in its relationship to the semantic structuredness of human experiencing generally, a point should first be emphasized which represents perhaps the most important gain provided by Dilthey's analyses of meaning and significance in the context of experiencing. That is the fact that Dilthey's descriptions offer an understanding of meaning and significance according to which these do not stem from a bestowal of meaning by the human subject but proceed from the relationships of life itself, that is, from the relationships of its submoments to the whole of the life-context. Viewed in this way, life events already have meaning and significance. This applies also to the events of history, which do not need to have a meaning subsequently conferred upon them through human interpretation. Historical events have in and of themselves meaning and significance according to their contribution to the whole of the life context to which they belong. To be sure, it is only relative to the standpoint of the historical consciousness that the meaning and significance of the individual events can be determined. Dilthey was thus able, through reflection on the historicity of the historical consciousness itself, to do justice to the multiplicity of semantic interpretations of historical occurrences, as well as to the unity of the significance which accrues to each but which cannot be fully determined once and for all until the end of history. Life's moments have a significance (*Bedeutung*) in themselves, but we can only grasp their significance through the medium of an interpretation (*Deutung*) which itself is conditioned by the perspective of a particular historical standpoint. This insight is valid for the life experience of the individual just as much as for history at large. Only from the end of history could we fully and completely comprehend the significance inherent in the events and forms of history. Only from the end of history, therefore, will a final decision concerning the truth or falsity of our convictions of meaning be made. The evidence which the contemporary experience of meaning provides has the form of faith and of an anticipatory representation of a meaning which has yet to appear with finality.

The relationship between Dilthey's description of the experiencing of meaning in an everyday life-context on the one hand, and the specifically religious consciousness of meaning on the other, has been in principle already elucidated by Schleiermacher. He described the everyday consciousness as oriented around finite objects and relationships, whereas the religious consciousness comprehends finite realities as grounded in the infinite and whole, intuiting thereby the infinite itself in the finite things. Paul Tillich wrote in 1925 in his philosophy of religion that all individual meaning is conditioned by a context of meaning which in turn rests on an unconditioned ground of meaning. This unconditioned ground of meaning, however, only becomes an explicit topic for the religious consciousness. The cultural consciousness, which is oriented around individual meaning, presupposes such an unconditioned meaning but does not occupy itself expressly with it: "Every cultural act contains the unconditioned meaning; it is based upon the ground of meaning; insofar as it is an act of meaning it is substantially religious." But it is not expressly religious: "Religion is directedness toward the Unconditional, and culture is directedness toward the conditioned forms and their unity."[4]

I gave expression to a similar determination of the relationship of the religious consciousness to the semantic structure of everyday experience in my 1973 book, *Theology and the Philosophy of Science*, linking myself more closely than Tillich, however, to the hermeneutical analyses of meaning propounded by Dilthey. I argued there that the religious consciousness has as its explicit theme that totality of meaning which is implicitly presupposed in all everyday experiences of meaning, oriented as they are around individual experiences of significance. Religion has above all to do with the divine reality that grounds and completes the meaning-totality of the natural and social world, and thus only indirectly with the totality of meaning of the world itself. Nevertheless, the truth claim made by the religious consciousness must authenticate itself by showing that the God (or gods) alleged by it can actually be understood as the creator and perfecter of the world as it is in fact experienced. The assertions made within the religious traditions, which are directed beyond formal meaningfulness to a positive fulfillment of meaning in human life, must prove themselves by being able to integrate the relations that are given implicitly in all everyday experience of meaning within an encompassing context of meaning that grounds all individual meaning. The urgent experiences of senselessness, suffering, and evil are among those life experiences which the religious consciousness of meaning must integrate. If the religious tradition is not able to do justice to human experience through such integration, its failure will lead to a crisis of the truth-consciousness of the tradition in question; it then becomes questionable whether the God proclaimed by this tradition can, as a matter of fact, be understood as and believed to be the creator and perfecter of the world as actually experienced by humans.

Christian truth claims about God must also face this question of a confirmation through the human experience of meaning and its implications for the understanding of reality as a whole. The feelings, so widespread today, of an all-pervading senselessness, together with the related questioning after meaning, indicate that, for many persons and for broad segments of the public consciousness in our secular culture, the traditional answers of Christianity are no longer adequately functioning as a comprehensive interpretation of the experience of the world's reality and of the life problems that contemporary people face. The individual reasons for this failure cannot be developed here. However, the contemporary question of meaning that arises out of the experience of the absence of meaning should not simply be dismissed by Christian theology as an idolatrous question.[5] Certainly theology must criticize the widespread tendency to reduce meaning to human action as self-destructive.[6] It is also correct that meaning and truth are not the same.[7] Seductive images may be experienced as most meaningful — that is the key to their seductiveness, since only for this reason can they lead astray.

Attention to the suffering from meaninglessness can awaken the false impression that the problem might be solved simply by providing humans with some sort of sense that life is meaningful, as if the content were a peripheral matter and the question of the truth or falsity superfluous and disruptive.[8] Yet if we were to approach the question of meaning that arises out of the experience of meaninglessness as if it were merely a demand to anesthetize nihilistic experience, we would have misunderstood it. Those who earnestly inquire into meaning are concerned with an *adequate* answer to the problems which have led to the forfeiture of the consciousness of meaning.

Thus the question of meaning, correctly understood, is inseparable from the question of truth. This is evidenced by the longing for an all-encompassing meaning. For to the concept of truth belongs the unity of all truth, that is, the simultaneous existence, without contradiction, of each individual truth with all other truths. From this insight alone it should be clear that the question of the meaning-context of reality as a whole is not theologically illegitimate.[9] To inquire into the total meaning of reality is not automatically an expression of human presumptuousness. It is a matter of fact that the individual is everywhere conditioned by the whole, and the consciousness of this state of affairs belongs essentially to the humanity of humankind. To be sure, the simultaneous awareness that we can never gain a definitive overview of the whole of reality is also a part of our humanity. Only when this is forgotten is it appropriate to speak of presumptuousness.

Knowledge about the whole of reality itself and the question of its basis must not be confused with this sort of presumptuousness. The presumption lies in alleging to command a definitive view over the whole, whereby persons forget their own finitude and place themselves in the position of God. The sort of knowledge of the whole of reality, on the other hand, that remains conscious at the same time of its own finiteness, reaches consummation in a knowledge of God as distinct from human subjectivity. The concept of God as such is always an answer to the question of the meaning of reality as a whole. Whoever wishes to forbid this question must also forbid that religious consciousness through which we honor God as the creator of ourselves and the world.

To a correct knowledge of God certainly belongs the allusion to divine inscrutability. Yet this allusion must not be understood as the avoidance of an answer to the question of the meaning-context of reality as a whole. Instead, it represents a phase in such an answer, insofar as it emphasizes the superiority of the God-based meaning of the life-world as a whole over and above the limitations of human understanding. Even negative theology, which refuses to go beyond the conception of the unknown God, is in this sense an answer to the human question of meaning. Of course, it is not the Christian answer, for Christianity confesses that in Jesus of Nazareth the divine Logos has become human, the one in whom all things have their being. The word *logos* connotes "meaning" as much as "word." The connection of the Old Testament concept of the divine Word with the Greek notion of *logos* means nothing less than that the context of meaning that encompasses the entire creation and its history up through the eschatological completion has appeared in Jesus Christ.

NOTES

1. Paul Tillich, *Religionsphilosophie* (1925); *Urban-Reihe* 63 (1962), pp. 42, 44ff. Translated as "The Philosophy of Religion," in Paul Tillich, *What is Religion?* ed. James Luther Adams (New York: Harper & Row, 1969), chap. 1.

2. Viktor E. Frankl, *The Will to Meaning: Foundations and Applications of Logotherapy* (New York: New American Library, Plume Books, 1969), p. 156; published in German as *Der Wille zum Sinn* (1972), p. 117. This was part of a series of lectures at the Perkins School of Theology, Southern Methodist University, Dallas, Texas, summer 1966.

3. Wilhelm Dilthey, *Gesammelte Schriften*, 16 vols. in 18 (Stuttgart: Tübner, and Göttingen: Vandenhoeck & Ruprecht, 1914–72), 7: 237.

4. Tillich, *Religionsphilosophie*, p. 44; "The Philosophy of Religion," p. 59.

5. Gerhard Sauter, *Was heisst nach Sinn fragen? Eine theologisch-philosophische Orientierung* (Munich: C. Kaiser, 1982), pp. 145, 163.

6. Ibid., pp. 39ff, 46ff, 56ff, 130f.

7. Ibid., pp. 61f, 88.

8. For a critique of this position, see Sauter, *Was heist nach Sinn fragen?* pp. 105, 107f.

9. Sauter comes at least very close to such a thesis, inasmuch as he flatly characterizes the meaning question (as a question concerning absolute meaning) as "immoderate and presumptuous" (p. 167). He brings the alleged avoidance of this question by Job and Kohelet into connection with the Old Testament prohibition of images of God. Nevertheless, Sauter also says that the question of meaning belongs to life itself (pp. 128f), and speaks of the "meaning that is communicated in the cross of Christ" (pp. 152ff).

11

Religion and Science
in an Advanced Scientific Culture
LANGDON GILKEY

MY SUBJECT IS THE creationist controversy as that came to a momentary boil in Arkansas in 1981. There a law had been passed requiring that creation science, for all intents and purposes a literal interpretation of the Genesis account, be taught in science classes alongside what they called "evolutionary science." This case provided a window into the complexity and therefore the opacity of an advanced scientific culture, and especially into the relations of religion and science in such a culture. The media, the scientific community, and the public-at-large viewed it as simply the latest battle in the continuing warfare between the benighted legions of religion and the enlightened forces of science. I shall seek to show that this is a part of the optical illusion that the reigning mythology of an advanced scientific culture helps to create whenever that culture seeks to understand itself.

The plaintiffs in the case — those who objected to the law forcing a teaching of creationism as a science — were largely churches, clergy, and ministerial associations, Protestant, Catholic, and Jewish; only one represented a scientific organization, the National Association of Biology Teachers. Half the witnesses on our side, the American Civil Liberties Union side, represented religion and religious studies; all but one of the witnesses on the other side represented one scientific discipline or another. Correspondingly, the leaders of the movement of creation science are scientists in the sense that most of them have advanced degrees in science from reputable universities and hold tenured positions in natural science.

This is enough to show that the situation is mixed, strangely confused, and therefore obscure. Surprisingly, there is a good deal of *religion* in the forces arrayed against creationism, and a good deal of *science* in the forces for it. These unexpected sorts of union of science and religion seem to be characteristic of an advanced scientific culture.

The first implication of this cultural situation is that science is now thoroughly "established." In practical circles this means that science is now utterly necessary for almost every aspect of our life: for the production of goods, agriculture, medicine, communication, travel, self-defense, and so on. The society unquestionably supports it and reveres it. In theoretical circles this means that science is "queen." Science represents that central form of knowledge that brings forth both truth and well-being. As a consequence, it has a sacral character in our common life, and it sheds a sacral aura on those who possess, embody, and further it.

We theologians ought to understand this — we once enjoyed the same role. Dominant groups should understand and recognize their own dominance and power, for only if they recognize their dominance can they use their power wisely. One cause of this controversy has been an irresponsible use of this power, that is, of the authority of science in the teaching of science. A vast number of scientists and teachers of science have identified their scientific knowledge with total knowledge, and thus have dismissed religious understanding as primitive, prescientific, and false. This assumption, that scientific inquiry represents the only relevant path to truth, has produced the creationist reaction.

A second consequence of an advanced scientific culture is that science shapes all the levels of modern society. In the previous two or three centuries of its life, empirical science was practiced and understood only by portions of the educated elite. It was located, therefore, only at the top and perhaps slightly outside a society actually determined by other established forces, especially the established force of class and of religion. This situation has radically changed. This permeation throughout society has long been true of technology: every class, every form of entertainment, every variety of religion is at home with the most contemporary instruments of modern technology. Similarly, fundamentalist groups operate faultlessly amid sophisticated commercial and financial matters and even direct large portions of our economic system. They also found universities. It is no surprise, therefore, that members of fundamentalist groups enter the laboratories and the graduate schools of our larger universities in pursuit of doctorates in science and that such doctorates now abound among these groups — though, note, no similar doctorates in theology or in biblical studies are found there. This participation in our technical and scientific culture has only recently become true of fundamentalism. At the Scopes trial the major forces of fundamentalism were anti-urban, anti-university, anti-science, anti-wealthy-capitalist. They represented a rural and small-town reaction to the more sophisticated areas of contemporary American life. This is no longer so. The change is especially evident in the creationists' repudiation of evolutionary science, *not* because it is science but because it is "bad science" or "false science" and their own view is "true science."

Thus appears the notion of "popular science," comparable to "popular religion" in a culture where a traditional religion has long been thoroughly established. An established religion takes on local, age-old, often deviant or bizarre, syncretistic forms as a result of its mingling with the whole range of the culture. Such forms of popular Christianity are still Christianity, however unpalatable to the Councils of Bishops or the National Council of Churches. What we here refer to are forms of modern science, however they may horrify the AAAS.

Different cultures, with different ideologies, have incorporated modern technology and science into their life and have produced variant forms of both. The forms which science takes shift interestingly as they become embodied in different social matrices. Many of these are strikingly deviant forms from the point of view of our own elite Western scientific culture. Nazi Germany was scientific, and it incorporated all the universities and laboratories of modern Germany with minimal resistance into its ideological life. Stalinist Russia did the same, as did Shinto Japan. Believing in the universality and necessity of our own form of science, we took each of these as mere aberrations and, in one sense, they were. Still, consider that Maoist China would have been another differently shaped example had it lasted, and possibly Khomeini's Iran will prove the most bizarre of all. Surely, we cannot be so naive as to think that the vast number of Sunni and Shi-ite students at our technological and engineering schools will return to their lands to reproduce there MIT and the Charles River Basin rather than to help create an *Islamic* form of modern culture and so of science.

Our liberal understanding of science and of technology thus reveals itself not as the one necessary or guaranteed form of scientific culture, but as *one* option, one developed by and indebted to the liberal, democratic, humanistic, and capitalistic culture of the European Enlightenment. Quite naturally it remains for us "true science." But we may be sure that it is not the only form of science that developments in the immediate future will produce.

Creation science represents one home-grown variety of a union between science and religion. The warfare is not between science and religion but between two different sorts of unity of science and religion: an "elite form" made up of elite science (the AAAS) and religion (the National Council); and a "popular form," constituted by fundamentalist religion and popular science. This illustrates the point frequently made before that scientific knowledge and technology add know-how and force to religious commitments. It has been, therefore, the liberal humanistic culture of elite science, not its scientific or technological components, that has made it liberal. There is little reason within science itself why it cannot associate itself with other nonliberal cultures, ideologies, and religious forms. The health of science as a social force depends on the persistence and the health of the wider liberal culture in which it is embedded.

Thirdly, most advanced cultures tend to be religious. At the close of Hellenistic culture and at the end of the medieval period new religious forms poured in from the outside, and older, traditional, indigenous forms of religion often became revitalized. This same process has taken place in our advanced scientific culture, only here the new vigorous religious movements have tended to take on a scientific form. Most of the new cults picture themselves as scientific. Even a resurgent fundamentalism, championing a literal interpretation of Scripture, claims to be science.

The establishment of science means that science represents the paradigmatic and so sacral form of knowing. Each form of sacred knowledge has for very understandable reasons a sacral aura, symbolized in our case by the white coat and by the super prizes bestowed on scientists. As the forms of religion in such a culture seek to be scientific, so science itself begins to manifest a religious dimension or religious attributes. An inflation of science takes place: from method or heuristic rules or canons to metaphysical, ontological, and theological substantive statements. Only scientific statements are now cognitive. Only the factors scientific inquiry uncovers and knows are to be the real and effective causes of things.

The belief that scientific explanations are total explanations dominated both sides of the creationist controversy. The creationists assumed it throughout their literature and their testimony. If the Genesis account was valid, then it was or must be science. If evolutionary science does not mention God then it follows that evolutionary science has excluded and so denied God. Note, too, that many if not all supporters of science have thoroughly agreed with this view. If, said they, science no longer makes use of the hypothesis of God in its tracing of origins, then religious explanations are anachronistic, outmoded, false. Both sides regarded natural science as providing a total explanation of origins.

Interestingly, despite their other differences, neither side envisioned the possibility that a religious understanding and a scientific understanding of origins were quite compatible and not mutually exclusive. The error that characterized both sides of the controversy was that truth is all of one kind. The consequences of this error are serious. For then the other aspects of culture— imaginative literature, art, rational speculation, morals, and religion— cease to be taken seriously. They are regarded as merely subjective, generated entirely out of the psyche, and so irrelevant for the fundamental business of life in its relation to reality.

Thus develops the myth that the scientific community need not understand the rest of culture. This myth has become embodied in the majority of graduate programs in science, which are quite bare of required courses in either the history of science or the philosophy of science. In fact, to my knowledge, science is the only university discipline taught without any substantial reference to its own history and to its own relations to the rest of life. As theology once thought that because of revelation it was quite independent of culture and of culture's relativities, so science has seen itself, because of its modes of objective inquiry, to be independent of ordinary cultural life. This view of itself is, of course, an illusory one. Science is also a fully human activity, appearing and developing within a given cultural and historical matrix. As in the cases of art, politics, and religion, therefore, to understand science one must understand the history of science and its relations to other aspects of culture.

The main consequence of the idolization of science is the ignoring of the logical limits of science. The canons of scientific method define the modes of explanation that are scientific. These canons support the reliability of scientific conclusions, but they also rule out as nonscientific clearly religious "doctrines," such as the concept of creation out of nothing embodied in creation science. I refer to such canons as (1) the *empirical* canon: no concept is permissible but one that grows out of and can be checked in sensible and so shareable experience; (2) the *naturalistic* canon: no supernatural explanatory cause is permissible in scientific explanation; only natural or human causes may be appealed to; and (3) the canon that scientific explanations are in terms of *universal* and so *necessary* relations and not purposes or intentions — and so on.

In the trial we used these rules of method to exclude creation science from the domain of science, since creation science inescapably referred to a transcendent God, to God's purposes, and to a quite transnatural action to explain the world. To speak, as they did, of a sudden and recent creation of all things *out of nothing*; to postulate an absolute beginning not only to the universe but to each "kind" within it; to refer to supernatural causes of geological formations such as the Flood — these concepts defy the canons of scientific method we have mentioned and transcend its mode of explanation.

Let us note, however, that these same rules clearly limit scientific explanations. When scientists look for origins, therefore, they can only ask, How did state A arise out of state B, and how can I interpret these changes in terms of natural processes? They cannot ask, How did the entire system originate and why? Nor can they ask, What other transnatural or even intentional factors may be at work? The scientific question of origins only concerns the question of proximate origins. By its very nature, scientific inquiry cannot ask about the ultimate origin or the ultimate ground of the natural process itself.

The same is true, interestingly enough, of the logical limits both of historical inquiry and of law. In neither case can God be appealed to as an explanation. I made this point about the latter in the trial: no defending lawyer can advance in court — even in the faithfully orthodox state of Arkansas — the hypothesis that God instead of the client is responsible for the murder under consideration. The judge firmly agreed: "God" is not an acceptable explanatory factor in terms of Arkansas law. These are thus *secular* disciplines, and this is the meaning of that term — not that they are atheistic or entail atheism, for surely in Arkansas God establishes and supports the law. Rather, these disciplines are confined by their logical rules to natural and historical causes. Scientific inquiry is distinct from any general consideration of the whole of things and from inquiry into knowing subjects as well as known objects. Scientific inquiry and reflection are enterprises different from reflection in metaphysics and theology. Science in this sense is limited; it is only an aspect of our contact with reality. For this reason scientific explanation neither excludes nor replaces a religious explanation or a metaphysical one, though it may well imply changes in the formulations of theories in either discipline.

But to creationists evolutionary science was essentially atheistic because it never mentioned God in its explanation or origins. They did not realize that the special sciences could not have mentioned God as an explanation and remained science; nor did they realize that their own religious statements, like metaphysical ones, functioned on a different level of discourse and of conceptuality than did the scientific ones they had learned in their training. After all, to speak of an object in its relation to other objects within the natural system represents a different mode of speech than to speak of God who is the author of all things.

Correspondingly the new scientific explanations of origins have simply replaced traditional religious explanations of origins. They understand Genesis and the doctrines of Christianity or Judaism as prescientific attempts to understand the world cognitively. Now that much more reliable information about the natural world has come to us, this whole panoply of religious understanding is out of date. Creationism is a reaction to the establishment of modern science insofar as science has claimed to provide a total explanation of our existence and of the world in which we exist. It has been the expansion of science from a reliable method into a speculative world view and a humanistic religion that has led to this controversy. It is, therefore, primarily the religious dimensions of modern or evolutionary science that the creationists have reacted to — and in that reaction they have been in their own way quite right.

Religion is not about to wither away, nor is science. Each culture, modern ones included, unites the ever-present factors of rational inquiry and of ultimate commitment in a wide variety of ways. To deal with the specific issues in this controversy concerning the relation of current scientific views of origins to Hebrew and Christian beliefs about origins requires an acquaintance with the philosophy of religion. Above all, a refashioning of the modes of training of the scientific community — a restoration of philosophy of science and the history of science — is absolutely vital if that community is to fulfill the creative role that its intellectual and social dominance forces upon it.

This critique of the scientific community should be balanced by a corresponding critique of our religious communities. Creation science is at base a religious movement, largely inspired and motivated by fundamentalist Protestant Christianity. But other more liberal religious communities have been more than lax in dealing forthrightly with the issues raised by a fundamentalist interpretation of Christian faith.

The rapprochement between science and theology has been an accomplished fact for two hundred years. Since 1790 the question has not been *whether* science and religion can be set into accord with one another, but *how* it is to be done. The intellectual contradiction between science and religion, while still apparent for some within Christianity and Judaism, has quite dissolved for most, and the unity of science and religion has frequently been fully thought through. It should, therefore, be as much common knowledge, for example, as is the fact that the Boston University School of Medicine no longer has a Department of Bleeding. Yet, astoundingly, almost no one knows of this accord of religious belief with science.

In speaking on this theme since December 1981 I have encountered over and over astonishment that — as a *Time* reporter challenged me at the trial — I, as a theologian, should have been there defending Darwin! Clearly the notion that the churches, their believers, and their theologians do not subscribe to fundamentalism and so to a creation science view of origins has not really dawned on widespread sections of the public. Perhaps we assumed, wrongly, that the issue had receded amid the progressive developments of history; perhaps we were afraid of initiating controversy. In any case, the cowardice in not dealing with this issue is the precise mirror image to the *hubris* of science in not dealing with *its* relations with the rest of culture. These two sins of omission have helped generate this controversy and the public's reaction to it.

The unexpected persistence of the religious in modern culture has been a surprise because it was long assumed that the "need" — as we liked to put it — for religion would recede. This has turned out to be wrong. Religions are on the increase. What did we *not* understand about the religious and society that led us to be wrong about the destiny of religion in the twentieth century?

First of all, every culture needs a unifying, organizing, and directing set of symbols that gives to all common experience an intelligible and meaningful pattern. The view that religion was an aspect of past, prescientific, and ignorant societies has been a part of our scientific self-understanding. This view understood the major cultural activities of the past as solely cognitive endeavors, either prescientific or pseudoscientific. The religious myths of the past were prescientific efforts to explain natural events. It was reasonable to believe that all forms of religious "knowing" would dissolve away as science itself developed and replaced it. However, every cycle of religious mythology takes care to interpet a *competing* cycle of myths as the direct opposite of itself — for example, as generated by satanic powers and not by the divine. Large portions of a scientific culture have also done this to that culture's early spiritual antagonists, orthodox Christianity and Judaism. For out of that culture's own advances have arisen dilemmas which raise religious questions and which call for religious answers. To sum up, then: even a scientific culture is established in part on a religious vision of what is really real, true, and good, a vision that animates, empowers, and directs each aspect of the culture.

The role of religion in cultural life shifts and becomes even more crucial in times of trouble. Such times of trouble appear when those structures which founded the culture's life turn and become destructive and so lead to the disintegration of the common life. In our time we have seen this beginning to happen with theoretical science and with capitalist and Marxist social theories. Naturally, in such times the most basic symbols become themselves shaken, and the assumed values of the culture suddenly appear vulnerable. Every basis for serenity itself seems now precarious. The Hellenistic period illustrates all of these modes of doubt, uncertainty, and anxiety about its cultural foundations, and as a consequence it tended to welcome a whole new range of religious cults.

It is, therefore, no surprise that in our period literalistic fundamentalism should be on the rise. Vast new anxieties have appeared in our time and must be appeased. These anxieties have arisen, not despite our scientific culture but precisely because of it. When each of us must now contemplate the possibility of a nuclear and so a secular apocalypse, it is not strange that some among us begin to find fundamentalist language and symbols viable and even necessary. Nor is it strange that such new modes of literalistic religion unite with and take on a scientific form. In unexpected ways in our century, science not only breeds religion but also finds itself united with religions old and new.

The uses of scientific knowledge and technological power depend on the character and intentions of their users. This fact has come home to us recently. Science has had vastly benevolent effects, but our predominant present awareness is of its devastating consequences. Any progressive and benevolent consequences of science and technology are subjectively utterly dependent on the moral and spiritual situation of the persons within a scientific culture. Objectively they are dependent on the legal, political, and educational health of that society. Ironically these aspects of culture are precisely those elements most ignored. A scientific culture cries out precisely for its sibling, the humanities, lest despite itself it destroy itself. The myth of an independent, self-sufficient, and yet creative scientific and technological tradition has vanished without a trace.

Correspondingly, religion as it appears in an advanced culture is itself by no means always creative. Religion too can be destructive, in fact, demonic. Whenever science generates evil consequences it is largely because of the *spiritual* ambiguity of the culture in which it is used. It is after all the claim to ultimacy and sacrality that breeds fanaticism, cruelty, and terror. The danger is that a scientific community be taken over by a rising religious movement, whether it be a traditional movement as in Japan or Iran, a secular one as in Germany, Italy, or Russia, or "home-grown religion" as with our own religious and political Right. The scientific community, conscious that it looks back with disdain on its own traditional forms of religion, has literally not believed this to be a possibility. But the evidence shows it is. They should look *forward* to the possibility of nationalistic, ideological, and cultural modes of religion, for the varieties of relevant religious commitments range far beyond their hometown's list of church services on Sunday. The relations of science and of technology to the religious, and of both to the humanistic aspects of our culture, are crucial to the health of both science and religion.

In a time of trouble such as we are in, the religious tends to expand and to become more and more fanatical. Science tends to become more and more positivist in theory and intensely specialized in inquiry, and to develop greater means for destruction in practice. Such a cultural existence, split at its center — long on theoretical knowledge and destructive know-how, and short on self-understanding, self-criticism, and a transcendent ground for love and hope — provides a sure recipe for self-destruction.

Let us stem this tide. Let us begin again to speak together — for unless religion and science unite in reasonable and humane ways, they will unite as partners in disintegration.

12

The Meeting of East and West: Paul Tillich's Philosophy of Religion

LEROY S. ROUNER

CHRISTIAN THOUGHT HAS belatedly discovered the problem of religious pluralism, and many of the best minds in the Christian world are now engaged in some form of dialogue with other religious traditions, especially the Buddhist and Hindu traditions of the East. Toward the end of his life Paul Tillich made a celebrated trip to Japan, became much interested in Buddhism, and wrote a popular little book on Christianity and other world religions. But he really knew too little of the history, intellectual substance, and cultural ethos of another religion to engage in significant comparative study. His substantive contribution to the comparative philosophy of religion had already been made, and lay at the heart of his method of correlation. There he tried to resolve the age-old metaphysical problem of the One and the Many, the conflict between monism and dualism. He was not, I think, entirely successful, but he took seriously — as most of his theological contemporaries, alas, did not — the fundamental difference between the qualified dualism inherent in Christian thought and the qualified monism inherent in most Hindu and Buddhist metaphysics.

Christianity and Hinduism have the most extensive and technically sophisticated metaphysical systems of all the world's great religious traditions. This fundamental difference is at the heart of basic conflicts in ethics as well as epistemology and metaphysics. First I offer a word of introduction to the problem of interreligious dialogue; secondly, an examination of Tillich's contribution, using the problem of evil as a paradigm; finally, a word of criticism and appreciation.

From 1800 to 1960 the people most aware of religious pluralism were Christian missionaries and scholars with an academic interest in the history of religion or comparative religion.[1] These scholars were usually Christian and regularly proved that Christianity was the best religion. The early Protestant missionaries were less generous than the scholars. Not only was their religion the best; the other world religions were the worst. The only way to salvation was the version of Christian faith in which they believed.

Unlike the scholars, however, the missionaries had the eventual advantage of vital contact. The scholars were taking the measure of other religions by reading sacred texts in German and British university libraries. The missionaries lacked leisure for such critical reflection but were forced by their vocation into living cheek-to-jowl with believers in other gods. As a result, they discovered that other religions are not sacred texts. They are common folk who may revere alien ideas but whose ethical instincts are often congenial and whose humanity may be winsome. Occasionally, a certain empathy resulted. In India, for example, the neo-Hindu movement of the nineteenth and early twentieth centuries had produced Ram Mohun Roy, Sri Ramakrishna, Swami Vivekananda, and Mohandas Gandhi — all of whom were in conversation with missionary thinkers and activists, and all of whom eventually cooperated with missionaries to bring about social and religious reform. The relation between Gandhi and the Christian missionary Charles Andrews was distinctive but not entirely unusual. The missionaries had gradually come to suspect that other religious folk knew something crucial about the God who was really God, and were living in devotion to that knowledge.

So at the International Missionary Conference in Jerusalem in 1928 there was a call for cooperation among the world's living religions. A few years later William Ernest Hocking published *Rethinking Missions*, reinforcing that call. In Germany, however, the collapse of the Weimar Republic and the rise of National Socialism was forcing a radical distinction between those who were prepared to fight for authentic Christian faith and those who capitulated to the Blood-and-Soil tribalism of the Third Reich. This was the crucible from which the New Reformation theology of Karl Barth emerged. His distinctive and triumphant Christianity stood over against all the powers of this world, including its religions. Among the missionaries, Hendrik Kraemer was Barth's most effective representative, and his study volume for the International Missionary Conference in Tambaram, India, ten years later, *The Christian Message in a Non-Christian World*, rejected Hocking's conciliatory thesis as lacking in authentic Christian faith.

But what had been so effective a rallying cry against Nazi tyranny soon seemed unappreciative of the spiritual depth in other religions and unmindful of the need for common spiritual ground in a world threatening to destroy itself. The global village had reconstituted the missionary experience for everyone. We were now *all* living cheek-to-jowl with folk who trust different gods. By the mid-fifties, the new question was how Christian faith might fare in the coming world civilization.

Paul Tillich was a philosopher as well as a theologian. He called himself an existentialist, but concern for the anguish and ambiguities of human experience did not keep him from metaphysical speculation in the tradition of German idealism. He had both a philosopher's doctrine of reason and a theologian's doctrine of revelation; he believed in both history and transcendent realms of being. He was not an Either/Or thinker, as Barth was; he was a Both/And philosopher in the tradition of Hegel and Schelling. He described himself as living and thinking on the boundary between different realities, especially between philosophy and theology. His message was that they are genuinely different, but that each needs the other in that dimension of depth where they are most themselves. Reason drives toward revelation because it asks questions which it cannot answer. Revelation seeks out reason because it provides an answer which it cannot articulate. So with history and the transcendent, and indeed, with all the fundamental differing opposites of human experience.

The method of correlation which he introduced in the first volume of his *Systematic Theology* is ultimately an attempt to resolve the conflict between monism and dualism. This metaphysical adventure makes Tillich important for comparative philosophy of religion. The problem was best stated by Whitehead; at least his statement of it is the one I like best because it is pithy and experiential. He and Ernest Hocking taught a seminar at Harvard on the question: What do you mean when you appeal to experience? John Dewey had made the famous comment that *experience* is a weasel word, and the seminar was an exercise in clarification. In the course of the seminar Hocking reported that Whitehead mused: "Sometimes I think that I am in the world; and sometimes I think the world is in me."

This seems to me to describe our experience. Our initial reaction to the world is a natural realism. Of course I am in the world. The world was here before I was and will be here after I am gone. We know that we are all *in* this room. We came in and we will go out, and if that is not real, nothing is. Further, this contact with the objective reality of a physical world which is there, no matter what I think or feel about it, is necessary to my sense of individual selfhood. I cannot know myself to be a self in any definitive way unless I can *place* myself. The fundamental differences which I experience in space between here and there; in time between now and then; in causality between this and that; are all real—and are part of my experience of my own reality. The vividness, sharpness, concreteness, and reliability of physical objects are not simply helpful for my own clarity of mind; these characteristics of my experienced world are necessary not only for my self-identity but for my sanity.

Whitehead's second comment is equally true. What I know is not the room in itself as it exists out there objectively for every possible perceiver, but the room as I perceive it. You and I have different rooms right now, but this we have in common: the room we each experience is the room given to us through our five senses. Your room supposedly comes from some objective room 'out there', but you don't have any individually independent way of establishing that. What you can authoritatively claim to know is your perception, and that room is in you. So our natural realism is in conflict with this subjectivism; and both have an authoritative basis in experience.

What we have here is not only a fundamental dilemma of human reflection, but a key to the two major options in metaphysics: some sort of monism and some sort of dualism. I say "some sort of" because the great metaphysical systems are always aware of this problem, so the result is a qualified monism, as in the Advaita Vedānta philosophy of the Hindu Śaṁkara; or a qualified dualism, as in the Christian philosophy of Saint Thomas. To be sure, there are dualistic philosophies within the Eastern traditions of Hindu and Buddhist philosophy; and there are monistic philosophies within the Western traditions of Christian, Jewish, and Muslim thought; but in neither case are they characteristic. What is characteristic of Eastern religious metaphysics is a qualified monism which discovers ultimate reality in the depths of selfhood, where the *ātman* of my inwardness is identical with the Holy World Power of Brahman. What is characteristic of Western religious metaphysics is a qualified dualism which affirms the reality of time, space, and causality, the real distinction between you and me, and the ultimate distinction between the world and God.

One can illustrate these two ways of thinking by comparing and contrasting the world-making myths of the Hindu tradition with the world-making myth in the Bible. In the Hindu tradition the world has no beginning in time. The endless cycle of birth and death, creation and destruction, spins off the activity of a dancing God at play. God's being emanates forth to form a world composed of God-stuff. In the biblical story, on the other hand, the world comes to be "in the beginning." A single history moves inexorably toward its conclusion. The Word of God works intentionally on that which is nothing apart from God to create a world which bears the *imago dei* and cannot finally be separated from God but which is nevertheless different from God. Play versus work; accident versus intention; dance versus speech; an eternal now versus time; pantheism versus monotheism; emanation versus creation; monism versus dualism.

Many argue that philosophers East and West are saying the same thing, and that only the terms and accents are different. On the contrary, I am persuaded that our philosophies have purchase in our culture because they reflect something we really believe. I like Ernest Hocking's definition of philosophy as the examination of belief. And our various cultures and beliefs are not essentially the same. As befits a modified dualist, my thesis is therefore that the distinction between East and West is real, and that exploration of the metaphysical issue is an important prelude to understanding differences concerning specific doctrines, practices, and ethical norms.

For example, an emanationist cosmology and the resulting monistic metaphysics demand a Stoic ethic. The reason for that is not very complicated. In a monism, however qualified, there is ultimately neither here nor there, now nor then, this nor that. If it is nondual, then two-ness, wherever it appears, must be only an appearance. Since there is ultimately no 'outside' to anything, but only a limitless 'inside', the only resources for moral action available to us are those 'inside' the self. A Stoic ethic, when confronted with the need for greater moral resources, digs down deeper, inside—whether one be Marcus Aurelius or Mahatma Gandhi.

On the other hand, a Christian ethic of obedience to God's will assumes an 'outside'. We cannot do what we ought to do on our own apart from the enabling grace of a God who helps us be who we really are. This fundamental distinction is easy to miss if one focuses on the details of doctrine, liturgy, or piety. Sarvepalli Radhakrishnan argued masterfully that Hinduism and Christianity were essentially the same, by quoting passages from the *Upaniṣads* which could indeed have come right out of the Gospel of Saint John. John Findlay's brilliant Gnostic interpretation of Saint John's Gospel serves the same argument.[2] But even a whole flock of these graceful philosophical swallows does not constitute a metaphysical summer. That would reduce our religious philosophies to a curious aberration in our cultural life. If our religious philosophies were essentially the same, our religious cultures would be essentially the same, but no one really argues that. By focusing on the metaphysical wood, rather than on the doctrinal trees, we can make some progress on a problem which is more recalcitrant than we are sometimes led to believe—which brings us to Tillich.

Tillich defines God as the ground of being, being itself, or the power of being—what German idealism had called the absolute. God is the possibility of both potentiality and actuality; the context of both essence and existence; the meaning of all events. God is not a person because God is not an individual. To be an individual would make God a particular, however great, in a world of particulars. This means that God does not exist, in the sense of being a particular, individual being. God is rather the ground and power of both being and nonbeing.

Tillich is less concerned with the abstract grandeur of explanation than he is with the intimate reassurance of existential understanding. Marx wanted philosophy to change the world. Tillich wants philosophy to heal the world — to overcome the *angst* which characterizes the human situation. The cosmological argument for God assumes an individual cosmic cause appropriate to the creative value effect which we experience in the world. For Tillich this makes God a stranger, far out on the rim of the cosmos, knowable only indirectly through the divine effects. But the existential human problem of anxiety about our being in the world is intense and immediate. The God who saves us cannot come to us as a stranger, but as the power of overcoming estrangement. Here Tillich echoes Augustine: "O Lord, Thou hast made us for Thyself, and our hearts are restless till they find their rest in Thee."[3] That estrangement is characteristic of our relation to ourselves, to the natural world, and to each other. Only a God who is an intimate participant in these realities can enable our reconciliation with them.

How, then, did this existential estrangement take place? Or, as the theologians put it, how did we fall from grace? In keeping with his method, Tillich deals with the problem of evil by correlating the biblical story of the Fall with Plato's myth of the Fall from essence to existence. Here his intellectual agility is on full display. He may not believe in a dancing God, but he is a dancing philosophical theologian. Reinhold Niebuhr, who thought the venture ill-advised, nevertheless admitted that Tillich was the great theological tightrope walker of his time.

The biblical story of the Fall is that once upon a time the man and woman created by God lived in a garden paradise in perfect moral and spiritual harmony with themselves, each other, the natural world around them, and God. Their only restriction was that God told them not to eat the fruit of the tree of the knowledge of good and evil. But a serpent tempted Eve, she ate, told Adam about these great apples, he ate, and the rest, as we say, is history. Biblical literalists have taken the story at face value, but Tillich does not take that view seriously. There are two alternative readings, however, which he does take seriously even though he rejects them. One is Hegelian idealism, where the fall is reduced to the difference between the ideal and the real, and where reality is then seen as pointing to the ideal. In this view "the Fall is not a break, but an imperfect fulfillment. It approximates fulfillment in the historical process or is fulfilled in principle in the present period of history."[4] The other alternative is a naturalism which announces that humankind "has no predicament" and that existence has no knowable essence. Evil is therefore not a problem for which humankind has responsibility but simply a fact of existence. Idealism does not take seriously the self-contradicting power of human freedom, or the demonic implications of human history. Naturalism leads logically to moral cynicism. This is usually avoided by adapting elements of Stoicism, but this cannot reach the full depth of Christian realism.

For Tillich the problem of the biblical story is that its once-upon-a-time literalism is not true. The power of the story, however, is that it contains a temporal element in dealing with the pervasive phenomenon of human evil. Human evil is not simply an occasional accident, but neither is it a created necessity of human life. Between the subjective idealism which tends to regard sin as only seeming to be a radical break with the Good, and the natural realism which tends to regard sin as only a fact of existence, there is a boundary line, a tightrope which locates sin in the moment of transition from essence to existence. The name of the tightrope, then, is this transition, and Tillich calls this approach a "halfway demythologization of the Fall." "Sin," he says, "is not created"[5] — that is to say, it is not a necessity of human existence, or a consequence of humankind's essential nature. On the other hand, the transition from essence to existence is a fact, "a story to be told and not a derived dialectical step."[6]

Reinhold Niebuhr made this same point by saying that sin is inevitable but not necessary. He quoted a *London Times* editorial writer who said that original sin is the only empirically verifiable doctrine in Christianity, but that was a joke. Empiricism can only tell you that there is a lot of bad stuff going on. Sin is an explanation as to why it is happening. If you asked Niebuhr how he knew sin was inevitable, he replied that it is part of the biblical revelation, and that only if you start there does the demonic dimension of human history make sense. He argued a rough pragmatism but was persuaded that any serious attempt at philosophical explanation would be drawn into the ontological quicksand of subjective idealism. He has a point. The most thoroughly consistent metaphysical solution to the problem of evil is the idealistic monism which shows it to be metaphysically unreal. That leaves life problems which can be dealt with only through the heroic Stoic disciplines of inner calm — Marcus Aurelius in his tent with the world crashing around him, or the Hindu yogi on his bed of nails, so intent on his inwardness that he feels no pain — but it solves the metaphysical problem. This heroic Stoicism, however, is only for the very few; it is not a solution to what Tillich calls the human situation. Perhaps more to the point, it requires radical detachment from the substance of one's own life. The Hindu yogi is an extreme case. But the Roman Stoics did not have friends; they only had people upon whom they practiced the virtue of friendship. Tillich is an existentialist and a Christian, and for him the substance of one's life is what philosophy and theology are all about. As an existentialist, dissolving pain in a purely metaphysical solution is inauthentic existence. As a Christian, it is disobedience to the God-with-us, who suffered, and died, and calls us to bear our cross faithfully. So on that issue he agreed with Neibuhr.

On the other hand, Tillich regarded Niebuhr's haphazard pragmatism as a failure of human reason to keep faith with itself. Tillich was not afraid of mysticism. There are limits to human knowledge, and he was more than ready to admit that the God who is really God is always the God above any conception we may have of God. If we say that sin is inevitable, however, we are responsible for explaining what we mean and why we say it. Niebuhr, always suspicious of pride, tended to think of metaphysics as intellectual arrogance. Again, Tillich was less concerned with the grandeur of metaphysical explanation than he was with the intimacy of existential understanding. Humankind is a philosophical animal; we are born with wonder, we need to know why; the question of being is a fundamental human question. Our existential suffering, our *angst*, is not just over our moral failure to do the good; it is also over our spiritual failure to know ourselves truly, and to understand why we are the way we are. So, call it a tightrope and warn against the ontological abyss. But for Tillich it is the inevitably human way to go.

He refers to the story of the Fall in Genesis 1–3 as the profoundest and richest expression of our existential estrangement. It is also a biblical myth which is unavoidably part of our experience. Demythologizers who don't like the virgin birth can set it aside, because we are not regularly surrounded by virgins giving birth. But a story about how we knew it was a bad thing and did it anyway, because we wanted to, is one in which we all recognize ourselves. The issue is first of all a matter of finite human freedom; that is to say, freedom within the limits of human destiny. Within this finite freedom the transition from essence to existence takes place. The state of essential being, in which the transition begins, is not a moment in time, for Tillich, any more than the Adam and Eve story is about a moment in time. Our essential nature, as potentiality, has no actual place or time. Yet this sense of our essential nature is present to us in all times and places as a consciousness of dreaming innocence, an idea which he adopts from Kierkegaard. This essential nature, or pure potential, is described as dreaming because, like potentiality, it is real and unreal at the same time. "Dreaming," he says, "anticipates the actual, just as everything actual is somehow present in the potential. In the moment of awakening, the images of the dream disappear as images, and return as encountered realities."[7]

The condition is one of innocence because non-actualized potentiality lacks experience, responsibility, and moral guilt. Adam before the Fall is the dreaming innocence of undecided potentialities. But God's command that they should not eat of the tree "presupposes that what is commanded is not yet fulfilled."[8] That is to say, the command presupposes a sin which is not yet a sin but which is also no longer innocence. It is the desire to sin, or what Tillich calls "aroused freedom." When finite freedom becomes conscious of itself it tends to do two things. Its first tendency is to actualize itself. Its second tendency is to draw back from the transition to existence in order to preserve the unity of its relation to destiny, since freedom and destiny are in harmony in the state of dreaming innocence. Humankind is caught "between the desire to actualize freedom and the demand (symbolized by God's command not to eat the fruit of the tree of the knowledge of good and evil) to preserve dreaming innocence. In the power of his finite freedom, he decides for actualization."[9]

In psychological terms the consciousness of freedom poses a double threat. One experiences the threat of losing oneself by not actualizing one's potential, and, at the same time, the threat of actualizing oneself and therefore losing the dreaming innocence in which the purity of one's essential being is preserved. In a rare illustration Tillich draws an analogy to adolescent male sexuality. The typical adolescent male confronts the prospect of losing himself, either by actualizing his sexual potential, or by failing to actualize it. Characteristically he actualizes it, and in so doing, experiences a loss of innocence. Tillich argues that the desire to actualize potential is temptation. But surely, we reply, to actualize our potential is what human creativity is all about. If that is all there is to sin, hasn't Tillich provided an excellent case for rejecting it? No; because it is not some external authority, or some internal neurosis which convicts us of sin. It is our own awareness that we have lost something of ourselves that creates our anxiety. And this essential being which has been lost was our harmony with the Ground of Being Itself. Tillich goes on to analyze this transition from essence to existence in terms of unbelief; hubris or pride; and concupiscence, the temptation to become centered in oneself. It is of the nature of essence to be pure; but existence is always mixed. Actualization is not a transition from the abstract to the concrete. Existence is a form of corruption. "Man," says Tillich, "in actualizing himself, turns to himself and away from God in knowledge, will, and emotion."[10]

And this brings us to the relation between Creation and the Fall. Humankind is held responsible for the Fall, but Tillich also argues that we must "simultaneously acknowledge the tragic universality of estrangement or sin."[11] This means that nature as well as humankind participates in alienation from the Ground of Being. It is not just individual people who are guilty. That is the Pelagian heresy, a form of the idealistic separation of innocent nature from guilty humankind. Tillich argues that there are analogies to human freedom in nature, and analogies to human good and evil in all parts of the universe.[12] Therefore it is not without cause that Isaiah prophesied peace in nature for the new age, and Paul spoke of nature's bondage to futility (Romans 8). Humankind and nature participate in each other, and cannot be separated from each other, thus making it possible to speak of a fallen world. In that sense Creation and Fall are identical.

It was at this point that Reinhold Niebuhr thought Tillich had fallen off the tightrope. For if "fallenness" is simply another name for existence, it is hard to make a case for humankind's moral responsibility. And since existence is not essence, and since essence is who we truly and most really are, the reality of existence is at best secondary, or derivative. And that was basically the message of Śaṁkara's Hindu Advaita Vedānta. Having criticized Hegel for not making a radical break between essence and existence in his view of the Fall, Tillich seems to have done much the same thing.

Tillich knows his critics, and raises the question himself. "Does not the preceding description 'ontologize away' the reality of the Fall and estrangement?" His defense is this:

> Creation and the Fall coincide in so far as there is no point in time and space in which created goodness was actualized and had existence. This is a necessary consequence of the rejection of the literal interpretation of the paradise story. There was no "utopia" in the past, just as there will be no "utopia" in the future. Actualized creation and estranged existence are identical.
>
> Creation is good in its essential character. If actualized, it falls into universal estrangement through freedom and destiny. . . . The leap from essence to existence is the original fact — that is, it has the character of a leap and not of structural necessity. In spite of its tragic universality, existence cannot be derived from essence.[13]

Let me sum up: My thesis was that metaphysical reflection begins from one of two basic experiences: sometimes I think that I am in the world; and sometimes I think the world is in me. Put simplistically, the first view implies a naturalistic realism which takes our experience of difference seriously, and results in a metaphysical dualism. The second view implies a subjective idealism which takes our experience of unity seriously, and results in a metaphysical nondualism, or ultimate monism. I suggested that the conflict between these two views was a key to the conflict between the characteristic religious metaphysics of the East and the West. But I noted that all great religious metaphysical systems attempt to do justice to both these fundamental human experiences, to the realities of our experienced life-world, where differences must be dealt with, and to the final unity of everything that is in the ultimate reality of the divine transcendence.

I have argued that Tillich's philosophy of religion makes a contribution to interreligious dialogue because it is one of the great contemporary systems of religious thought which takes this metaphysical conflict seriously. I have used his analysis of original sin as a paradigm case for two reasons. First, it makes explicit his search for a middle way between idealism and naturalism. Secondly, this is probably the most controversial issue in East-West religious dialogue. Hinduism, Buddhism, Taoism, and Confucianism have differences among themselves, but they are unanimous in rejecting the Christian notion of original sin.

So, a brief word of conclusion:

The name of the tightrope, you will recall, is "the transition from essence to existence." Tillich doesn't really fall off it, as Reinhold Niebuhr claimed. He does something more interesting. With a touch of metaphysical magic, he makes it disappear, thus leaving himself the Rudolf Nureyev of philosophical theology, suspended in his Kierkegaardian leap, without any place to land. For consider: the transition is real only if the distinction between essence and existence remains real. But if creation and Fall coincide, then the essential character of creation's goodness and the existential character of the fallen world's evil also coincide, since goodness is part of the essential character of creation and evil is part of the existential character of the fallen world. And in such a scheme, not only *can* existence be derived from essence, existence *must* be derived from essence if one is to argue that the real creation is really good. In other words, Śaṁkara and the Hindu tradition of Advaita Vedānta are right that all existence is derived from the ultimate essential reality of the One.

But is there any real objection to that? Yes, it makes the idea of God redundant. *God* becomes just another name for the way things are. It is only when one has a reality which is in some sense more than, greater than, other than the way things ultimately are that one is close to the characteristic Western notion of God. But in fairness to Tillich, God is not just being. God is the ground of being, or being itself, or the power of being. God is not just essence as opposed to existence. God is beyond both being and nonbeing, the ground of both essence and existence. The difficulty is that these metaphors cannot function effectively in any specific doctrine, as we have seen. Eastern notions of the Holy World Power of Brahman, or the Tao, are all interpretations of 'being'. The Western notion of God, while it includes 'being', is also beyond 'being'.

I think it was Tillich's intention that the terms *power* of being, or being *itself*, or the *ground* of being, should indicate that. But if that is the case, the intention is not philosophically operational, and the question for Tillich's philosophy of religion is whether such a God can, in fact, heal the world.

The method of correlation emphasizes "the real interdependence of things or events in structural wholes."[14] This kind of holistic thinking is increasingly popular in interreligious dialogue, especially in its process form where Whiteheadian Christians and Zen Buddhists find common methodological ground. But at one such consultation John Hick reminded his Christian colleagues that "we are stuck with God." He was raising the same question about Whitehead's God that I have raised about Tillich's. If Tillich's method were more dialectical — that is to say, had he maintained the clear distinction between essence and existence — then the God we Christians are stuck with would have been more clearly visible. The structure of Tillich's metaphysical system would be less complete, but that might not be a loss. There is a mysticism in Tillich's metaphysics which is partly obscured by metaphors like "ground of being." With that mysticism exposed and dealt with philosophically, Tillich's philosophy of religion would have greater power. Even with its inconsistencies, it is one of the major achievements of recent philosophy, and a substantive contribution to the meeting of East and West.

NOTES

1. These paragraphs on the missionary movement include much of the preliminary discussion from my "Introduction," in *Religious Pluralism*, vol. 5, Boston University Studies in Philosophy and Religion (Notre Dame, Ind.: University of Notre Dame Press, 1984), pp. 1–3.

2. Ibid., pp. 180–92.

3. Augustine, *Confessions*, trans. R. S. Pine-Coffin (Baltimore: Penguin Books, 1961), p. 9.

4. Paul Tillich, *Systematic Theology*, 3 vols. (Chicago: University of Chicago Press, 1951–63), 2: 29–30.

5. Ibid.

6. Ibid., 2: 33.

7. Ibid.

8. Ibid., 2:35.
9. Ibid.
10. Ibid., 2:47.
11. Ibid.
12. Ibid., 2:43.
13. Ibid., 2:44.
14. Ibid., 1:60.

13

Messianic Atheism

JÜRGEN MOLTMANN

EUROPE HAS LOST ITS ability to hope for great things. The European spirit is like a landscape of burned-out craters, covered by a dull layer of lava. Ideologies, utopias, hopeful designs, plans for a better future have become caricatures. A general resignation in the face of the dictatorship of the facts, of the *fait accompli*, rules over the positivism of an intelligentsia which only manipulates things on a technical level. Helmut Schelsky once illustrated the intellectual situation of the skeptical generation in the words of an American student: "What all of us under thirty lack is a guiding passion, a moral vision if you will. We are unable to weave a grandiose pattern out of the loose threads of our experience— and we know it." This is not just the sincere feeling of a particular age-group; it concerns all of humanity in all areas of knowledge, thought, and action, Christian theology and the church not excepted.

One is tempted to ask where the hope of the kingdom, inspired by the gospel, has gone. Where is the theology based on this hope which is capable of grasping the problems of the world and of history? Isn't the institutionalization of the Christian hope —the reduction of apocalyptic to the eschatological moment and the defamation of cosmic eschatology as "myth"— simply justification for a Christian-bourgeois, individualist culture which through existentialist resolution and a situation ethics can be mobilized only insignificantly and subjectively?

It is therefore no wonder that the Marxist and Jewish philosopher Ernst Bloch was greeted with so much admiration and applause in West Germany when Suhrkamp published his life's work, *Das Prinzip Hoffnung*, in 1959, thereby forcing the Aufbau publishing house in East Berlin to bring out there the disturbing, indeed heretical, third volume of the work in the German Democratic Republic as well. Bloch reawakened stifled and repressed hopes in both parts of our divided country. He injected a note of uneasiness into both party-line Marxism and the Western consumer world, a note which in its best exemplifications could be described as messianic. His principle of hope may as *principle*, that is, as an ideology coming out of the school of Hegel and Marx, seem rather conventional. Beneath this outer garment a messianic passion is hidden, however, so this principle is a challenge to both East and West, and in particular to Jewish and Christian theology.

One year before Ernst Bloch emigrated from Leipzig to Tübingen I attempted to present *Das Prinzip Hoffnung* under the title "Messianismus und Marxismus." Although it was his humanistic, democratic socialism which in the sixties led students and middle-class people, trade unions and parties, churches and schools to a fundamental reform of life and life's relationships, I was increasingly more fascinated by his messianism. At that time I asked the question: "In Bloch's *Das Prinzip Hoffnung* does messianism win out over Marxism or is it defeated by it?"[1] Today I wouldn't put the question in quite such an either/or way. Messianism seems to me to be the overarching perspective and inner impulse for his socialism, and democratic socialism the historical form which messianism must take given the present poverty of capitalism and its democracies. The messianic spirit shakes both socialism and democracy out of their torpidity and opens both up to broader perspectives. It puts both in a state of suspension, mediating between their hitherto unreconciled opposition and enmity—but only when seen in this suspended state.

In the field of messianism today, Judaism, Christianity, and Bloch's philosophy of hope encounter each other. It is a field of surprising variations, of conflicting possibilities. Only in a discussion among Jews, Christians, and socialists can the meaning of *messianism* be more precisely determined.[2] And the moment has come for such a discussion among the different messianic movements, for it is only out of the experience of the messianic *élan vital* and its concrete disappointments that a hope is born which acquires knowledge through experience without discrediting itself.

The messianism of the founder religions

In chapter 53 of *Das Prinzip Hoffnung*, Bloch offers a messianic interpretation of the great religions, especially of the earlier, so-called founder religions. According to Bloch, their special significance lies in the fact that besides the religious mystery and together with it, the "founder's placing of himself into the religious mystery" is also venerated. To the concept of transcendence itself belongs the exceptional human transcending of the world with which every religious act begins. Thus, in the founder religions, the unique religious act of the founder is regarded as a first-time event, an example to be exacted and imitated and, further, to be celebrated as a sacrament of the mediation of the transcendence experienced in it. Of course, the mediator is not what is mediated. Yet because it is only mediated through him or her, the mediator is seen as "the way." Thus the founder acquires an intrinsic significance for the goal and a guiding power for all those who search for it.

Block speaks in a history-of-religions sense of a "growing" extent to which founders place themselves into the religious mystery. This idea of an evolution in religious development is, admittedly, a construal based on religions which advertise themselves as the "absolute religion." Bloch takes this claim over from Hegel. If he does not declare Christianity the "absolute religion," as does Hegel, he nevertheless does inquire about the consummation of the history of religion. This yearning after the consummation of the history of religion is messianic. It leads to an absolutization of one's own religious experience and to a relativization of all other experiences, as well as to a relegation of all self-willed, premature consummations to the realm of historical incompleteness.

This ambivalence is easily recognizable in Bloch's presentation. He finds this "placing of oneself into the religious mystery" consummated in Moses and Jesus. Through his religious act Moses made God the "Exodus-light" of the people. Out of the "God over us" comes the "God before us"; out of the high lord of heaven comes the future kingdom of God's glory on earth. Through his sacrifice Jesus penetrates the transcendent understood as human tribune and transforms it into the kingdom.[3] This is all still constructed along the lines of Hegel's "absolute religion" with, to be sure, the difference that the history of human consciousness of God in no way counts already as the history of the divine consciousness of itself, but rather only aims at the final exposition of the messianic hope in totality.

Bloch's key phrase, "Where hope is, there is religion,"[4] leads to his idea of Christianity as the essence of religion, to the extent that in Christianity the "human-eschatological, in which a messianism ready to explode is set," appears.[5] At the same time the opposite is also valid: "Where hope is, there is atheism," to the extent that in atheism and its criticism of religion is intended this same human-eschatological, in which a messianism ready to explode is set. This is the ambivalent mystery of Bloch's "religion in inheritance," hope in totality, for this "religion in inheritance" can mean an inheritance of dead sayings and in this respect be irreligious. It can also mean the fulfillment of what is only promised in religion and in so doing be more than religious. Thus Bloch refers to it at one point as "without religion" and two pages before as "not simply no religion."[6] This double meaning is a typical sign of the messianic pathos of fulfillment. It must, in the same breath, terminate and fulfill. Hence, Bloch's atheism must also come out against "God" for God, if he wants to be consistent and to reject easy substitutes.

Messianism and utopias

Toward what is Bloch's messianism aimed? The symbols of the goal that he uses are variable, suspended, unstable, and vague: "totality," "exploding consummation, "ens perfectissimum," "home of identity," "habitableness in existence," "transfiguration of nature," and, over and over again, "the kingdom," signified astral-mythically (and with Dostoyevsky) as "crystal," or seen in a biblical sense as "glory." Over against the laws and customs of this world, these symbols demand a "rebirth," a "leap into the totally other." Bloch likes to speak in these contexts of the "most unconditioned utopia," of the utopia of the absolute, of the not presently existing, the not-yet-become. It announces itself in various signs and signals but is not yet known by anyone. It is mystically experienced in the darkness of the lived moment but cannot be seen and understood in the as-yet-unchanged world. This messianism of the totum, the kingdom, the glory, or the identity Bloch considers to be "the salt of the earth and also of heaven."[7] The messianism which proclaims such a future in history must make known that this future, even in the best possible society, is unattainable by pressing its thorn in the "unabolished intransigence of the surrounding nature."

As is well known, Bloch dealt extensively with the social utopias of happiness and their realization through scientific socialism and with the legal utopias of human dignity and their political realization through human rights and democracy. But these are for him only partial utopias, utopias taken out of the "totum of utopia" and looked at in an isolated, narrow-minded, one-sided way. Outside of the totum of utopia they lose their context and their best intentions. In this totum of utopia an absolute is anticipated "wherein still other conflicts besides the social ones are resolved, wherein also the understanding of all former frameworks changes."[8] Bloch does not attempt to reduce the messianic utopia or indeed any religious images of hope to actual, real-world social or political utopias. He attempts exactly the opposite, that is, the integration of these partial utopias into the totum of utopia. In so doing he is not just a metaphysician but also a metaethicist, metasocialist, metareligionist.

Those who assumed that in the classless society religion would simply be buried and forgotten will be disappointed by the ending of Bloch's *Naturrecht und menschliche Würde*.

> Certainly a no longer antagonistic society would hold all worldly destinies fast in its hand, determining an economic-political conformity. But for just this reason the triviality of existence rises in a much more noticeable way to the surface, from the jaws of death up to the level of boredom, of satiety. The messengers out of the nothingness have lost the simple values they carried in the class society, but have a new, still largely unimaginable face and indeed the series of necessities which they interrupted also consumes again in a new way.[9]

Thus Bloch's utopian view of the classless society ends with a vision of a new religion as the "reconnecting of a total dream forward to our needy patchwork"[10] and the vision of a new church which "with friendliness takes the deeply urgent and with brotherhood the difficulties seriously," a catholicity in solidarity, an ecumenical community, "so that it doesn't live for its time, but over and beyond its time"—a "church without superstition and on its way."[11]

Those who assumed that Bloch must stylize Jesus of Nazareth as a social rebel or political revolutionary will be no less disappointed. The idea of the messianic kingdom in the preaching of Jesus did indeed begin as a social movement among the miserable and heavy-laden, the humiliated and wronged, because it gave them an impulse, a feeling of worth, a hope. But in its intended content and scope it in no way coincided with just any social utopia. The liberating gospel for the poor anticipates as historically necessary a form among these invisible people which in itself has yet to appear and which will explode the entire system of heaven and earth according to Revelation, namely, the kingdom.[12]

The absolute, total hope content of messianism is claimed in the symbols of God and the kingdom of God. It stimulates ever new social and legal utopias related to specific situations and is the driving force behind liberation movements and people's struggles for justice. Hope itself, however, goes beyond this. It leads people through these utopias. It contains a concrete utopia and more than utopia. It is a real revolution and more than revolution. This superabundance of messianic hope becomes, despite the transformations of the God-hypostasis under the eschatological impulse — indeed because of this transformation — that which is no longer itself transformed and which thus again and again transforms even the transformations. Messianism becomes concrete through its production of real utopias and their mediation with the subjectively and objectively possible. It transcends continually into the immanent. But it also continually puts its own realizations into a state of suspension, the suspension of the compelling not-yet, and becomes immanent in the transcendent. Whoever begins to live messianically comes ever closer, but never quite makes it all the way home.

Messianism and atheism

"Without atheism, there is no place for messianism"[13] — so goes Bloch's thesis. But what in this context do *theism* and *atheism* actually mean? We read: "The existence of God, indeed God in any sense as essence, is superstition."[14] Religion itself is superstition when it is not hope and its symbols are not symbols of that most absolute utopia, inviting one to the moment of hope. Bloch's atheism is decidedly against any hope symbol of the totum hypostatized as *God*, that is, an essence existing for itself. When God is thought of and worshiped in such an absolute way, then hope is paralyzed. Thus all the representations of God as creator and ruler of the world, as heavenly power or enthroned authority, fail for Bloch.

> God becomes the kingdom of God, and the kingdom of God no longer contains a God, that is, this religious heteronomy and its thing-oriented hypostasis dissolve completely in the theology of the community, but as a theology which itself has crossed over the threshold of the hitherto existing creature and its anthropology and sociology.[15]

As with Feuerbach, so it also goes with Bloch, rather monotonously: God hypotheses are "nothing other than. . . ." Nevertheless, the messianic bond of atheism doesn't allow religious symbols to be reduced to the level of any anthropology of presently existing humans or the sociology of the present society. *God* and the *kingdom of God* converge on a practical level only in the going beyond of the past and present form of the creature and will finally converge only in the eschatological leap of the "Behold, I make all things new" (Rev. 21:5). It is the "religious intent of the kingdom as such with which, in the final analysis, atheism is involved,"[16] and nothing else. If, then, there is no place for messianism apart from atheism, so atheism is also powerless without messianism.

Grasping the messianic intention of atheism and of Bloch's critique of religion is necessary to a correct understanding of his thought. His atheism is not a reductionist atheism, not a simplistic explanation, much less a limitation to the merely banal. And despite the similarities with Feuerbach's thought it is not about some reductionist atheism of the future. As in the best parts of Marx's thought, so it is with Bloch: He is merely concerned with a functional criticism of religion, not with a critique of the essence of the religious. He is simply looking for a new functional interpretation of theism in the light of messianism. Theism is superstition when it causes superstition. And it can't effect hope until its functions have been interpreted in a new, messianic way. Theism has an alienating, imprisoning effect on people when it puts a religious hold on experience and hinders messianic transcending. If experience, practice, and analysis had shown that belief in God had had a liberating, stimulating, mobilizing effect toward a real transcending of poverty, then this functional criticism would have been unnecessary. The criticism of the old praxis of belief in God can only be overcome through new praxis. This is the level at which Marx's and Bloch's functional criticism of religion operates.

Behind this is another level. It is the impulse behind Moses' commandment against graven images which Bloch, like Adorno before him, applies to the Judaic and Christian religions, to Christian theology, and to the metaphysical imaging of reality itself. When the Yahweh religion became too influenced by Baal-worship, the Old Testament prophets used the commandment against graven images to sharpen the differences between Yahweh and the Baalim. Within the political religions of Christianity, the idolatries of the Christian faith have also been criticized in a similar way by the theology of the cross and the discipleship of the cross. Bloch's atheism is influenced by this commandment against images which is radicalized in the Jewish prohibition against speaking the name of God or representing the being of God, and to a large degree is a carrying out of this commandment. Religious symbols built upon religious experience must not dogmatize this experience, or they will harden it, fix it, and thus end the pilgrimage. They ought rather to invite one on to further experiences and discoveries, to the movement of transcending; to do this they must remain open and under way.

Symbols of the origin always guide people back to the same starting point. They form the *restitutio in integrum*. Eschatological symbols, on the other hand, invite people to break away from the same old thing and to an experience of new life. As signs of the change, they are themselves changeable signs of a journey which does not turn back. In Bloch's symbolism is found his preference for symbols of the *incipit vita nova*. His demythologization for the purpose of the eschatologization of religious symbols has support in the messianic tradition of Judaism. When the messianic era breaks in, the oppressive idols and demons will disappear from the world.[17] The earth will become human and liveable. One of the ideas of messianism is that the messianic era will, among other things, fulfill the commandment against graven images worldwide. The messianic era will so transform the world that human understanding will be able to abandon its doubled, alienating world of images.

Behind this level of the commandment against graven images stands then a third — the messianic level. According to cabbalistic tradition the messianic world will be a world without images. In this world the image and the imaged must no longer be somehow related to each other because in it appears a mode of being which no longer needs to be, indeed is not capable of being, imaged.[18] The difference between God and creation, faith and experience, consciousness and being will disappear.

Does not Pauline eschatology also contain this vision? When all dominion has been done away with and death has been destroyed, then God will be "all in all" (1 Cor. 15:28). And if God is all in all, then the historical difference between God and the world which had to be bridged with symbols, images, representations, and hypostases no longer exists. The foreignness of God over against the world and the alienation of human beings from God are abolished in God's glory which lives in all, permeating all. Thus also ended are all symbols and images of the Other which in history take part in God's foreignness and humanity's alienation because they can point to that home only in a historical way. They are "the song of the Lord in a foreign land" (Ps. 137:4) sung by the imprisoned people of God. "God all in all" is no longer capable of being imaged; nor is this any longer necessary, because God doesn't need to be represented by anything else or mediated through a third party. This vision is of the immediate nearness of God which makes pictures, symbols, signs, and codes superfluous.

This also applies to theological concepts. That which in history and in alienation is called *God* is grounded in the Exodus experiences of history and refers to the glory which will permeate all, but it is itself part of the foreignness and slavery which must still be overcome. The glory shines forth in a light that up to now has not yet (according to Jewish messianism) or has already (ac-

cording to the Christian faith in the paradoxical form of the resur-
rected crucified one) come forth from its source. That which no
one has yet seen or heard, which has only made an appearance
in the unseemly and unassuming figure of Christ, shall in the kingdom transform and transfigure the world. With respect to the historically necessary alienation of the theisms, the kingdom of God
will be "atheistic." Thus these historically limited theisms can be
interpreted messianically, namely, in their making of themselves
superfluous in the unmediated presence of God.

Bloch remains messianic insofar as his statements in this area
remain equivocal and double-edged. "*God* becomes the *kingdom
of God* and the *kingdom of God* no longer contains *God*"—this
thesis is, if not simply frivolous, highly paradoxical in its contradictory use of the word *God*. If a simple reduction were implied,
then the kingdom ought not to be called the "kingdom of God."
If the messianic interpretation is correct, then God as an essence
existing-for-itself outside of the world in the coming kingdom becomes the glory indwelling the world. The kingdom of God, then,
really no longer contains a *God* existing-for-itself separated from
and outside the world. The following phrase also contains this paradox: "This religious heteronomy and its thing-oriented hypostasis
dissolve completely in the *theology* of the community. . . ." They
dissolve not in the autonomy of humanity but in the "theology of
the community." This can only refer to, as the closing phrase about
a crossing over of the "threshold of the hitherto existing creature"
shows and the similarity to Hegel implies, God's indwelling of God's
people through the power of the Holy Spirit, the "God in us" and
"with us." In the Spirit-presence of God and in the new creation
the religious heteronomies and objectified hypostases are, in fact,
dissolved. The phrase about the "fulfillment of the Exodus-God
in the kingdom, in the dissolving of Yahweh in this glory"[19] is also
to be understood messianically. The Exodus-God is fulfilled in the
God of the kingdom, and this fulfillment is, at the same time, the
dissolving of the historically manifested and historically limited
Yahweh-form in the form of that glory of which, according to the
vision of the prophet, "the whole earth is full" (Isa. 6:3). Of course,
alongside these, one also finds in Bloch many statements which,
à la Feuerbach, make it sound as if the mystery of God is "nothing
other than" the mystery of humanity.[20] With such statements, how-

ever, Bloch falls below the standard of messianic thought and of his own better insights.

The cost of messianism

Gershom Scholem, at the end of his tract on "The Messianic Idea in Judaism," named the price which the Jewish people have had to pay and which they continue to pay even today for this idea which they themselves gave to the world. The greatness of the messianic idea directly corresponds to the weakness of the Jewish Diaspora which was not prepared, in exile, to enter into the historical plane because it dreamed of returning home. The messianic hope kept the Jewish people alive during the time they were scattered among other peoples. One lived from year to year with the thought, "next year in Jerusalem." But for just this reason one did not live with a heartfelt commitment to the present. The messianic idea has the weakness of the preliminary and provisional which does not give of itself but preserves itself, which cannot die because it refuses to live. "To live in hope is something great, but it is also something highly inauthentic."[21] The messianic idea forced upon Judaism "a *life-in-deferment* in which nothing can be done or executed in a conclusive way."[22]

It was not until after Auschwitz, in its return home to Zion, that Judaism found itself ready to enter irrevocably into the concrete world — certainly a move accompanied by the messianic overtones of Zionism, but without the commitment to some sort of metahistory. Whether it can maintain this effort without foundering on the rocks of the messianic demand is a life-or-death issue for Israeli Judaism. Jewish messianism becomes concrete in Zionism. But Zionism has also put the messianic hope in a crisis situation, a situation of self-defeating fulfillment, so that either the messianic hope must be put in terms of the Sinai and the Golan or else the transcendent element of messianism must be reborn.[23]

Bloch's philosophical messianism also puts the world in a state of suspension: "Such a conscientiousness . . . mindful of being hope-in-totality comprehends simultaneously the essence of the world in a state of tremendous suspension, towards the Tremendous — a situation which hope believes in, which active hope urges on, as being a good thing."[24] Bloch uses a rich variety of symbols to characterize this state of suspension into which the messianic idea brings the world and the experience of the world, symbols such as "open world-process," "process matter," and "experimentum mundi." On the one hand this sounds encouraging: nothing is conclusive; everything is open; "Poland is not yet lost." Hope can be disappointed — otherwise it would not be hope — but it cannot be destroyed by any disappointment because no disappointment is final. This contains within itself, however, the weakness which Gershom Scholem pointed out. Nothing is done in a conclusive way. Everything remains preliminary, provisional. Life in this "tremendous suspension" of hope in "the Tremendous" can only be a life of continual deferment. Every word remains open, every thought remains fluid, every act revocable. Everything is an experiment. The core of existence cannot be pinned down because it has yet to appear. It is unable to come out in the open.

But where and in what way does the conclusive, the entering into the concrete without reservation or possibility of evasion, the complete sacrifice, the ability to die, come into this continually preliminary-because-hopeful messianic life and thought? Even when this messianic life in hope is not interpreted negatively as a "life-in-deferment" but positively as a "life-in-anticipation," even when life in the dynamic of the preliminary is not defined by the continual "not yet real" but rather by the "now already possible," this question persists as a criticism of the theory and practice of the hope principle.

If we attempt to overcome the weakness of messianism and Bloch's principle of hope without destroying them both, then we must introduce the paradoxical elements of the ultimate into the dialectical categories of the preliminary.[25] Otherwise, we can scarcely avoid the danger of considering the world an always possible but always unreal world of appearance, and of not living or not yet living or only experimentally living our lives in this world.

Dietrich Bonhoeffer wrote along his road of no turning back, in his final prison cell, and under the influence of his reading of the Old Testament:

It is only when one apprehends the unspeakability of the name of God that one may also speak the name of Jesus Christ;

it is only when one so loves life and the earth that with them all seems to have been spent and have come to an end that one may believe in the resurrection of the dead and in a new world.[26]

Now of course Bonhoeffer earlier, in his *Ethics*, drew a careful distinction between the "next-to-last" and "the last,"[27] but in the face of death he recognized that both — love and death as well as resurrection and a new world — are "last things." The sacrifice of life in love and the irrevocable entering into the concrete can only be accomplished with the same absolute passion that one has in hoping for the resurrection and the kingdom of God. Sacrifice and hope, death and resurrection do not harmonize with each other in some middle position between death and life, neither in the friendly, undecided world-process nor in a life-in-deferment. Sacrifice and hope can only occur in a final, ultimate way. They are not brought into any sort of "suspension" without losing the point of their thrust.

According to Jewish and Christian traditions, the messianic era begins with the death pains of the old and the birth pains of the new world. It began, from a Christian perspective, with Christ's passion and death on the cross. It was not Jesus' placing of himself in a transcendent mystery, "even death on a cross" (Phil. 2:8), which inaugurated the messianic era and the messianic life. For this reason, hope can only be put into practice through a complete placing of oneself into the concrete world. This is no state of suspension, no open process, no merely experimental mode of conduct, but rather the paradox of living and dying in light of the cross and resurrection of the Messiah. There is then no transcending of hope without the paradoxical countermovement of the incarnation of love, no breaking out to new horizons without the sacrifice of life, no anticipating of the future without first investing in it. It is in the incarnational movement even unto passion and death that, paradoxically, the kingdom of God can even now be lived and not just hoped for. The real life of hope in fellowship with the crucified Messiah will not manifest itself in any other way for "as dying . . . behold we live" (2 Cor. 6:9). Without this paradox of the real, the dialectic of the possible remains inauthentic.

NOTES

1. Jürgen Moltmann, "Messianismus und Marxismus," in Jürgen Moltmann, *Gespräch mit Ernst Bloch. Eine theologische Wegbegleitung* (Munich: Chr. Kaiser, 1976), p. 31.

2. For this see Gershom Scholem, *Die jüdische Mystik in ihren Hauptströmungen* (Frankfurt am Main: Suhrkamp, 1957); Gershom Scholem, *Von der mystischen Gestalt der Gottheit* (Zurich: Rhein-Vorlag, 1973); Gershom Scholem, *Judaica* (Frankfurt am Main: Suhrkamp, 1963); Schalom Ben-Chorin, *Die Antwort des Jona* (Hamburg-Volksdorf: H. Reich, 1956); Schalom Ben-Chorin, *Jüdischer Glaube* (Tübingen: Mohr, 1975).

3. Ernst Bloch, *Das Prinzip Hoffnung* (Frankfurt am Main: Suhrkamp, 1959), p. 1402.

4. Ibid., p. 1416.

5. Ibid., p. 1404.

6. Ibid., pp. 1416 and 1414.

7. Ibid., p. 1415.

8. Ibid., p. 1411.

9. Ernst Bloch, *Naturrecht und menschliche Würde* (Frankfurt am Main: Suhrkamp, 1961), pp. 310f.

10. Ibid., p. 312.

11. Ibid., pp. 312, 314.

12. Bloch, *Das Prinzip Hoffnung*, pp. 1493ff.

13. Ibid., p. 1413.

14. Ibid.

15. Ibid., p. 1408.

16. Ibid., p. 1415.

17. Ben-Chorin, *Die Antwort des Jona*, p. 112.

18. Scholem, *Judaica*, pp. 72ff.

19. Bloch, *Das Prinzip Hoffnung*, p. 1493.

20. See, for example, ibid., pp. 1515ff.: "God as utopian hypostatized Ideal of the unknown human being."

21. Scholem, *Judaica*, p. 73.

22. Ibid., pp. 73ff.

23. Jochana Bloch, "Selbsthauptung. Zionistische Aufsätze," *Zeitstimmung* 61/62 (1972).

24. Bloch, *Das Prinzip Hoffnung*, p. 1409.

25. Hermann Deuser, *Sören Kierkegaard. Die paradoxe Dialektik des politischen Christen* (Munich and Mainz: Chr. Kaiser and Matthias-Grünewald, 1974).

26. Dietrich Bonhoeffer, *Widerstand und Ergebung* (Munich: Chr.

Kaiser, 1951), pp. 112f. Translated as *Letters and Papers from Prison*, trans. and ed. Eberhard Bethge (New York: Macmillan, 1971).

27. Dietrich Bonhoeffer, *Ethik* (Munich: Chr. Kaiser, 1949), pp. 75ff. Translated as *Ethics*, trans. N. H. Smith, and ed. Eberhard Bethge (New York: Macmillan, 1965).

Author Index

Subject Index

210